· The · Illustrated ·
Escoffier

Beef Tenderloin Saint-Germain

· THE · ILLUSTRATED ·
ESCOFFIER

RECIPES FROM THE CLASSIC FRENCH TRADITION

Selected and Edited by Anne Johnson

CONSULTANT EDITORS
H. L. CRACKNELL AND R. J. KAUFMANN

INTERNATIONAL CULINARY SOCIETY
NEW YORK

This 1987 edition published by
International Culinary Society
Distributed by Crown Publishers, Inc.
225 Park Avenue South
New York
New York 10003

h g f e d c b a

Adapted from:
The Complete Guide to the Art of Modern Cookery
by A. Escoffier
translated by H. L. Cracknell and R. J. Kaufmann
(London: Heinemann, 1979)

ISBN 0 517 63342 6

Printed in Hong Kong

Acknowledgements
Editors Andrew Jefford, Norma MacMillan
Art Editor Alyson Kyles
Designer Bob Gordon
Production Sara Hunt, Maryann Rogers

Photography by Martin Brigdale
Martin Brigdale was assisted by Philomena O'Neill

Food prepared for photography by Nichola Palmer (all photographs excluding those listed below)
Anne Hildyard (pages 11, 15, 27, 35, 51 and 67)
Nichola Palmer was assisted by Juliet Brigstocke and Angela Drake

Stylist Andrea Lambton

The publishers would like to thank the following companies for their kindness in providing materials and equipment used in the photography for this book:

Harrods
Knightsbridge
London SW1X 7XL

Josiah Wedgwood and Sons Limited
Barlaston
Stoke-on-Trent ST12 9EF
and at
Wedgwood House
32–34 Wigmore Street
London W1H 0HV

Gallery of Antique Costume and Textiles
2 Church Street
London NW8 8ED

NOTE
Words printed in *italics* in the recipe methods indicate that the word is included in the short Glossary on pages 188–189.

CONTENTS

AUGUSTE ESCOFFIER

INTRODUCTION

One may wonder as to the motive in producing a selected and illustrated version of Escoffier's *Guide to Modern Cookery*, when the book in its original form is still selling well worldwide.

The reason, I believe, is revealed in the foreword and introductions that Auguste Escoffier himself wrote to the first and subsequent editions of the *Guide*.

"My intention is to offer my colleagues a tool rather than merely a recipe book . . . something to be placed on a nearby shelf for easy reference . . . [but that would] leave them free to develop their own methods and follow their own inspiration. . . . The art of cooking, which in many ways is similar to that of fashion design, will evolve as society evolves. . . . Only basic rules remain unalterable. . . . It may be feared that in order to satisfy the requirements of an ever-more hurried clientele, cooking would be simplified to such a degree that our art would become merely a trade. This will not take place because simplicity does not exclude beauty. I am convinced that the ability to give the supreme touch to a modest dish, presenting it in an elegant yet appropriate manner, will always be the indispensable compliment to technical expertise."

This is all well and good, but it should not be forgotten that Escoffier was addressing himself to professional chefs. Today, when interest in refined cooking is spreading rapidly through society, new presentation of the *Guide* seemed called for. Of the 5,000 or so recipes in the *Guide*, a number are seldom prepared today as their ingredients have disappeared or become outmoded or outpriced. In *The Illustrated Escoffier*, a careful selection of recipes has been made, ingredients or methods have been adapted where necessary, and beautiful color photographs have been painstakingly taken of many of the dishes.

However, this new version should be used exactly as the *Guide* itself was intended to be, with readers free to adapt according to their own inspiration, in order to present the results to their guests in an elegant, genuine manner.

It is the hope of all those who have contributed to *The Illustrated Escoffier* that it will be welcomed and appreciated by those for whom the adaptation has been made: enthusiastic home cooks wishing to take part in the best tradition of French classic cooking.

PIERRE P. ESCOFFIER

Stocks & Sauces

Brown Stock

Fonds Brun

3½ lb beef shank
3½ lb veal shank or lean veal trimmings
¼ lb carrots, peeled and roughly chopped
1 onion, peeled and roughly chopped
6 tablespoons clean fat, such as strained drippings
1 fresh pork hock, blanched
¼ lb fresh pork rind, blanched
1 bouquet garni
4½ quarts water

Bone the beef and veal, break the bones up small and lightly brown them in the oven. Fry the carrot and onion in half the fat until nicely browned.

Place the bones, vegetables, hock, pork rind and bouquet garni in a stockpot, then add the cold water. Bring to a boil, skim and simmer gently for at least 12 hours, adding water as required to keep the liquid at the same level throughout.

Cut the beef and veal meat into large dice, heat the remaining fat and fry until brown. Place in a pan, cover with some of the prepared stock and boil until reduced to a glaze. Repeat this process 2 or 3 times.

Add the rest of the prepared stock, bring to a boil, skim to remove all fat, and allow to simmer gently until all the flavor has been extracted from the meat; maintain the level of the liquid with water as required.

Strain and reserve for use.

Makes approximately 2½ quarts

Game Stock

Fonds de Gibier

2 lb game, to include a variety selected from rabbit, pheasant, venison or hare, preferably older animals and birds, but fresh
2 carrots, peeled and sliced
2 leeks, green part only, sliced
1 small onion, peeled and sliced
1 large celery stalk, sliced
⅔ cup sliced mushrooms or mushroom trimmings
2 tablespoons butter
1 clove garlic
large bunch of parsley stalks
1 pinch chopped fresh thyme
1 bay leaf
good pinch salt
15 juniper berries and 1 clove, tied together in cheesecloth

Cut the game into pieces and brown in a hot oven (425°F). Place the vegetables in the bottom of a heavy pan and fry until brown in the butter with all the flavoring ingredients except the juniper and clove. Add the browned pieces of game.

Deglaze the roasting pan with a little water and add to the other ingredients. Cover all with water, add the juniper and clove and bring to a boil. Skim carefully. Allow to simmer very gently, skimming as and when necessary, for 3 hours, maintaining the level of the liquid with water as required.

Strain and reserve for use.

Makes approximately 1½ quarts

White Stock

Fonds Blanc

3½ lb veal shank, veal trimmings and veal bones
4 raw chicken carcasses, with giblets
1 teaspoon salt
¼ lb carrots, peeled and roughly chopped
1 small onion, peeled and roughly chopped
1 small leek, chopped
½ celery stalk, chopped
1 bouquet garni

Bone the shank and chop the bones very small. Place all the bones and meat in a stockpot, cover well with cold water and add the salt. Bring to a boil, skim carefully and add the vegetables and bouquet garni. Allow to simmer gently, uncovered, for 3 hours, removing scum and fat and adding boiling water as required to keep the liquid to the same level for half the cooking time. Add no more liquid thereafter. Strain and reserve for use.

Chicken Stock (Fonds Blanc de Volaille)
Chicken stock is made exactly the same way, but with more chicken in proportion to veal. This can be achieved by using more giblets or carcass, or by using a whole, quartered stewing chicken in place of an equal weight of veal.

MAKES APPROXIMATELY 1½ QUARTS

Fish Stock

Fumet de Poisson

3½ lb bones and trimmings of sole or flounder
1 small onion, peeled and sliced
⅓ cup chopped button mushrooms
1 pinch salt
a few parsley stalks
1½ quarts water
½ bottle good dry white wine
a few drops lemon juice
5 peppercorns

Put the fish bones and trimmings, onion, mushrooms, salt and parsley stalks into a pan and cover with the water. Add the wine and lemon juice. Bring to a boil quickly, skim and allow to simmer very gently for 20 minutes. Add the peppercorns and continue cooking for 10 more minutes.

Strain and use as required.

MAKES APPROXIMATELY 1½ QUARTS

Meat Glaze

Glace de Viande

A meat glaze is used to impart a brilliant shine and an unctuous coating to finished dishes, to reinforce the quality of a sauce, or to strengthen a preparation of which stock is too weak. It is usually made using a Brown Stock, page 8, though a lighter-colored glaze can be made using a White Stock, left. Chicken and game glazes can be prepared by the same method using Chicken Stock, left, or Game Stock, page 8.

Place 2 cups of stock in a large pan and allow it to reduce. Skim carefully as the reduction takes place. When an appreciable degree of reduction has taken place, strain the stock into a smaller pan and repeat this process from time to time, skimming and straining carefully and reducing the heat each time. The glaze is ready when it adheres to the back of a spoon in the form of a glossy coating.

Light Gravy

Jus de Veau Lié

4 quarts Brown Stock, page 8
3 tablespoons arrowroot

Reserve ½ cup of the cold stock for use later. Bring the rest of the stock to a boil, then allow it to reduce to a quarter of its original volume.

Dilute the arrowroot in the reserved cold stock, stir into the boiling stock and allow to cook gently for 1 minute. Pass through a fine strainer. The resultant gravy should be transparent and light brown in color, and have a fresh, clean taste.

MAKES APPROXIMATELY 1 QUART

Velouté Sauce

Sauce Velouté

4 tablespoons butter
½ cup flour, sifted
5 cups White Stock or Fish Stock, page 9, depending on the flavor of the dish in preparation

First prepare a *white roux* by mixing the butter and flour together in a heavy pan and placing over a moderate heat for just a few minutes, stirring frequently, to eliminate the raw flavor of the flour. Allow to cool.

Gradually stir the stock into the roux, making sure that you obtain a smooth consistency. Bring to a boil, stirring continuously, and allow to simmer very gently for 1½ hours, skimming carefully from time to time. Strain and use as required.

MAKES APPROXIMATELY 1 QUART

Espagnole Sauce

Sauce Espagnole

4 tablespoons clarified butter
½ cup flour, sifted
2½ quarts Brown Stock, page 8
2 slices bacon, chopped
1 large carrot, peeled and roughly chopped
½ small onion, peeled and roughly chopped
1 sprig thyme
1 small bay leaf
¼ cup dry white wine
½ cup tomato paste or ½ lb fresh tomatoes, roughly chopped

Start making this sauce at least one day before you need it. First make a *brown roux* by mixing the *clarified butter* and flour together in a heavy pan and place over a moderate heat to cook, stirring frequently, until an even light brown color is obtained. When cooked, the roux should be smooth and smell of hazelnuts or baked flour.

Place 1½ quarts of the Brown Stock in a heavy pan and bring to a boil. Add the roux, mix well with a wooden spoon or whisk, and bring to a boil, stirring continuously. Turn down the heat and allow to simmer gently.

Meanwhile, place the bacon in a dry pan and fry to render the fat. Add the vegetables and herbs and fry until golden brown. Carefully drain off the fat and add these ingredients to the sauce. Deglaze the pan with the white wine, reduce by half and add to the sauce. Allow to simmer gently for 1 hour.

Pass the sauce through a conical strainer into another pan, pressing lightly. Add a further 2 cups of the Brown Stock, bring to a boil and allow to simmer gently for a further 2 hours. Strain and stir the sauce occasionally until completely cold.

The following day, add the remaining stock and the tomato paste or fresh tomatoes. Bring the sauce to a boil stirring continuously with a wooden spoon or whisk. Allow to simmer gently for 1 hour, skimming carefully.

Pass through a fine strainer and stir occasionally until the sauce is quite cold.

MAKES APPROXIMATELY 1 QUART

Demi-glace Sauce

Sauce Demi-glace

1 cup Espagnole Sauce, left
½ cup Brown Stock, page 8
6 tablespoons Meat Glaze, page 9
1 tablespoon sherry, port or Madeira (optional)

This sauce is made by bringing Sauce Espagnole to a final stage of perfection by carefully adding the Brown Stock, mixing, simmering and skimming until reduced to about scant 1 cup. It is then finished at the last moment with a small quantity of meat glaze.

Demi-glace can be flavored with various fortified wines, such as sherry, port or Madeira. This addition should be made at the very end and the sauce should not be allowed to boil again after this addition. For a tomato-flavored Demi-glace, either increase the proportion of tomato or tomato paste in the Espagnole Sauce used, or add 1 tablespoon of tomato paste with the Brown Stock, before making the final reduction.

MAKES APPROXIMATELY 1 CUP

Poivrade Sauce

Sauce Poivrade

2 tablespoons oil
1 large carrot, peeled and diced
½ small onion, peeled and diced
a few parsley stalks
1 small pinch chopped fresh thyme
½ bay leaf, crushed
¼ cup wine vinegar
1 cup reserved marinade from dish in preparation
2 cups Espagnole Sauce, left
4 peppercorns, crushed
2 tablespoons butter

Heat the oil in a pan, add the vegetables and herbs, and fry gently until lightly colored. Add the wine vinegar and ½ cup of the reserved marinade and reduce by two-thirds. Add the Espagnole Sauce and simmer gently for 45 minutes, adding the crushed peppercorns after 35 minutes.

Strain, pressing firmly to extract all the flavor, then add another ½ cup of the reserved marinade. Bring to a boil, skim and simmer gently for 35 minutes to reduce. Pass again through a fine strainer, this time without pressing, and finish with the butter.

MAKES APPROXIMATELY 2 CUPS

Consommé Carmen

Chasseur Sauce

Sauce Chasseur

1 stick plus 2 tablespoons butter
2 cups sliced button mushrooms
2½ tablespoons finely chopped shallot
½ cup dry white wine
1 tablespoon tomato paste
1 cup Demi-glace Sauce, page 10
1 tablespoon chopped fresh tarragon and chervil or parsley, mixed

Melt 2 tablespoons butter in a small pan, add the mushrooms and fry gently. Add the shallot and cook together for a few more minutes.

Add the white wine. Reduce by half and add the tomato paste and the Demi-glace Sauce. Bring to a boil, allow to simmer gently for a few minutes and finish by whisking in the remaining quantity of butter and the chopped fresh tarragon and chervil. Do not re-boil.

MAKES APPROXIMATELY 2 CUPS

Duxelles Sauce

Sauce Duxelles

½ cup dry white wine
½ cup mushroom cooking liquid
2 tablespoons chopped shallot
1 cup Demi-glace Sauce, page 10
1 tablespoon tomato paste
1 pinch chopped fresh parsley

Dry duxelles
1 tablespoon butter
1 tablespoon chopped onion
½ cup finely chopped mushrooms

Place the wine and *mushroom cooking liquid* in a pan with the chopped shallot and reduce to one third of its original quantity.

Meanwhile, prepare the dry duxelles by heating the butter and frying the onion gently for a few minutes. Add the mushrooms and cook gently until all the moisture has evaporated.

Add the Demi-glace Sauce to the reduced white wine and mushroom liquid, then add the tomato paste and dry duxelles. Allow to simmer gently for 5 minutes and finish the sauce with the chopped parsley.

MAKES APPROXIMATELY 2 CUPS

Béchamel Sauce

Sauce Béchamel

5 tablespoons butter
½ cup flour, sifted
1 quart boiling milk
1 onion, peeled and finely sliced
1 sprig thyme
salt
pepper
1 pinch grated nutmeg

First prepare a *white roux* by mixing together 4 tablespoons of the butter and the flour in a heavy pan and placing over moderate heat for just a few minutes, stirring frequently, to eliminate the raw flavor of the flour. Allow to cool.

Gradually stir the milk into the roux so as to obtain a smooth sauce and bring to boiling point. Fry the onion gently in the remaining butter but do not allow to brown, then add the thyme, salt, pepper and grated nutmeg. Add this mixture to the sauce and simmer for 1 hour. Pass through a fine strainer.

If you are not going to use the sauce immediately, coat the surface with a little butter to prevent a skin forming. For the thick or very thick Béchamel Sauce required for certain recipes, allow to simmer and reduce considerably before straining and using. For a light Béchamel Sauce, thin with a little boiling milk before straining and using.

MAKES APPROXIMATELY 1 QUART

Suprême Sauce

Sauce Suprême

1 quart Velouté Sauce made with Chicken Stock, pages 9–10
1 quart Chicken Stock, page 9
½ cup mushroom cooking liquid
1½ cups heavy cream
5 tablespoons butter

Place the Velouté Sauce, Chicken Stock and *mushroom cooking liquid* in a heavy pan. Bring to a boil and reduce quickly, while simultaneously adding two-thirds of the cream, a little at a time, and stirring the sauce continuously with a straight-edged wooden spatula.

When the sauce has been reduced by one-third, pass it through a fine strainer. Finish the sauce with the remaining cream and the butter.

MAKES APPROXIMATELY 1½ QUARTS

Mornay Sauce

Sauce Mornay

½ cup Fish Stock, page 9, or cooking liquid
1 quart Béchamel Sauce, page 12
¼ cup grated Gruyère cheese
¼ cup grated Parmesan cheese
4 tablespoons butter

Add the fish stock, or the cooking liquid from the fish with which the sauce is to be served, to the Béchamel Sauce. (If the sauce is required for a dish other than fish, the fish stock or cooking liquid should be replaced by the cooking liquid from the dish under preparation, or by milk.) Reduce by a third and add all the grated cheese.

Reheat for a few seconds, mix well to ensure that the cheese is melted, and finish with the butter.

MAKES APPROXIMATELY 1 QUART

Hollandaise Sauce

Sauce Hollandaise

2 tablespoons vinegar
5 tablespoons water
salt
coarsely ground pepper
5 egg yolks
1 lb (4 sticks) unsalted butter, softened or melted
a few drops lemon juice

Place the vinegar with 4 tablespoons water in a pan with a pinch each of salt and pepper. Reduce by two-thirds and transfer to a *bain-marie.*

Add another tablespoon water and the egg yolks to the reduction and whisk continuously over a gentle heat, while very gradually adding the butter. The sauce will thicken as the temperature rises and the yolks are cooked, but great care should be taken that the mixture does not overheat or it will separate. Add a few drops of water from time to time so as to ensure the sauce remains light.

Check the seasoning and add a few drops of lemon juice. Pass through a fine strainer and keep at a lukewarm temperature until the sauce is required, to prevent it from separating.

Note: It is best to avoid the use of an aluminum pan in the preparation of this sauce because of the risk of discoloration.

MAKES APPROXIMATELY 2 CUPS

Mayonnaise

Sauce Mayonnaise

2 egg yolks
salt
white pepper
½ tablespoon wine vinegar or lemon juice
1¼ cups olive oil
2 tablespoons boiling water

Whisk the egg yolks in a bowl with the seasonings and a little of the vinegar or lemon juice.

Add and whisk in the oil, drop by drop to begin with, then faster in a stream, as the sauce begins to thicken. Adjust the consistency occasionally by adding a few more drops of vinegar or lemon juice.

Lastly, add the water, which ensures that the emulsification holds, even if the sauce is not used immediately.

MAKES APPROXIMATELY 1¾ CUPS

Béarnaise Sauce

Sauce Béarnaise

½ cup dry white wine
½ cup tarragon vinegar
2 tablespoons chopped shallot
6 peppercorns, crushed
2 tablespoons chopped fresh tarragon
1 tablespoon chopped fresh chervil or parsley
4 egg yolks
2½ sticks butter, softened
salt
cayenne pepper

Place the wine and the vinegar in a small pan with the shallot, peppercorns and half of the herbs. Bring to a boil and reduce to a quarter of its original volume. Allow to cool.

Whisk the egg yolks into the wine and vinegar reduction and, over a gentle heat, gradually whisk in the butter.

When all the butter has been incorporated and the sauce is very thick, pass through a fine strainer, correct the seasoning and add a little cayenne pepper. Finish by stirring in the remaining tarragon and chervil. Do not allow the sauce, at any time, to reach a temperature much higher than blood heat, or it will curdle.

Note: It is best to avoid the use of an aluminum pan in the preparation of this sauce because of the risk of discoloration.

MAKES APPROXIMATELY 1¾ CUPS

Butter Sauce

Sauce au Beurre

3 tablespoons flour
2 sticks butter
2 cups boiling water
salt
3 eggs yolks
$\frac{1}{4}$ cup heavy cream
a few drops lemon juice

Melt 2 tablespoons of the butter. Mix the flour and melted butter together in a pan. Add the boiling water gradually, whisking thoroughly after each addition, and season. Make a *liaison* of the egg yolks, cream and lemon juice, and add this to the sauce.

Reheat to thicken, pass through a fine strainer and finish away from the heat, just before serving, with the butter.

MAKES APPROXIMATELY 3 CUPS

Tomato Sauce

Sauce Tomate

1 tablespoon butter
2 slices bacon, diced and blanched
$\frac{1}{2}$ small onion, peeled and roughly diced
1 carrot, peeled and roughly diced
1 bay leaf
1 sprig thyme
3 tablespoons flour
3 lb ripe tomatoes, squashed
1$\frac{3}{4}$ cups White Stock, page 9
1 clove garlic, peeled and minced
salt
pepper
1 pinch sugar

Melt the butter in a flameproof casserole, then add the bacon and fry gently. Add the vegetables and herbs and fry until golden brown. Sprinkle with the flour and stir. Cook until golden brown and allow to cool. Add the rest of the ingredients, then bring to a boil, stirring continuously.

Cover with a lid and place in a moderate oven (350°F) for 1$\frac{1}{2}$–2 hours, then strain into a clean pan. Stir and return to a boil for a few minutes. If you are not using this sauce immediately, coat the surface with butter in order to prevent a skin from forming on the top.

MAKES APPROXIMATELY 1 QUART

Tomato Fondue

Fondue de Tomate

1 onion, peeled and finely chopped
2 tablespoons butter or 1 tablespoon olive oil
1$\frac{1}{2}$ lb tomatoes, peeled, seeded and chopped
1 clove garlic, peeled and minced
salt
pepper
1 pinch sugar (optional)

Fry the chopped onion gently in the butter or oil and add the tomato flesh, minced garlic, seasoning and optional sugar. Allow to simmer gently until all the liquid has evaporated.

MAKES APPROXIMATELY 2 CUPS

Provençale Sauce

Sauce Provençale

$\frac{1}{2}$ cup olive oil
1$\frac{3}{4}$ lb tomatoes, peeled, seeded and roughly chopped
salt
pepper
1 pinch sugar
1 clove garlic, peeled and minced
1 tablespoon chopped fresh parsley

Heat the oil in a pan until almost smoking hot. Add the chopped tomato flesh and season with salt, pepper and sugar. Add the minced garlic and parsley. Cover with a lid and allow to simmer gently for 30 minutes.

MAKES APPROXIMATELY 2 CUPS

Apple Sauce

Sauce aux Pommes

1 lb apples, peeled, cored and sliced
1 tablespoon sugar
1 pinch cinnamon
$\frac{1}{4}$ cup water

Place the apples in a pan with the sugar, cinnamon and water. Cover with a lid and cook gently until soft, then make into a smooth sauce by beating with a whisk.

This sauce should always be served lukewarm.

MAKES APPROXIMATELY 1 CUP

Shrimp Bisque

Consommes & Soups

Consommé Carmen

Consommé Carmen

1 lb very lean boneless beef, trimmed and chopped
1 carrot, roughly chopped
2 leeks, roughly chopped
½ large sweet red pepper
5 tablespoons tomato paste
1 egg white
1½ quarts White Stock, page 9

To garnish
1 tomato
½ sweet red pepper
1 tablespoon boiled long-grain rice
6 sprigs chervil or parsley

Place the chopped meat, vegetables, red pepper, tomato paste and egg white in a small stockpot, mix well and add 5 cups of the White Stock. Bring to a boil, keeping the bottom of the pan clean using a flat-ended spatula and taking great care that the consommé is disturbed as little as possible. After boiling point has been reached, simmer very gently for 1½ hours without disturbing the consommé in any way.

Meanwhile, prepare the garnish. Peel the tomato by placing it in boiling water for a few seconds so that the skin can be removed easily. Remove the seeds, cut the flesh in dice, and poach for 7–8 minutes in the rest of the White Stock along with the red pepper, cut into *julienne*. Remove and cool.

When the consommé is cooked, ladle it out gently without disturbing the crust of ingredients on the top, and pass it through clean cheesecloth. Place the poached tomato and pepper and the boiled rice directly into the hot consommé just before serving and garnish each bowl with a sprig of chervil. *See photograph on page 11.*

Serves 6

Game Consommé

Consommé au Chasseur

1 lb lean mixed game meat, chopped
1¼ lb fresh game bones, roasted
1 small leek, roughly chopped
1 oz dried ceps or porcini
1 sprig sage
1 pinch dried rosemary
2 crushed juniper berries
pepper
1 egg white
1½ quarts Game Stock, page 8

To garnish
1 tablespoon julienne of mushrooms, stewed in a little butter and lemon juice
5 tablespoons port wine
6 sprigs chervil or parsley

Place the chopped meat and roasted bones, vegetables, herbs, flavorings and egg white in a small stockpot, mix well together and add the game stock. Bring to a boil, keeping the bottom of the pan clean using a flat-ended spatula and taking great care that the consommé is disturbed as little as possible. After boiling point has been reached, simmer very gently for 1½ hours without disturbing the consommé in any way.

Meanwhile prepare the garnish. When the consommé is cooked, ladle it out gently without disturbing the crust of ingredients on the top, and pass it through clean cheesecloth. Stir the mushrooms and port into the hot consommé just before serving and garnish each bowl with a sprig of chervil.

Serves 6

Shrimp Bisque

Bisque de Crevettes

1 carrot, peeled and diced
½ small onion, peeled and diced
2 parsley stalks, chopped
1 sprig thyme
½ bay leaf
1¼ sticks butter
1 lb raw shrimp in shell, washed
salt
pepper
1 tablespoon brandy
1 cup dry white wine
1 quart White Stock, page 9, or Chicken Stock, page 9
⅔ cup long-grain rice
5 tablespoons heavy cream
cayenne pepper

Fry the vegetables and herbs in 2 tablespoons of the butter until golden brown, then add the shrimp and cook together for a few minutes. Season with salt and pepper, sprinkle with the brandy and wine and allow to cook gently to reduce. Add ¾ cup of the stock and allow to cook gently for 10 minutes. Cook the rice in another 2 cups of the stock.

Shell some of the shrimp and reserve for garnishing. Finely pound the remainder of the shrimp in shell and add the rice and its cooking liquid together with the cooking liquid from the shrimp. Pass through a fine sieve and dilute with the remaining 1¼ cups of stock. Bring to a boil, pass through a fine strainer and keep warm in a *bain-marie*.

Finish the bisque before serving with the rest of the butter and the cream. Correct the seasoning and add a little cayenne pepper.

Garnish with the reserved shelled shrimp. *See photograph on page 15.*

SERVES 6

Creamed Fish Soup

Velouté d'Eperlans

2 cups soft white bread crumbs
2½ cups boiling milk
¼ lb fillets of smelt
½ lb fillet of whiting, cod or sole
1 small onion, peeled and finely chopped
2 tablespoons lemon juice
1½ sticks butter
½ cup Fish Stock, page 9
4 egg yolks
½ cup heavy cream
cayenne pepper

Make a light *panada* by simmering the bread crumbs in the boiling milk for about 10 minutes. Meanwhile, stew together the fish and the onion with the lemon juice and 6 tablespoons of the butter for a few minutes, then add the milk panada.

When all the ingredients are cooked, pass them through a fine sieve or process in a blender and then sieve. Adjust the consistency with the fish stock, strain and reheat without boiling.

Finish with a *liaison* of egg yolks and cream, and blend in the remaining butter. Season lightly with cayenne pepper.

SERVES 6

Endive, Leek and Potato Soup

Soupe à l'Ardennaise

1¼ sticks butter
¾ lb Belgian endive, shredded
2 leeks, white part only, shredded
¼ lb potato, peeled and cut into small square slices
1 quart boiling milk
salt
pepper

Melt half the butter in a pan, add all the vegetables and cook gently for a few minutes. Then add the boiling milk, season and simmer gently until the vegetables are cooked.

Finish at the last minute by adding the remaining butter. Serve with thin slices of French bread.

SERVES 6

Vegetable Soup with Milk

Soupe à la Dauphinoise

¼ lb turnip, peeled
¼ lb summer squash flesh (scant 1 cup)
¼ lb potato, peeled
3 tablespoons butter
2 cups water
2 cups milk
salt
pepper
4 leaves of chard or mustard greens, shredded
1 oz vermicelli
6 sprigs chervil or parsley

Cut the vegetables into small square or round slices and cook them gently with the butter. Add the water and milk, season and, when the vegetables are half-cooked, add the shredded leaves of chard or mustard greens.

About 15 minutes before the soup is cooked, sprinkle in the vermicelli. Garnish each bowl with a sprig of chervil.

SERVES 6

Carrot and Brussels Sprout Soup

Soupe à la Nevers

½ lb very small Brussels sprouts, trimmed
1 stick butter
½ lb carrots, peeled and sliced
5 cups White Stock, page 9
salt
pepper
1 oz vermicelli

To garnish
6 small sprigs chervil

Blanch the Brussels sprouts and stew them in half the butter for about 20 minutes or until almost cooked. Meanwhile stew the carrots in the remaining butter for about 20 minutes. Add a little of the stock to the carrots, season and finish cooking them in the stock.

About 20 minutes before serving, add the sprouts to the carrots, along with the remaining stock. Sprinkle in the vermicelli and finish cooking everything together.

Check and adjust the seasoning. Garnish each bowl of soup with a small sprig of chervil.

SERVES 6

Garlic Soup

Soupe à l'Ail

1½ quarts water
40 small cloves garlic, peeled and crushed
2 small sprigs sage
2 cloves
salt
pepper
1 loaf French bread
¾ cup grated cheese
olive oil

Bring the water to a boil with the garlic, sage, cloves and seasoning, and allow to simmer gently for 15 minutes. Meanwhile, cut 12 small slices of French bread, sprinkle with grated cheese and place them in a moderate oven (350°F) to bake for a few minutes and melt the cheese. Place these melted cheese croûtons in a warmed soup tureen, sprinkle with a little olive oil and pour the soup over them through a fine strainer, lightly pressing the ingredients as you do so. Allow the bread to soak and swell for 2 minutes before serving.

SERVES 6

Artichoke Cream Soup

Crème d'Artichauts à la Noisette

6 medium artichoke bottoms
3 tablespoons butter
2½ cups light Béchamel Sauce, page 12
4 hazelnuts, inner skin removed, lightly roasted and crushed
salt
pepper
½ cup White Stock, page 9
1 cup heavy cream

Blanch the artichoke bottoms, and stew them in the butter until they are soft, taking care not to allow them to color. Slice 5 of them.

Reserve the whole artichoke bottom for the garnish and add the others to the béchamel sauce, together with the hazelnuts and seasoning. Allow to cook gently for 10 minutes, then pass through a fine sieve or process in a blender. Adjust the consistency with the stock, strain and reheat.

Finish just before serving by stirring in the cream. Garnish with the reserved artichoke bottom cut into small dice.

SERVES 6

Vegetable Soup with Milk

Mushroom Soup Agnès Sorel

Crème Agnès Sorel

1 lb fresh white mushrooms
2 cups thin Béchamel Sauce, page 12
2 cups hot Chicken Stock, page 9
1¼ cups light cream

To garnish

¾ cup mushrooms cut into julienne and stewed in butter
3 tablespoons cooked chicken breast meat cut into julienne
6 tablespoons salted beef tongue cut into julienne

Wash the mushrooms and pass through a fine sieve or work in a food processor. Add the mushroom to the Béchamel Sauce and simmer very gently for 7–8 minutes. Pass through a fine sieve. Dilute to the required consistency with the hot stock. Strain again, reheat without allowing to boil and finish at the last moment with the cream.

Garnish each bowl of soup with a little of the cooked *julienne* of mushroom and the julienne of chicken and tongue.

SERVES 6

Cream of Lettuce Soup

Crème Choisy

1½ lb lettuce (about 3½ heads)
6 tablespoons butter
1 pinch sugar
2½ cups thin Béchamel Sauce, page 12
6 tablespoons hot White Stock, page 9
1½ cups light cream

To garnish

6 small sprigs chervil
3 cups small cubes of bread
4 tablespoons butter

Blanch the lettuce and refresh under cold running water. Drain and squeeze out all the moisture. Roughly shred the lettuce and stew with the butter, sugar and a little stock. Add the Béchamel Sauce and simmer gently for about 30 minutes. Pass through a fine sieve and adjust the consistency of the soup with the hot stock. Strain. Reheat the soup without allowing it to boil and finish at the last moment with the cream.

Garnish each bowl with a small sprig of chervil and the cubes of bread fried in the butter.

SERVES 6

Jerusalem Artichoke Soup

Potage Palestine

1 lb Jerusalem artichokes, peeled, sliced and placed
in acidulated water until ready to use
1¼ sticks butter
2 tablespoons shelled hazelnuts, inner skin removed, lightly
roasted and crushed
2½ cups White Stock, page 9
3 tablespoons arrowroot
½ cup cold milk

Cook the artichokes gently in 4 tablespoons of the butter for 5–10 minutes without browning, then add the hazelnuts, stock and a little seasoning. Heat to boiling point, reduce the heat and simmer gently until the artichokes are soft.

Purée the vegetables either by rubbing through a fine sieve or by processing in a blender. Adjust the consistency by thickening the soup with the arrowroot, previously mixed with the cold milk. Bring back to a boil and strain finely.

Reheat and finish with the remaining butter.

SERVES 6

Chicken and Okra Soup

Potage Okra

½ small onion, peeled and finely chopped
3 tablespoons butter
6 slices lean bacon, diced
¾ lb raw chicken meat, diced (about 2 cups)
5 cups Chicken Stock, page 9
¼ lb okra, sliced
⅔ cup roughly chopped tomato flesh
salt
pepper
Worcestershire sauce
2 tablespoons boiled long-grain rice

Fry the chopped onion gently in the butter without coloring it and add the bacon. Fry for a few more minutes until golden in color. Add the diced raw chicken meat and fry this also until golden, stirring frequently.

Add the Chicken Stock, bring to a boil and allow to simmer gently for 25 minutes without a lid. Then add the okra and tomato flesh and continue cooking gently for another 25 minutes. Skim, then season to taste with salt, pepper and a little Worcestershire sauce. Add the boiled rice and serve.

SERVES 6

Shepherd's Soup

Potage Pastorelle

3 cups sliced white of leek
½ small onion, peeled and sliced
1 cup sliced mushrooms
1 stick plus 2 tablespoons butter
3 cups White Stock, page 9
salt
pepper
1 lb potatoes, peeled and sliced
1¼ cups boiling milk

To garnish
¾ cup sliced small white mushrooms
6 tablespoons butter
⅓ cup peeled and diced potato

Stew the leek, onion and mushrooms in 4 tablespoons of the butter. Add the stock, season, add the sliced potato and simmer gently until soft. Pass through a fine sieve. Use the milk to adjust the consistency of the soup. Finish at the last moment with the rest of the butter.

To garnish, stew the mushrooms in half the butter and sauté the diced potato in the remaining butter until soft and golden brown. Garnish the soup with the mushrooms and potato.

SERVES 6

Soup Dubarry

Potage Dubarry

1 lb cauliflower, blanched
½ lb potatoes, peeled and sliced
1 quart milk
salt
1 stick butter

To garnish
6–8 sprigs fresh chervil
3 cups small cubes of bread
4 tablespoons butter

Cook the blanched cauliflower and the sliced potatoes in 3 cups of the milk. Season, then sieve finely.

Bring the remaining milk to a boil and use it to adjust the consistency of the soup. Finish with the butter. Garnish with sprigs of chervil and croûtons fried in butter.

SERVES 6–8

Green Bean Soup

Potage Cormeilles

1 lb fine green beans
1½ sticks butter
¾ lb potatoes, peeled and sliced
2½ cups White Stock, page 9
salt
pepper
1 cup boiling milk

Reserve about one-eighth of the beans to cook later, for the garnish, and blanch the rest of them in boiling water for 5 minutes. Drain then stew them together with 5 tablespoons of the butter and the potatoes. Add the stock, season and allow to simmer gently for about 30 minutes or until cooked. Pass through a fine sieve, or process in a blender and then sieve, and adjust the consistency with the boiling milk.

Finish with the remaining butter, then check the seasoning, adjusting if necessary. Garnish with the reserved green beans, freshly cooked and cut into diamond shapes.

SERVES 6

Creamed Pumpkin Soup

Potage Bressane

1½ lb (about 4–5 cups) pumpkin flesh
3 cups milk
salt
1 pinch sugar
10 cups white bread cubes
2 sticks butter
½ cup heavy cream

To garnish
¼ cup small Italian pasta shapes
milk

Cut the pumpkin into large pieces and put in a pan with the milk, salt and sugar. Bring to a boil.

Meanwhile fry the bread cubes in half the butter. Add these to the pan containing the pumpkin flesh and the milk and simmer all together gently for about 20 minutes. Pass through a fine sieve or process in a blender and then sieve.

Finish with the remaining butter and the cream, then check the seasoning, adjusting if necessary. Garnish with the small Italian pasta shapes cooked in milk.

SERVES 6–8

Fresh Pea Soup

Potage Saint-Germain

$1\frac{1}{2}$ lb (about 5 cups) shelled fresh peas
$1\frac{1}{4}$ sticks butter
2 leeks, green part only, sliced
$\frac{2}{3}$ cup shredded lettuce leaves
1 pinch salt
1 pinch sugar
1 pinch chopped fresh chervil or parsley
6 tablespoons water
$2\frac{1}{2}$ cups White Stock, page 9
6 sprigs chervil or parsley

Reserve some of the smallest peas for a garnish, then stew the rest of the peas gently together with 4 tablespoons of the butter, the leek, lettuce leaves, seasonings and water until they are cooked.

Pound them well or process in a blender, then pass through a fine sieve. Adjust consistency with the stock, reheat to boiling point and strain.

Reheat before serving. Cook the reserved peas in 1 tablespoon of the butter. Finish the soup at the last moment with the remaining butter. Garnish each bowl with a few of the reserved peas and a sprig of chervil.

SERVES 6

French Onion Soup

Potage Garbure-Cooper

$\frac{3}{4}$ lb onions, peeled and finely sliced
1 stick butter
1 quart White Stock, page 9
French bread, thinly sliced
1 cup grated Cheddar cheese

Fry the onions gently in half the butter until soft and golden brown. Add the stock and allow to simmer gently for 10 minutes.

Rub through a fine sieve or process in a blender and then sieve, then pour into a shallow ovenproof tureen or flat, individual ovenproof soup bowls. Cover the surface with thin slices of French bread and sprinkle the bread with the grated cheese. Melt the remaining butter and pour this over the top of the cheese.

Gratinate quickly in a very hot oven (500°F) and serve immediately.

SERVES 6

Fresh Tomato Soup

Potage Portugaise

$1\frac{1}{4}$ sticks butter
3 slices lean bacon, diced
$\frac{1}{2}$ small onion, peeled and chopped
1 carrot, peeled and chopped
1 sprig thyme
1 small bay leaf
$1\frac{1}{4}$ lb fresh ripe tomatoes, peeled, seeded and roughly chopped
1 clove garlic, peeled and minced
1 pinch sugar
$\frac{1}{2}$ cup long-grain rice
3 cups White Stock, page 9

To garnish
2 tablespoons diced tomato flesh lightly cooked in butter
2 tablespoons boiled long-grain rice

Heat 4 tablespoons of the butter in a pan and add the bacon, vegetables and herbs. Fry gently until golden brown. Add the roughly chopped tomato flesh, the minced clove of garlic, the sugar, rice and $2\frac{1}{2}$ cups of the stock.

Simmer gently until tender, then pass through a fine sieve or process in a blender. Adjust the consistency with the remaining stock, strain and reheat.

Finish at the last minute with the remaining butter. Garnish each bowl with a small quantity of cooked diced tomato flesh and boiled rice.

SERVES 6

Chicken, Leek and Potato Soup

Potage Réjane

2 leeks, white part only, cut into julienne
2 tablespoons butter
$\frac{1}{4}$ lb cooked white chicken meat, cut into julienne (scant 1 cup)
$2\frac{1}{2}$ cups boiling White Stock, page 9
$\frac{1}{4}$ lb potatoes, peeled and cut into julienne

Cook the leek gently in the butter until soft but not colored. Add the *julienne* of chicken and leek to the stock and simmer gently for 10 minutes, taking care that the soup does not become cloudy.

Then add the potatoes and simmer all together gently until cooked. Serve immediately.

SERVES 6

Fresh Pea Soup

Hors d'Oeuvre

Mussel and Celery Salad

Salade de Moules et Céleri

2 quarts mussels, cleaned
1 onion, sliced
large bunch of parsley stalks
pinch crushed peppercorns
1 cup water
1 small bunch crisp celery, very finely sliced

Mustard Sauce
1½ tablespoons dry mustard
juice of ½ small lemon
¾ cup heavy cream
salt
freshly ground black pepper

Place the mussels in a deep pan with the onion, parsley stalks, crushed peppercorns and water, then cover and cook at high heat for 5–7 minutes until the shells have opened. Remove the mussels from the shells and remove the beards. Use only the mussels which have opened during cooking.

Meanwhile make the Mustard Sauce. Mix the mustard and lemon juice in a bowl then add the cream, blending thoroughly together. Season with salt and flavor well with freshly ground black pepper.

Place the cooked mussels in a bowl with the finely sliced celery and toss lightly with the prepared sauce. The salad can either be served as it is in an hors d'oeuvre dish, or the mussels can be replaced in the half shells before arranging with the salad in the dish.

Serves 6

Dorzia Salad

Salade Dorzia

2 cucumbers
1 teaspoon salt
½ lb cooked white chicken meat
1¾ cups cold cooked long-grain rice

Vinaigrette
½ cup olive oil
2 tablespoons wine vinegar
1 teaspoon prepared mustard
1 teaspoon chopped capers
½ tablespoon chopped fresh parsley
½ tablespoon chopped fresh tarragon, chervil and chives, mixed
1½ tablespoons finely chopped onion
salt
pepper

Peel the cucumber, cut in half lengthwise, remove the seeds then cut into short *bâtons*. Place these in a colander, lightly salt and leave for 10–15 minutes to drain. Rinse and remove from the colander, pat dry with a clean dishtowel or paper towels and put the bâtons in a salad bowl.

Cut the chicken into short *julienne* and add these to the cucumber along with the cooked rice.

Make the vinaigrette by whisking all the ingredients together thoroughly. Pour over the salad and mix lightly.

Serves 6

Celeriac Salad

Salade de Céleri-rave

1 lb celeriac, peeled
1½ tablespoons dry mustard
a few drops lemon juice
⅔ cup heavy cream
1 pinch salt
freshly ground black pepper

Cut the raw celeriac into thick *julienne*. Make a Mustard Sauce according to the instructions given in the recipe for Mussel and Celery Salad, page 24, but using the ingredients listed above. Mix the julienne of raw celeriac well with the sauce.

SERVES 4–6

Salt Cod Croquettes

Croquettes de Morue à l'Américaine

1½ lb dried salt cod
1½ lb potatoes, peeled and cut into pieces
salt
6 tablespoons butter
pepper
grated nutmeg
2 egg yolks
2 tablespoons very thick Béchamel Sauce, page 12
flour
1 beaten egg
dry white bread crumbs
oil for deep frying

Soak the fish in cold water for 24 hours, changing the water 2–3 times. Poach it gently in water for 10–15 minutes and flake it, removing any skin and bones.

Cook the potatoes quickly in salted water until they are just cooked. Drain, dry out in the oven, and pass them through a sieve. Replace in the pan, add the butter, salt, pepper and grated nutmeg to taste, and beat well over heat. Then remove from the heat and mix in the egg yolks.

Mix the flaked fish with the mashed potato and add the thick Béchamel Sauce. Mold the mixture into walnut-sized balls on a well-floured surface, then roll each one in the beaten egg and bread crumbs and fry them in hot or very hot deep oil (350°–375°F) until golden brown. These croquettes are best served with Tomato Sauce, page 14.

SERVES 6

Marinated Herring

Harengs à la Dieppoise

6 fresh herrings, cleaned
2 tablespoons butter

Marinade
2½ cups dry white wine
1¼ cups wine vinegar
2 carrots, peeled, fluted and thinly sliced
4 small onions, peeled and cut into rings
2 shallots, peeled and sliced
1 sprig thyme
2 bay leaves
4 parsley stalks
10 peppercorns
salt

To garnish
1 lemon, fluted and sliced

Prepare the marinade in advance by mixing all the ingredients together, seasoning with salt, bringing the marinade to a boil and simmering gently for 10 minutes. Arrange the herrings in a shallow, buttered pan and cover with the boiling marinade.

Poach the herrings gently for 12 minutes and allow them to cool in the liquid. When cool, chill them further in the refrigerator.

Serve the herrings very cold with a spoonful or two of the cooking liquid. Garnish with some of the carrot slices and onion rings and slices of *fluted lemon*.

SERVES 6

Shrimp Canapés

Canapés aux Crevettes

Canapés, or toasts, are made from white bread cut into various shapes and no more than ¼ inch thick. These are then either fried in *clarified butter* or, more usually, toasted.

To make these Shrimp Canapés, coat round toasts with a pink shrimp butter, made by pounding cooked shrimp to a fine paste, then mixing this paste with an equal quantity of well-softened butter and passing the mixture through a fine sieve.

Then pipe a border around each round toast using the pink shrimp butter in a pastry bag with fancy tubes. Fill the centers with a rose pattern of shrimp and finish each canapé with a caper in the middle. *See photograph on page 27.*

Niçoise Beignets

Beignets à la Niçoise

A beignet is any food or mixture of foods which has been dipped in a fritter batter and then deep fried.

Niçoise Beignets are made using round slices of raw fresh tuna fish, about 1–1½ inches in diameter and ¾ inch thick. Wrap each slice with thin strips of anchovy fillet marinaded in oil.

Dip in light Fritter Batter (see below) and deep fry immediately in very hot oil (375°F). Arrange on a napkin in neat piles and garnish with a border of deep-fried parsley.

Fritter Batter

Pâte à Frire

scant 1 cup flour, sifted
1 pinch salt
2 tablespoons olive oil or melted butter
1 cup lukewarm water
2 egg whites

If the batter is required for immediate use, place all the ingredients except for the egg whites in a bowl and mix by turning them over gently with a wooden spoon. This prevents the batter from becoming elastic (an elastic batter will not stick to the items dipped into it). If the batter is prepared in advance, all the ingredients except for the egg whites can be mixed well and then allowed to rest for a while, during which time the batter will lose its elasticity.

Whisk the egg whites stiffly and fold these into the batter immediately before use.

MAKES APPROXIMATELY 2 CUPS

Spinach Barquettes

Barquettes de Laitances à la Florentine

Barquettes differ from tartlets only in their shape, which is a sort of pointed oval as opposed to round. Barquette tins are generally lined with either Basic Pie Pastry (opposite) or Puff Pastry, page 28, and baked blind (unfilled) to a golden color.

These particular barquettes are filled with roughly chopped spinach, which has been gently cooked with a little butter. Poach some soft herring roe lightly in dry white wine, and place a slice of roe on top of each filled barquette. Coat with well-seasoned Mornay Sauce, page 13, sprinkle with Parmesan and gratinate lightly under a hot broiler.

Anchovy Medallions

Médaillons d'Anchois

Wrap fillets of anchovy, marinaded in oil, around the edges of thick slices of cooked potato or baked beet. Then fill the centers, according to taste, with chopped hard-boiled egg, caviar or a purée of cooked soft herring roes.

Danish-style Cucumber

Concombres à la Danoise

3 cucumbers
½ lb smoked salmon
½ lb smoked herring
3 hard-boiled eggs

To garnish
a little grated horseradish

Cut the cucumbers into halves, and then into sections; scoop out the seeds from the middle of each section, then trim each section into rounded boat-shaped barquettes. Purée the smoked salmon, dice the herring and finely chop the hard-boiled eggs: mix together carefully. Then fill the centers of the cucumber cases with this mixture and sprinkle the surface of the stuffed cucumbers with a little grated horseradish.

SERVES 6

Basic Pie Pastry

Pâte à Foncer

2 cups flour, sifted
1 pinch salt
1¼ sticks butter, softened
4–6 tablespoons water

Make a well in the flour and place the salt, butter and water in the center. Mix the flour gradually into the butter and water until it is incorporated and forms a paste. Mix the pastry dough together for a moment, then press it firmly between the palm of the hand and the worktop, pushing small pieces away from the main ball with the heel of the hand, thus assuring the complete blending of all the ingredients. Do this twice.

Form into a ball then wrap in a cloth and place in the refrigerator, preferably for a few hours, before use.

MAKES APPROXIMATELY ¾ LB

(from left to right)
Chicken and Mushroom Bouchées, Danish-style Cucumber, Shrimp Canapés

Chicken and Mushroom Bouchées

Bouchées à la Reine

Bouchées (or vol-au-vent or patty shells) which are being served as an hors d'oeuvre are normally slightly smaller than usual, ideally only a mouthful each. Their shape often varies according to the type of filling.

To make Chicken and Mushroom Bouchées, prepare some fancy, round vol-au-vent cases using Puff Pastry (see below). The classic filling for these is a creamed chicken purée but modern practice is to use a *salpicon* of diced cooked white chicken meat, mushrooms and truffles. This is then mixed with a Velouté Sauce, pages 9–10, enriched with *mushroom cooking liquid* and egg yolks, flavored with lemon juice and black pepper, and finished with a little extra butter. (This variation on velouté is known as Allemande Sauce or Parisienne Sauce.) Use the pastry tops as lids. *See photograph on page 27.*

Puff Pastry

Feuilletage

2 cups flour
1 pinch salt
$\frac{1}{2}$–$\frac{3}{4}$ cup cold water
2 sticks butter

Sift the flour and salt together and make a well in the center. Add the cold water and mix to a paste. Roll into a ball without working it too much and leave to rest for 20 minutes. Meanwhile, work the butter until it has the same texture as the dough. Roll the paste out evenly to form a 6-inch square of even thickness. Place the well-kneaded butter in the center and fold over the edges of the paste to enclose it completely, thus forming a square block. Allow to rest for 20 minutes.

Roll out the paste and give it two turns, as follows. First of all, roll it out to form an oblong 16 inches long by 6 inches wide, then fold it in three. Turn this package through 90° and roll out and fold as before. Turn the package through 90° again.

Allow the paste to rest for 10 minutes in the refrigerator, then roll the dough out twice more, turning the package through 90° after each folding. Allow to rest for another 10 minutes in the refrigerator and repeat the procedure.

After six turns, and 30 minutes' rest in the refrigerator, the puff pastry is ready for use. Trimmings left over after use should be reassembled into a ball and kept in the refrigerator. They can then be used to make small tartlet and barquette cases.

MAKES APPROXIMATELY $1\frac{1}{4}$ LB

Poached Red Mullet

Rougets au Safran

6 small red mullets or snappers, cleaned
olive oil
6 tomatoes
$2\frac{1}{2}$ cups dry white wine
1 pinch salt
6 peppercorns
4 parsley stalks
1 tablespoon chopped fresh fennel
1 sprig thyme
1 bay leaf
1 clove garlic, peeled and minced
10 coriander seeds
1 large pinch saffron threads

To garnish
1 lemon, fluted and sliced
sprigs of fennel

Put the fish in a well-oiled flameproof dish. Peel and core the tomatoes, remove the seeds and chop the tomato flesh roughly. Place this around the fish. Cover with white wine and add all the flavorings.

Bring to a boil, cover and place in a moderate oven (350°F). Monitor the oven temperature so as to ensure that the fish simmers very gently for 10–12 minutes, then remove from the oven and allow the fish to cool fully in the cooking liquid.

Serve with a little of the cooking liquid, vegetables and flavorings and garnish with slices of carefully *fluted lemon* and sprigs of fennel.

SERVES 6

Poached Red Mullet

EGG DISHES

Scrambled Eggs with Kidneys

Oeufs Brouillés d'Aumale

4 tablespoons butter
½ lb ripe, red tomatoes, peeled, seeded and chopped
½ veal kidney
salt
pepper

Madeira Sauce
½ cup Espagnole Sauce, page 10
5 tablespoons Brown Stock, page 8
½ tablespoon Meat Glaze, page 9
1 tablespoon dry Madeira

Scrambled Eggs
8 eggs
1 stick butter
2 tablespoons heavy cream
1 pinch chopped fresh parsley

Heat 2 tablespoons of the butter in a pan, add the tomato flesh and cook gently and carefully to a smooth, almost dry paste. Keep warm.

Meanwhile, skin, core and cut the kidney into small dice, season and sauté quickly in the remaining 2 tablespoons of butter, then drain and place in a clean saucepan. Place the Espagnole Sauce and Brown Stock in another saucepan and reduce by approximately one-third. Add the meat glaze, season well and pass through a fine strainer over the diced and sautéed kidney. Reheat but do not re-boil, then add and shake in the Madeira and keep warm.

To make the scrambled eggs, first beat the eggs carefully with a whisk without making them frothy, then season lightly. Gently heat half of the butter in a small heavy pan (not aluminum) and add the beaten eggs. Place over a moderate heat. Stir continuously with a wooden spoon, taking care that the heat remains even; cooking the eggs too rapidly will cause lumps to form which impare the essential quality of the dish.

When the eggs have obtained a light, smooth texture, and before they become over-set and hard, remove the pan from the heat. Now quickly mix in the remaining butter, then the prepared tomatoes and the heavy cream and place in a deep, warmed serving dish. Make a hollow in the center of the eggs and fill this with the mixture of kidney and Madeira sauce. Sprinkle the kidney with a pinch of chopped parsley and serve.

SERVES 4–6

Eggs Brittany-style

Oeufs à la Bretonne

6 eggs
⅔ cup sliced mushrooms
6 tablespoons butter
1 small onion, peeled and finely sliced
1 large leek, white part only, finely sliced
½ cup White Stock, page 9
1¼ cups Béchamel Sauce, page 12

Hard-boil the eggs. Meanwhile, sauté the mushrooms in 2 tablespoons of the butter and put to one side.

Stew the onion and leek gently for a few minutes in the remaining butter and finish cooking them by adding the stock and simmering gently until quite soft. Then add the cooked mushrooms and the Béchamel Sauce.

Cut the hard-boiled eggs in half lengthwise. Pour a third of the vegetable and béchamel mixture into the bottom of a serving dish and arrange the eggs on top. Cover with the remaining vegetables and sauce.

SERVES 6

Baked Eggs Montmorency

Oeufs sur le Plat Montmorency

4 heaped tablespoons creamed asparagus tips
4 eggs

To garnish
4 artichoke bottoms
2 tablespoons butter
16 asparagus tips

Place a tablespoon of creamed asparagus tips in four individual ovenproof dishes, break in the eggs and bake in a moderate oven (375°F) for about 8–10 minutes. Meanwhile, blanch the artichoke bottoms, slice them and fry in the butter.

When the eggs are cooked, garnish each one with 4 green asparagus tips and the fried slices of artichoke bottom.

SERVES 4

Poached Eggs in a Cradle

Oeufs Pochés en Berceau

4 medium potatoes
½ lb cooked white chicken meat
3 tablespoons heavy cream
4 eggs

Aurora Sauce
1¼ cups Velouté Sauce, pages 9–10, warmed
2 tablespoons Tomato Fondue, page 14, warmed
2 tablespoons butter

Bake the potatoes and keep warm. Meanwhile, finely chop the cooked chicken meat and warm through in the cream.

To make the Aurora Sauce, add the Tomato Fondue to the Velouté Sauce and finish with the butter. Poach the eggs.

Cut off a third from the tops of the cooked potatoes and scoop out some of the insides, leaving the potatoes in the shape of a crib or cradle. Put the chicken and cream mixture inside the potatoes. Coat the eggs with the Aurora Sauce and place an egg on top of each potato.

SERVES 4

Eggs Portuguese-style

Oeufs à la Portugaise

4 eggs
4 large firm tomatoes
salt
pepper
2 tablespoons olive oil
1 tablespoon coarsely chopped fresh parsley

Sauce Portuguese
2 tablespoons olive oil
1 small onion, peeled and very finely chopped
¾ lb tomatoes, peeled, seeded and roughly chopped
1 clove garlic, peeled and minced
salt
pepper
1 pinch sugar
½ tablespoon tomato paste

First make the Portuguese Sauce. Heat the oil in a pan, add the onion and fry quickly until golden. Add the roughly chopped tomato flesh along with the garlic, seasoning, sugar and tomato paste. Cover the pan with a lid and allow to simmer gently until well flavored and fairly thick.

Hard-boil the eggs. Meanwhile, cut the 4 large firm tomatoes in half and hollow out their centers. Season lightly and fry them very gently in the oil until slightly softened.

Place half a hot hard-boiled egg on each half tomato. Coat with the hot, thick sauce. Place a pinch of the chopped parsley on each and serve.

SERVES 4

Baked Eggs Savoyarde

Oeufs sur le Plat à la Savoyarde

¾ lb potatoes, peeled and thinly sliced
4 tablespoons butter
¾ cup grated Gruyère cheese
4 eggs
½ cup heavy cream

Fry the thin slices of potato gently in the butter until just soft. Then divide them between four individual ovenproof dishes and sprinkle with the grated cheese. Break in the eggs, coat each one with 2 tablespoons of cream, and bake in a hot oven (425°F) for about 5 minutes.

SERVES 4

Baked Eggs Mirabeau

Oeufs sur le Plat Mirabeau

4 anchovy fillets
4 tablespoons butter, softened
4 eggs

To garnish
4 large black olives, halved and pitted
2 tablespoons fresh tarragon leaves, blanched
8–10 thin strips of anchovy fillet

Pound the anchovy fillets to a fine paste, then add and mix in three quarters of the softened butter and pass through a fine sieve. Coat four individual ovenproof dishes with this anchovy butter, break an egg into each dish and bake in a moderate oven (375°F) for about 8–10 minutes.

When the eggs are ready, garnish each one with two large halves of black olives filled with the rest of the butter mixed with some finely chopped tarragon leaves. Surround each yolk with thin strips of anchovy fillet, and decorate with the remaining blanched tarragon leaves.

SERVES 4

Baked Eggs with Endive

Oeufs à la Bruxelloise

½ lb Belgian endive, washed
6 tablespoons butter
½ cup Chicken Stock, page 9
½ cup Béchamel Sauce, page 12
4 eggs
2 biscottes, finely crushed, or dry bread crumbs

Braise the whole endive heads in a single layer in a covered dish with half of the butter and all of the Chicken Stock in a moderate oven (325°F) for about an hour. Then slice the endive and reheat it in the remaining butter and the Béchamel Sauce.

Cover the bottom of four ramekins or custard cups with the endive, make an indentation with the back of a spoon in each and break one egg into each indentation. Sprinkle lightly with the finely crushed *biscottes* and bake in a hot oven (425°F) for about 5 minutes or until the eggs are lightly set. Serve immediately.

SERVES 4

Baked Eggs Maximilian

Oeufs Maximilienne

2 large tomatoes
1 tablespoon olive oil
2 tablespoons chopped fresh parsley
1 clove garlic, peeled and minced
4 eggs
¾ cup grated Parmesan cheese
1 tablespoon fried bread crumbs

Cut the tomatoes in half, discard the seeds and fry the halves gently in the oil. Sprinkle the insides with 1 tablespoon of the chopped parsley mixed with the minced garlic.

Break an egg onto each half tomato. Sprinkle with the grated cheese, mixed with the rest of the chopped parsley and the fried bread crumbs.

Place them in a moderately hot oven (400°F) for about 8–10 minutes to cook and gratinate at the same time. Serve immediately.

SERVES 4

Baked Eggs Florentine

Oeufs en Cocotte à la Florentine

½ lb spinach leaves, lightly cooked and roughly chopped
3 tablespoons butter
2 tablespoons heavy cream, heated to boiling point
4 eggs
¼ cup grated Parmesan cheese

Stew the lightly cooked and roughly chopped spinach leaves in most of the butter, reserving a little to grease four ovenproof egg *cocotte* dishes or custard cups. Line these dishes with the stewed spinach and add ½ tablespoon of boiling cream to each one.

Break in the eggs and sprinkle with the grated Parmesan. Cook in a *bain-marie* in the oven, without a lid, so that the eggs cook and the tops become glazed at one and the same time. This will take about 8–10 minutes in a moderate oven (375°F). Serve immediately.

SERVES 4

Baked Eggs Mirabeau

Egg and Chicken Tartlets

Oeufs à la d'Orléans

½ lb cooked chicken breast meat
¼ cup fresh Tomato Sauce, page 14
4 cooked tartlet cases
¼ cup shelled pistachios, freshly skinned
2 tablespoons butter, softened
½ cup hot Béchamel Sauce, page 12
4 eggs

Cut the cooked chicken meat into small dice and bind it with the tomato sauce. Fill the tartlet cases (made using Basic Pie Pastry, page 26) with this *salpicon* of chicken. Keep warm.

Pound the pistachios until fine or grind them in a food processor, moistening with a few drops of water to form a paste. Add the softened butter, mix together and pass through a fine sieve. Add this to the béchamel before using as below.

Meanwhile, poach or soft-boil the eggs. Coat them with the pistachio-flavored béchamel and place one on each prepared tartlet.

SERVES 4

Eggs Serbian-style

Oeufs à la Serbe

1 medium eggplant, diced
4 tablespoons olive oil
4 slices lean bacon
4 eggs

Pilaff

1 small onion, peeled and chopped
6 tablespoons butter
⅔ cup unwashed Patna rice
1½ cups White Stock, page 9

To prepare the rice, fry the onion gently in half the butter until golden brown. Add the rice and continue to fry. Add the stock, cover with a lid and cook in a moderate oven (350°F) for 18 minutes.

Meanwhile, fry the diced eggplant gently in half the olive oil. As soon as the rice is cooked, turn it on to a serving dish. Fork in the remaining butter and add the fried eggplant.

Broil or fry the bacon. Heat the remaining oil and quickly fry the eggs on both sides until the whites are crisp. Arrange the eggs and bacon on top of the prepared rice.

SERVES 4

Egg and Vegetable Tartlets

Oeufs Froids à la Niçoise

4 cooked tartlet cases
½ cup diced tomato flesh
¼ lb cold cooked green beans, diced
¼ lb cold boiled potatoes, diced
4 eggs
½ cup Mayonnaise, page 13
2 tablespoons puréed tomato flesh

Fill the tartlet cases (made using Basic Pie Pastry, page 26) with a mixture of tomato, beans and potato. Poach the eggs, then cool, drain and dry them. Place one on top of each prepared tartlet. Mix the mayonnaise with the fresh tomato purée and use this to coat the eggs.

SERVES 4

Poached Eggs Chivry

Oeufs Mollets Chivry

¼ lb spinach leaves
2 oz sorrel leaves
1 oz watercress leaves (about ½ cup)
⅔ cup Béchamel Sauce, page 12
2 tablespoons butter
6 eggs
6 cooked tartlet cases

Chivry Sauce

5 tablespoons dry white wine
2 large sprigs chervil and parsley, chopped
2 pinches chopped fresh tarragon, chives and shallot
1¼ cups Velouté Sauce, pages 9–10, heated to boiling
2 tablespoons butter, softened

Blanch the spinach, sorrel and watercress leaves. Refresh, drain and squeeze out all the moisture. Pound with the béchamel, then sieve and reheat with the butter.

To make the Chivry Sauce, bring the wine to a boil in a pan, add half quantities of each of the herbs and all of the shallot and allow to infuse for 10 minutes. Strain. Add to the velouté and finish, away from the heat, with the butter, flavored and colored with the remaining herbs.

Soft-boil the eggs. Place a little of the green vegetable purée in each tartlet case (made using Basic Pie Pastry, page 26) and set an egg coated with Chivry Sauce on top.

SERVES 6

Egg and Chicken Tartlets

Omelettes

The theory of the preparation of an omelette is both straightforward and, at the same time, complicated, for the simple reason that people's tastes for this dish are very different – some like their omelettes firm and well done, while others prefer them runny and underdone. The important thing is to know – and respect – the preferences of your guests.

The actual method of preparation of the omelette – which is, after all, no more than a special type of scrambled egg enclosed in a coating of coagulated egg – is a question of practice and manual dexterity. The eggs should be seasoned with a small pinch of fine salt and a touch of pepper, and then well beaten until the yolks and whites are thoroughly blended. Heat a little butter – 1 tablespoon for 3 eggs – until it is just beginning to turn brown. This will not only give an excellent flavor to the omelette but will also provide the required amount of heat necessary to ensure the correct setting of the eggs. Pour in the beaten, seasoned eggs, shake the pan and stir briskly with a fork to ensure even cooking.

If the omelette is to be stuffed with a garnish, this should be placed in the center at this stage, and the omelette should then be quickly folded, rolled into shape and turned over on to a serving dish. When the omelette is on the dish and ready for the table draw a piece of butter, held on the point of a knife, over it in order to make its surface glossy.

Chicken Liver Omelette

Omelette Chasseur

3 eggs
1 pinch fine salt
pepper
2 chicken livers, each cut in half
4 tablespoons butter
¼ cup Chasseur Sauce, page 12
1 pinch chopped fresh parsley

Beat the eggs and season. Gently fry the chicken livers in half the butter, drain and mix with one tablespoonful of the Chasseur Sauce. Make the omelette in the usual way (see above) using the remaining butter, and fill and roll with half of the chicken liver mixture. Run a knife lengthwise along the top of the omelette and place the rest of the chicken liver mixture in this opening. Sprinkle with chopped fresh parsley.

Surround the omelette with a *cordon* of the remaining Chasseur Sauce.

SERVES 1 OR 2

Omelette Durand

Omelette Durand

3 eggs
1 pinch fine salt
pepper
¼ cup sliced mushrooms
2 tablespoons blanched and sliced artichoke bottom
4 tablespoons butter
2 slices truffle, cut into julienne
1 tablespoon sliced asparagus tips
1 tablespoon Velouté Sauce, pages 9–10
¼ cup tomato-flavored Demi-glace Sauce, page 10

Beat the eggs and season. Fry the mushroom and artichoke bottom in half the butter until soft, then add this mixture to the beaten eggs.

Make the omelette in the usual way (see left) and fill and roll it with the *julienne* of truffle and sliced asparagus tips mixed with the Velouté Sauce. Surround the finished omelette with a *cordon* of tomato-flavored Demi-glace Sauce.

SERVES 1 OR 2

Omelette with Herring Roe

Omelette à la Boulonnaise

3 eggs
1 pinch fine salt
pepper
1 herring roe
2 tablespoons butter

Maître d'Hôtel Butter
2 tablespoons butter, softened
1 teaspoon chopped fresh parsley
salt
pepper
a few drops lemon juice

Beat the eggs until whites and yolks are thoroughly blended and season. Fry the herring roe gently in half the butter. Prepare the Maître d'Hôtel Butter by mixing together all the ingredients listed.

Make the omelette in the usual way (see above left) then fill and roll the omelette with the cooked herring roe and a pat of the prepared butter. Draw any remaining Maître d'Hôtel Butter over the top of the omelette before serving.

SERVES 1 OR 2

Tuna Omelette

Omelette au Thon

3 eggs
pepper
2 heaped tablespoons canned tuna fish in oil, flaked
6 anchovy fillets
5 tablespoons butter

Beat the eggs and season with pepper. Add the flaked tuna fish. Finely pound the anchovy fillets and soften 4 tablespoons of the butter. Mix the butter and anchovy fillets together, pass through a fine sieve, melt and reserve.

Make the omelette in the usual way (see page 36) using the remaining butter. Pour 2 tablespoons of melted anchovy butter over the omelette and serve.

SERVES 1 OR 2

Bacon and Sorrel Omelette

Omelette Jurassienne

3 eggs
1 pinch fine salt
1 pinch chopped fresh chives
1 pinch chopped fresh chervil or parsley
1 tablespoon shredded sorrel leaves
1 tablespoon butter
2 slices bacon, cut in small bâtons

Beat the eggs, season and add the chopped chives and chervil. Stew the sorrel gently in the butter.

Fry the bacon gently in the omelette pan until the fat runs, add the beaten egg mixture and cook the omelette in the bacon fat. Fill and roll the omelette with the sorrel leaves.

SERVES 1 OR 2

Mexican Omelette

Omelette Mexicaine

3 eggs
1 pinch fine salt
pepper
$\frac{1}{3}$ cup sliced mushrooms
3 tablespoons butter
1 tablespoon chopped sweet red pepper
$\frac{1}{4}$ cup Tomato Fondue, page 14

Beat the eggs and season. Gently fry the mushroom slices in half the butter and add these to the egg mixture, along with the chopped red pepper. Make the omelette in the usual way (see page 36), using the rest of the butter, and fill and roll with the thick Tomato Fondue.

SERVES 1 OR 2

Pea and Lettuce Omelette

Omelette Clamart

3 tablespoons fresh peas
2 shredded lettuce leaves
4 tablespoons butter
3 eggs
1 pinch fine salt
pepper

Cook the peas with the shredded lettuce leaves, then toss both with half the butter. Meanwhile, beat the eggs well and season with fine salt and pepper.

Make the omelette in the usual way (see page 36) using the remaining butter, and fill and roll with 2 tablespoons of peas and lettuce. Slit the top of the omelette and arrange the remaining peas and lettuce in this. Serve immediately. *See photograph on page 39.*

SERVES 1 OR 2

Brussels Omelette

Omelette à la Bruxelloise

3 eggs
1 pinch fine salt
1 tablespoon butter
1 small head Belgian endive, braised and shredded
2 tablespoons heavy cream

Cream Sauce

$\frac{1}{4}$ cup hot Béchamel Sauce, page 12
$\frac{1}{2}$ tablespoon heavy cream
a few drops lemon juice

Beat the eggs, season and make the omelette in the usual way (see page 36). Fill and roll with the braised endive mixed with the cream. Surround the omelette with a *cordon* of hot Cream Sauce, made by mixing all the ingredients together.

SERVES 1 OR 2

Carrot Omelette

Omelette Crécy

3 eggs
1 pinch fine salt
pepper
1 small carrot, peeled and finely sliced
4 tablespoons butter
1 small pinch sugar

Cream Sauce
¼ cup hot Béchamel Sauce, page 12
½ tablespoon heavy cream
a few drops lemon juice

Beat the eggs and season. Stew the carrot slices very gently until soft in the butter with a little sugar, then pass half of them through a fine sieve.

Make the omelette in the usual way (see page 36) and fill and roll with the carrot purée. Garnish the omelette with the remaining slices of carrot and surround with a *cordon* of hot Cream Sauce, made by mixing all the ingredients together.

SERVES 1 OR 2

Fresh Herb Omelette

Omelette aux Fines Herbes

3 eggs
1 pinch fine salt
pepper
1 tablespoon chopped fresh fines herbes*: parsley, chives, chervil and tarragon*
1 tablespoon butter

Beat the eggs, season and add the tablespoon of mixed herbs. (It is quite incorrect to consider an omelette made with only one of these herbs – such as parsley – as a real herb omelette. Authenticity requires the combination specified above.)

Heat the butter in the omelette pan and cook the omelette in the usual way (see page 36).

SERVES 1 OR 2

Brittany Omelette

Omelette Bretonne

3 eggs
1 pinch fine salt
pepper
½ tablespoon shredded onion
½ tablespoon shredded white of leek
½ tablespoon very finely sliced mushroom
2 tablespoons butter

Beat the eggs well until the whites and yolks are thoroughly blended, then season. Stew the vegetables in ½ tablespoon butter and add them to the beaten, seasoned eggs. Heat 1 tablespoon butter in an omelette pan until it just begins to turn brown.

Pour in the egg mixture, shake the pan and stir the egg briskly with a fork to ensure even cooking. Cook to taste, then fold the omelette quickly, roll into an oval shape and turn on to a suitable dish. Rub the remaining butter over the omelette's surface to make it glossy.

SERVES 1 OR 2

Soufflé Omelette

Omelette Mousseline

3 eggs
1 small pinch fine salt
1 tablespoon heavy cream
2 tablespoons butter

Separate the eggs and stiffly beat the egg whites. In a bowl, mix the egg yolks with the salt and cream. Fold in the stiffly beaten egg whites.

Heat the butter in the omelette pan and pour in the egg mixture when very hot. Shake the pan briskly and keep swirling the eggs quickly from the side of the pan to the center and back again. When the omelette is evenly set, fold it in the usual way and turn it on to a plate to be served immediately.

SERVES 1 OR 2

Pea and Lettuce Omelette

Fish & Shellfish

Fish Aspic

Gelée de Poisson

1½ quarts cold Fish Stock, page 9
3 oz fillet of whiting, ground
1 egg white
4 envelopes unflavored gelatin, softened
1¼ cups dry white wine or Champagne

Skim and decant the cold fish stock, discarding any sediment. Place the whiting and egg white in a thick-bottomed pan and add the stock, mixing well with a whisk or spatula. Slowly bring to a boil, stirring very gently and occasionally to ensure that the bottom of the pan is kept clean. Allow to simmer gently for 15 minutes without disturbance, then add the gelatin and simmer for a further 5 minutes. Pass through cheesecloth.

Finally, add the wine when the aspic is almost cold. It is advisable, though, to check the consistency of the aspic while simmering following the addition of the gelatin, as the later addition of the wine will dilute the aspic. This can be done by putting a little on a plate and placing it in the refrigerator until chilled. If the gel is insufficient, or is likely to be after the wine is added, a little extra gelatin may be used.

Makes approximately 1½ quarts

Court-bouillon with Vinegar

Court-bouillon au Vinaigre

Whole salmon and large cuts of salmon or trout are usually cooked in a prepared vinegar or wine court-bouillon, started from cold. They should be covered and brought slowly to a boil, then allowed almost to finish cooking over a very gentle heat without further boiling (this will take between 10 and 15 minutes for a 1½ lb piece of salmon). Cool fully in the liquid.

1 quart water
¼ cup white wine vinegar
1 tablespoon coarse salt
¼ lb carrots, sliced
1 onion, sliced
1 sprig thyme
½ bay leaf
⅓ cup chopped fresh parsley
a few peppercorns

Place all the ingredients in a pan except for the peppercorns. Bring to a boil and simmer gently for about 1 hour. Add the peppercorns 10 minutes before the end, then strain. The court-bouillon is now ready for use.

Makes approximately 1 quart

Court-bouillon with White Wine

Court-bouillon au Vin Blanc

1 quart water
1 quart dry white wine
2 onions, peeled and sliced
large bunch of parsley stalks
1 sprig thyme
1 small bay leaf
3 tablespoons coarse salt
1 tablespoon peppercorns

Place all the ingredients except for the peppercorns in a pan, bring to a boil and simmer gently for 20 minutes. Then add the peppercorns, simmer for a further 10 minutes and strain. The court-bouillon is now ready for use.

Makes approximately 7 cups

Fine Stuffing for Fish

Farce Fine Pour Poissons

1 lb fish, such as salmon, trout, whiting or sole,
free from skin and bone
small pinch salt
small pinch white pepper
2 large egg whites
2½ cups heavy cream

Pound the fish with the seasonings, then add the egg whites one at a time. Beat well with a spatula between additions of egg white, then pass through a fine sieve. Alternatively, process in a food processor.

Place the fish purée in a shallow pan or bowl, smooth it over with a spatula and refrigerate for at least 2 hours. Then mix in the cream gradually and carefully until it has been completely incorporated. The stuffing is now ready to use.

MAKES APPROXIMATELY 1½ LB

Carp with Garlic

Carpe à la Juive

1 medium carp, weighing about 3½ lb
1 onion, peeled and finely chopped
¼ cup finely chopped shallot
1 cup olive oil
6 tablespoons flour
2 cups dry white wine
2 cups Fish Stock, page 9
1 small pinch cayenne pepper
5 cloves garlic, peeled and minced
1 bouquet garni
1 tablespoon coarsely chopped fresh parsley

Cut the carp into steaks, on the bone, about ½ inch thick. Fry the chopped onion and shallot very gently in ⅓ cup of the oil, without allowing them to color.

Put the fish steaks, onion and shallot in a fish kettle, cover with the lid and place over a moderate heat to start it cooking in its own juices for a few minutes. Sprinkle with the flour and cook for a few more minutes, without allowing the flour to color. Then add the white wine and the fish stock.

Season with salt and cayenne pepper and add the garlic, bouquet garni and another ⅓ cup of oil. Bring to a boil, cover and simmer very gently for 25 minutes.

Remove the pieces of fish and arrange them on a long dish in such a way as to give the appearance of a whole fish. Reduce the cooking liquid to one-third of its original volume, and gradually add the remaining oil, away from the heat, so as to thicken the liquid to the consistency of a sauce. Pour this over the carp and allow it to become quite cold and set.

Sprinkle with the coarsely chopped parsley before serving.

SERVES 6

Poached Pike with Sorrel

Grenadins de Brochet à l'Oseille

2½ lb fillets of pike, skinned and cut into thick slices
3 large gherkins, cut into thin strips 2 inches long
¼ lb carrots, peeled, cut into thin strips 2 inches long and blanched
6 tablespoons clarified butter
1¼ cups fish stock, made using the trimmings of the pike
⅔ cup Velouté Sauce, made using
fish stock, pages 9–10
1¼ sticks butter

Sorrel Purée

4 tablespoons butter
1 lb sorrel, stalks removed, washed
¼ cup thick Béchamel Sauce, page 12
2 tablespoons heavy cream

Remove any bones from the slices of pike carefully, then *lard* the pike with strips of gherkin and carrot, alternating the two colors. Heat the *clarified butter* in a flameproof dish and put the slices of pike in it to set the flesh.

Add the fish stock, cover loosely with a lid and poach in a hot oven (400°F) for about 20 minutes, basting from time to time. When the fish is almost cooked, remove the lid so as to allow it to glaze a little. Drain the fish slices and arrange them in a circle on a serving dish to keep warm.

Strain the cooking liquid, allow it to settle and then skim off the fat. Reduce the liquid to about one-third of its original volume. While the cooking liquid is reducing, make the sorrel purée by heating the butter in a pan, adding the sorrel and cooking it until all the moisture has evaporated. Pass through a sieve and reheat in a pan with the Béchamel Sauce and cream; season with salt and pepper.

When the pike cooking liquid is sufficiently reduced, thicken with the Velouté Sauce made from fish stock, enrich with the butter, and pour the sauce on to the serving dish over the fish slices. Serve accompanied by the puréed sorrel. *See photograph on page 43.*

SERVES 6

Cold Poached Salmon with Montpellier Butter

Saumon Froid au Beurre de Montpellier

1½ lb poached middle cut of salmon, on the bone, cold
2½ cups liquid Fish Aspic, page 40
6 oz truffles
4–6 hard-boiled eggs

Montpellier Butter
1 cup mixed fresh herbs, to include equal quantities of parsley, chervil, tarragon, chives and watercress
½ cup roughly chopped spinach leaves
2 tablespoons finely chopped shallot
2 small gherkins
½ tablespoon capers, drained
½ clove garlic, peeled and minced
4 anchovy fillets
2 sticks butter
2 hard-boiled egg yolks
1 raw egg yolk
½ cup olive oil
salt
1 pinch cayenne pepper

First, prepare the Montpellier butter: blanch the herbs and spinach leaves, refresh, drain and squeeze out all the moisture. Blanch the chopped shallot separately, drain and squeeze. Pound the herbs and shallot together finely.

Add the gherkins, capers, garlic and anchovy fillets and pound to a fine paste or process in a food processor. Add the butter and egg yolks, mix together and then add the oil, drop by drop. Pass through a fine strainer and, if necessary, mix together with a whisk until quite smooth. Season with salt and a small pinch of cayenne. Coat the salmon with this butter as described below, then put the remainder in the refrigerator to harden fully.

Remove the skin from the salmon and discard. Arrange the salmon on a flat dish before coating with Montpellier butter and decorating with cut crescents of truffle in graded sizes to simulate the scales of the fish. Coat with fish aspic, then place on a dish, the bottom of which has also been coated with a layer of fish aspic.

Surround the fish with halves of hard-boiled eggs, standing up, and with the yolks facing outwards. Garnish the edge of the dish with an assortment of shapes cut from the remaining very firm Montpellier butter.

SERVES 4–6

Salmon Steaks Danish-Style

Darne de Saumon à la Danoise

6 salmon steaks, about 5–6½ oz each
salt

Rich Butter Sauce
2 sticks butter
3 tablespoons flour
2½ cups boiling water
1 pinch salt
4 egg yolks
¼ cup heavy cream
a few drops lemon juice
1½ cans anchovy fillets, drained and pounded

Poach the salmon steaks carefully in lightly salted water. Meanwhile, make the Rich Butter Sauce. Melt 2 tablespoons butter in a pan and mix in the flour. Add the boiling water, whisking thoroughly, and add a pinch of salt. Mix in a *liaison* consisting of the egg yolks, cream and lemon juice. Reheat gently to thicken and finish, away from the heat, with the remaining butter, softened and mixed with the pounded anchovy fillets. Strain finely.

Drain the poached salmon steaks and serve with boiled potatoes and the Rich Butter Sauce.

SERVES 6

Salmon Mayonnaise

Mayonnaise de Saumon

1 head lettuce
salt
pepper
1 small piece of salmon, about 2½ lb, poached in Court-bouillon with Vinegar, page 40, and allowed to cool
1¼ cups Mayonnaise, page 13

To garnish
canned anchovy fillets, capers, olives, hard-boiled eggs, radishes

Cover the bottom of a large salad bowl with lightly seasoned shredded lettuce and put the flaked cold salmon on this, taking care to remove all skin and bone. Mound the salmon pieces into a domed shape, then coat with mayonnaise and decorate with strips of anchovy, capers, pitted olives, slices of hard-boiled egg and thin slices of radish.

SERVES 6–8

Poached Pike with Sorrel

Cold Poached Trout on a Tomato Mousse

Truite Saumonée Froide sur Mousse de Tomates

1 sea or lake trout weighing about 3½ lb
Court-bouillon with White Wine, page 40
2½ cups liquid Fish Aspic, page 40

Tomato Mousse
1 tablespoon chopped onion
1 tablespoon butter
½ cup dry white wine
3 cups coarsely chopped red ripe tomato flesh
salt
pepper
1 pinch paprika
1 sprig parsley
1¼ cups Velouté Sauce, pages 9–10
4 envelopes unflavored gelatin, softened
½ cup heavy cream, lightly whipped

To garnish
fresh tarragon leaves
fresh chervil or parsley leaves
hard-boiled egg white

Poach the whole trout in Court-bouillon with White Wine for about 15–20 minutes. Allow to cool in the liquid.

Meanwhile, make the tomato mousse. Fry the onion gently in the butter until golden, moisten with the white wine and reduce by half. Add the tomato flesh, seasoning, paprika and parsley. Cover and simmer gently for 25 minutes.

Add the Velouté Sauce and gelatin. Allow to boil for 2 minutes and pass through a fine strainer. Adjust the seasoning and allow to cool. When almost cold, add the cream. Pour onto a long serving dish, about 2 inches deep, and leave in the refrigerator to set.

Remove the skin from the fish, then carefully lift the two fillets from the central bone. Arrange the fish fillets side by side on the tomato mousse and decorate with leaves of tarragon and chervil and with hard-boiled egg white. If desired, put the head and tail back at each end of the fish.

Coat the whole fish with fish aspic when it is almost at setting point. Allow the aspic to set and present the dish on a bed of crushed ice.

SERVES 6

Salmon Meunière

Saumon à la Meunière

1½ lb salmon fillet, skinned
salt
pepper
flour
½ cup clarified butter
½ lemon
2 tablespoons blanched and coarsely chopped fresh parsley
1 stick butter

Cut the salmon into slices about ¾ inch thick. Season them and coat lightly with flour. Fry quickly on both sides in the very hot *clarified butter*.

When the fish is just cooked, transfer it to a hot serving dish. Squeeze the lemon over the fish, season again and sprinkle the surface with the parsley.

Finally, heat the butter quickly in a pan until it turns brown (or *à la noisette*), then immediately coat the salmon pieces with this. Serve while the butter is still sizzling against the moist parsley.

SERVES 4–6

Fried Trout with Parsley Butter

Truites Persillées

6 trout, cleaned
salt
pepper
flour
6 tablespoons clarified butter
juice of 1 lemon
2 tablespoons chopped fresh parsley
1 stick butter
½ cup fine soft white bread crumbs

Season the trout and coat lightly with flour. Fry quickly in the very hot *clarified butter*, turning once. When they are just cooked, arrange the trout on a hot serving dish and sprinkle with lemon juice and chopped parsley.

Cook the second quantity of butter until it starts turning a nut brown color (or *à la noisette*). Then add the very fine white bread crumbs and cook until they turn a golden brown colour and are frothing well.

Pour the bread crumb and butter mixture over the trout and serve immediately.

SERVES 6

Cold Poached Trout on a Tomato Mousse

Trout Hussar-style

Truites à la Hussarde

6 medium trout, boned and gutted from the back
1 onion, peeled and chopped
1¾ sticks butter
1 lb Fine Stuffing for Fish, page 41
1 large onion, finely sliced
¾ cup Chablis
1 bouquet garni
3 tablespoons flour

To bone and gut a trout from the back, make two deep incisions down each side of the backbone. Cut the backbone at head and tail, and remove the bone, together with the innards. The cavity left can now be used for stuffing the fish.

Fry the chopped onion gently in 2 tablespoons of the butter and mix with the prepared stuffing. Stuff the trout cavity carefully with this mixture.

Fry the finely sliced onion gently in 2 tablespoons of the butter without allowing it to brown. Butter an ovenproof dish, using another 2 tablespoons of butter, and cover the bottom of the dish with a layer of fried onion.

Arrange the trout on top and dot with 6 tablespoons of butter, the wine and the bouquet garni. Poach in a moderate oven (350°F), without a lid, for about 45 minutes, basting frequently.

When the trout are cooked, arrange them on a dish and pass the cooking liquid and onion through a fine strainer or blend in a food processor. Lightly thicken this with *beurre manié*, made using the rest of the butter and the flour. Coat the fish with this sauce and brown quickly under the broiler.

SERVES 6

Mackerel Boulonnaise

Maquereaux à la Boulonnaise

6 mackerel, cut into large sections (on the bone)
2 quarts Court-bouillon with Vinegar, page 40
30 mussels, poached until opened
1¾ cups Butter Sauce, page 14

Poach the mackerel sections in the court-bouillon. When they are cooked, drain, remove the skin and arrange on a dish surrounded by the poached mussels.

Coat with Butter Sauce, made using some of the strained court-bouillon instead of water.

SERVES 6

Mackerel Fillets Rosalie

Filets de Maquereau Rosalie

12 mackerel fillets
salt
pepper
flour
1 cup olive oil
1 small onion, peeled and chopped
2½ tablespoons chopped shallot
1½ cups chopped mushrooms
1 clove garlic, peeled and minced
1 tablespoon white wine vinegar
1 tablespoon chopped fresh parsley

Season and flour the mackerel fillets and shallow fry them in half the oil. Arrange on an oval serving dish to keep warm.

Add the rest of the oil to the pan and quickly fry the onion, shallot, mushroom and garlic in it. Pour over the fish fillets.

Finally, heat the vinegar in the pan, pour this over the fillets as well and sprinkle with the chopped parsley.

SERVES 6

Deep Fried Skate

Fritot de Raie

1½–2 lb small, young skate wings
1 tablespoon lemon juice
1 tablespoon olive oil
1 medium onion, peeled and thinly sliced into rings
1 pinch chopped fresh thyme
1 bay leaf
4 parsley stalks
salt
pepper
Fritter Batter, page 26
oil for deep frying
flour
few sprigs of parsley, fried

Cut the skate wings into small slices and marinate for 3 hours in the lemon juice, oil, onion rings, herbs and seasoning.

Dip the pieces of skate into batter and deep fry in hot oil (375°F), then flour the onion rings from the marinade and deep fry also. Drain and arrange the skate on a napkin on a dish with fried parsley on one side and the deep-fried onion rings on the other.

SERVES 4

Stuffed Herrings Baked in Paper

Harengs à la Calaisienne

6 fresh herrings, boned and gutted from the back
12 herring roes
$1\frac{1}{2}$ sticks butter
$2\frac{1}{2}$ tablespoons chopped shallot
1 tablespoon chopped fresh parsley
$\frac{3}{4}$ cup chopped mushrooms
salt
pepper
a few drops lemon juice

Open the herrings from the back and remove the backbones (see page 46, top left). Mix the herring roes with all the other ingredients and stuff the fish, in the cavity left by the removal of backbone and innards, with this mixture.

Enclose each fish in a well-oiled baking paper and cook gently in the oven (325°F) for about 20–25 minutes.

Serve the herrings on a dish *en papillote* (still wrapped in their individual paper packages).

SERVES 6

Whiting Dieppoise

Merlans à la Dieppoise

4 small whiting
$\frac{1}{2}$ cup dry white wine
$\frac{1}{2}$ cup mushroom cooking liquid
2 tablespoons butter

White Wine Sauce

$1\frac{1}{4}$ cups Velouté Sauce made with fish stock, pages 9–10
1 egg yolk
4 tablespoons butter

Dieppoise garnish

1 cup cooked shelled medium shrimp
20 mussels, poached until opened

Slit the whiting along their backs so as to facilitate their cooking. Poach them, covered, with the white wine, *mushroom cooking liquid* and butter in a moderate oven (350°F), basting from time to time until cooked.

Drain well, reserving the cooking liquid for the white wine sauce. Arrange on a dish and keep warm.

Make the sauce by straining and reducing the reserved cooking liquid to $\frac{1}{4}$ cup and heating this in a pan with the fish velouté. Add the egg yolk and reduce by one-third. Finish the sauce with the butter.

Surround the fish with the Dieppoise garnish and cover with the White Wine Sauce.

SERVES 4

Parisian Bouillabaisse

Bouillabaisse à la Parisienne

$\frac{1}{2}$ cup olive oil
1 onion, peeled and chopped
2 leeks, white part only, chopped
$1\frac{1}{2}$ cups dry white wine
$2\frac{1}{2}$ cups water
salt
pepper
1 pinch saffron threads
1 bouquet garni
2 cups roughly chopped tomato flesh
2 cloves garlic, peeled and minced
3 lb 6 oz fish, to include sole, red mullet or snapper, whiting and spiny lobster, trimmed and cleaned
1 quart mussels, cleaned
$2\frac{1}{2}$ tablespoons coarsely chopped fresh parsley
2 tablespoons butter
1 tablespoon flour
French bread, sliced, toasted and lightly rubbed with a cut clove of garlic

Place half the oil in a deep saucepan, then add the chopped onion and leek and cook gently without allowing the vegetables to color. Add the wine, water, salt, pepper, saffron, bouquet garni, tomato and garlic, bring to a boil and cook gently for 20 minutes.

Cut the seafood into large pieces, place them in a clean pan and put the mussels on top. Add the rest of the oil, sprinkle with the parsley and pour on the reserved cooking liquid and its garnish. Bring back to a boil and cook rapidly for 15 minutes. Remove the bouquet garni and, at the last moment, thicken the cooking liquid slightly by stirring in a *beurre manié* made from the butter and flour.

Arrange the fish and shellfish in a deep dish or in individual serving dishes. Place the slices of toasted French bread lightly rubbed with garlic in separate dishes, and ladle some of the cooking liquid over the bread to soak it thoroughly. *See photograph on page 49.*

SERVES 6

Cod Steaks Portuguese-style

Cabillaud à la Portugaise

1 onion, peeled and chopped
1 stick butter
6 cod steaks, weighing about ½ lb each
salt
pepper
½ cup olive oil
1 small clove garlic, peeled and minced
½ teaspoon coarsely chopped fresh parsley
1½ lb tomatoes, peeled, seeded and roughly chopped
⅔ cup cold three-quarters-cooked long-grain rice
1 cup dry white wine

Lightly fry the chopped onion gently in 2 tablespoons of the butter. Arrange the cod steaks in a shallow pan, season and add the olive oil, lightly fried onion, garlic, parsley, tomato flesh, partially cooked rice and white wine.

Cover the pan and cook quickly for 10 minutes, then remove the lid and cook for a further 8 minutes or so to reduce the liquid and to finish cooking the fish.

Arrange the fish on a serving dish. Pour the cooking liquid over the top and cover with the vegetable and rice mixture.

SERVES 6

Dover Sole Bonne Femme

Sole Bonne Femme

1½ sticks butter
1½ cups sliced mushrooms
2 tablespoons finely chopped shallot
½ teaspoon chopped fresh parsley
4 small Dover sole, trimmed and with black skin removed
1 cup dry white wine
1 cup thin Velouté Sauce made with fish stock, pages 9–10

Butter an ovenproof dish, using 2 tablespoons of the butter, and sprinkle the bottom with the mushrooms, shallot and parsley. Place the fish on top (white side up), and add the equal quantities of wine and thin fish velouté. Cover and poach in a moderately hot oven (400°F) for 12–15 minutes, basting from time to time.

When the sole are cooked, drain off the cooking liquid. Reduce it a little and enrich with the remaining butter. Pour the sauce over the sole and brown quickly under a hot broiler.

SERVES 4

Dover Sole Deauville

Sole Deauvillaise

2 onions, peeled and finely sliced
1¼ sticks butter
4 small Dover sole, trimmed and with black skin removed
1¼ cups heavy cream

To garnish
small lightly baked diamonds of Puff Pastry, page 28

Fry the onion gently, without allowing it to color, in 2 tablespoons of the butter. Butter an ovenproof dish, using another 2 tablespoons of the butter, and add the fried onion, the prepared fish (white side up) and the cream and dot with another 2 tablespoons butter. Cover, place in a moderately hot oven (400°F) and baste from time to time until cooked (about 12–15 minutes). Place on a serving dish and keep warm.

Pass the cream and onion through a fine strainer and enrich the resulting sauce with the remaining butter. Coat the sole with the sauce and garnish with small lightly baked diamonds of puff pastry.

SERVES 4

Dover Sole Florentine

Sole à la Florentine

1¼ sticks butter
4 small Dover sole, trimmed and with black skin removed
1¼ cups Fish Stock, page 9
½ lb fresh bulk spinach, blanched and roughly chopped

To finish
1¾ cups Mornay Sauce, page 13
¾ cup grated Parmesan cheese

Butter an ovenproof dish, using 2 tablespoons of the butter. Poach the sole (white side up), covered, in a moderately hot oven (400°F) with the fish stock and another 4 tablespoons of the butter, basting from time to time, for about 12–15 minutes.

Meanwhile, stew the blanched spinach in the remaining butter and transfer it to a suitable serving dish. Drain the cooked sole and place them on top of the spinach.

Coat with the Mornay Sauce, sprinkle with grated cheese and gratinate quickly in a hot oven (425°F) or under the broiler.

SERVES 4

Parisian Bouillabaisse

Dover Sole Rochelaise

Sole à la Rochelaise

1 stick butter
1 small onion, peeled and finely chopped
4 small Dover sole, trimmed and with black skin removed
1 cup red wine
1 cup Fish Stock, page 9

To garnish
8 soft herring roes, poached
16 oysters, shucked, poached and bearded
16 mussels, poached, shucked and bearded
$\frac{1}{2}$ cup Demi-glace Sauce, page 10

Butter an ovenproof dish, using 2 tablespoons of the butter, and fry the onion gently in another 2 tablespoons of butter. Poach the sole, covered with the fried onion, wine and fish stock in a moderately hot oven (400°F), basting from time to time until cooked (about 12–15 minutes).

Drain the sole, reserving the cooking liquid, and place on a warmed serving dish, surrounded by the poached herring roes, oysters and mussels. Keep warm.

Reduce the cooking liquid by two-thirds and strain. Add the Demi-glace Sauce and remaining butter. Coat the sole with this sauce and serve.

SERVES 4

Dover Sole Jouffroy

Sole Jouffroy

1 stick butter
4 small Dover sole, trimmed and with black skin removed
$1\frac{1}{4}$ cups dry white wine
$1\frac{1}{2}$ cups sliced white mushrooms

White Wine Sauce
$1\frac{1}{4}$ cups Velouté Sauce made with fish stock, pages 9–10
1 egg yolk
4 tablespoons butter

To garnish
8 small vol-au-vent (patty shells) filled with buttered asparagus tips and topped with a slice of truffle

Butter an ovenproof dish, using 2 tablespoons of the butter. Poach the sole (white side up), covered, in a moderately hot oven (400°F) with the wine and another 4 tablespoons of the butter. Baste from time to time until cooked (about 12–15 minutes).

Meanwhile, fry the mushrooms gently in another 2 tablespoons of the butter. When the fish is cooked, drain, reserving the cooking liquid for the sauce. Arrange the sole on a suitable dish, surrounded by slices of mushroom, and keep warm.

Make the wine sauce by straining and reducing the cooking liquid to $\frac{1}{4}$ cup and heating this in a pan with the fish velouté and egg yolk. Reduce by one-third and finish by enriching with the butter. Cover the prepared fish with the sauce and brown quickly in a hot oven (425°F) or under the broiler. Garnish with dainty little vol-au-vent filled with buttered asparagus tips and topped with a slice of truffle.

SERVES 4

Dover Sole Murat

Sole Murat

4 small Dover sole, trimmed and with black skin removed
salt
pepper
flour
8 tablespoons clarified butter

To garnish
$\frac{2}{3}$ cup peeled and diced potato
2 raw artichoke bottoms, diced
4 tablespoons butter
salt
pepper
flour
2 large tomatoes, cut into 4 thick slices each
1 tablespoon oil
a few drops lemon juice
1 tablespoon roughly chopped fresh parsley
1 stick butter

Shallow fry the diced potato then the artichoke in the butter. When cooked, drain and mix together. Season the fish, flour and fry in hot clarified butter, turning once.

When they are cooked, place the fish on a hot serving dish and surround with the prepared potato and artichoke bottoms. Season, flour and shallow fry the 8 thick slices of tomato in very hot oil and place two slices on each sole.

Sprinkle the sole with a few drops of lemon juice and the parsley, and cover with the butter which has been cooked until it is brown in color (or *à la noisette*). Serve immediately.

SERVES 4

Dover Sole Rochelaise

Dover Sole Meunière with Grapes

Sole Meunière aux Raisins

4 small Dover sole, trimmed and with black skin removed
salt
pepper
flour
8 tablespoons clarified butter

To garnish
1 lemon
salt
pepper
1 tablespoon blanched and coarsely chopped fresh parsley
1 stick butter
¼ lb Muscatel grapes, peeled, seeded and well chilled

Season the fish, lightly coat with flour, and fry in very hot clarified butter, turning just once.

When it is cooked, place the fish on a hot serving dish. Squeeze the lemon over it, season with salt and pepper and sprinkle with the blanched and coarsely chopped parsley. Finally, coat with butter which has been cooked until it is brown in color (or *à la noisette*). Serve immediately so that the hot butter sizzles against the moist parsley. Surround with the peeled and well-chilled Muscatel grapes.

SERVES 4

Sole Fillets Lady Egmont

Filets de Sole Lady Egmont

6 tablespoons butter
8 fillets of Dover sole, approximately 3 oz each
1 cup Fish Stock, page 9
¾ cup sliced mushrooms
a few drops lemon juice
salt
pepper
5 tablespoons heavy cream
¼ cup asparagus tips, freshly cooked and drained

Butter an ovenproof dish, using a third of the butter. Fold the fillets of sole in half top to bottom, with the head end placed over the narrow end, then place them in the dish and poach them in the fish stock, covered, in a moderately hot oven (400°F), basting from time to time. Meanwhile, quickly cook the mushrooms with 2 tablespoons of the butter, the lemon juice and seasonings. Drain, reserving the liquid.

When the fish is cooked (after about 12–15 minutes), drain and reserve the cooking liquid. Add this to the reserved mushroom cooking liquid and reduce by half. Add the remaining butter, the cream, the cooked mushrooms and the asparagus tips.

Arrange the fish in an oval gratin dish, cover with the sauce and the garnish, and brown quickly under the broiler.

SERVES 4

Sole Fillets Nelson

Filets de Sole Nelson

8 fillets of Dover sole, approximately 3 oz each
2 tablespoons butter
1 cup Fish Stock, page 9

White Wine Sauce
1¼ cups Velouté Sauce made with fish stock, pages 9–10
1 egg yolk
4 tablespoons butter

To garnish
¾ lb potatoes, cut into balls the size of large hazelnuts, using a melon baller
salt
pepper
4 tablespoons butter

Fold the fillets of sole in half top to bottom, with the head end placed over the narrow end, then place them in a buttered ovenproof dish and add the fish stock. Cover and poach in a moderately hot oven (400°F), basting from time to time.

When the fish is cooked (after about 12–15 minutes), drain, reserving the cooking liquid, and arrange the fillets, overlapping in a circle, on a suitable serving dish to keep warm.

Make the sauce by straining and reducing the cooking liquid to ¼ cup. Heat this in a pan with the fish velouté, add the egg yolk and reduce by one-third. Finish the sauce with the butter.

Coat the fish with this sauce and brown quickly in a hot oven (425°F) or under the broiler. Fill the center of the dish with a pile of potatoes, cut into balls the size of large hazelnuts, seasoned and fried in butter.

SERVES 4

Sole Fillets Burgundy-style

Filets de Sole à la Bourguignonne

2 onions, peeled and thinly sliced into rings
$1\frac{1}{4}$ sticks butter
$1\frac{1}{2}$ cups sliced mushrooms
8 fillets of Dover sole, approximately 3 oz each
freshly ground black pepper
salt
$1\frac{1}{4}$ cups red wine
$1\frac{1}{2}$ tablespoons flour

Fry the sliced onion gently in 2 tablespoons of the butter. Fry the sliced mushrooms, separately, in another 2 tablespoons of the butter. Butter an ovenproof dish, using yet another 2 tablespoons of butter, and place the fried onion in the dish with the flat fillets of sole on top. Surround the fish with the mushrooms, sprinkle with pepper and a little salt and add the red wine.

Cover and poach the fish in a moderately hot oven (400°F), basting from time to time. When the fillets are cooked (after about 12–15 minutes), drain off the cooking liquid and reduce to one third of its original volume. Thicken with *beurre manié*, made using 2 tablespoons of butter and the flour, and finish with the remaining butter. Adjust the seasoning if necessary. Coat the fillets with the sauce and brown quickly under the broiler.

SERVES 4

Sole Fillets Véronique

Filets de Sole Véronique

8 fillets of Dover sole, approximately 3 oz each
6 tablespoons butter
salt
pepper
1 cup Fish Stock, page 9

To garnish
$\frac{1}{4}$ lb Muscatel grapes, peeled, seeded and well chilled

Lightly flatten the fillets of sole and fold them in half top to bottom, with the head end placed over the narrow end. Butter an ovenproof dish, using 2 tablespoons of the butter. Place the fillets in it, season and add the fish stock. Cover and poach in a moderately hot oven (400°F).

When the fillets are cooked (after about 12–15 minutes), drain them and reserve the cooking liquid. Return them to the dish to keep warm, arranging them in an overlapping circle. Reduce the reserved cooking liquid to the consistency of a light syrup and add the remaining butter. Pour this sauce over the fish fillets and brown them quickly in a hot oven (425°F) or under the grill.

Just before serving, put the peeled and well-chilled Muscatel grapes in the center of the dish.

SERVES 4

Sole Fillets with Mushrooms

Filets de Sole aux Champignons

4 tablespoons butter
8 fillets of Dover sole, approximately 3 oz each
1 cup mushroom cooking liquid
16 very white mushrooms

Mushroom Sauce
$\frac{1}{4}$ lb tiny button mushrooms
6 tablespoons butter
$1\frac{1}{4}$ cups Demi-glace Sauce, page 10

Butter an ovenproof dish, using 2 tablespoons of the butter. Fold the fillets in half top to bottom, with the head end placed over the narrow end, and place them in the dish. Poach them, covered, in the *mushroom cooking liquid*, in a moderately hot oven (400°F), basting from time to time. Meanwhile, lightly fry the mushrooms in the remaining butter.

When the fish is cooked (after about 12–15 minutes), drain and reserve the cooking liquid. Arrange the fillets of fish in a circle on a suitable serving dish and place the lightly fried mushrooms in the center. Keep warm.

To make the mushroom sauce, place the reserved cooking liquid in a pan and reduce by half. Meanwhile, fry the tiny button mushrooms gently in 2 tablespoons of the butter. Add the Demi-glace Sauce to the reduced cooking liquid and allow to simmer gently for a few minutes. Strain, add the remaining butter, and finish by adding the tiny fried mushrooms. Pour over the fillets of sole and serve.

SERVES 4

Scallops au Gratin

MEAT DISHES

Beef Tenderloin Berrichonne

Filet de Boeuf à la Berrichonne

3 lb 6 oz beef tenderloin roast, trimmed
¼ lb slab bacon, cut into thin strips approximately 3 inches long
Brown Stock, page 8
beurre manié

To garnish
braised cabbage cooked with slices of bacon
small glazed onions
large braised chestnuts

Lard the beef with the strips of slab bacon and roast it, preferably keeping it slightly rare and pink in the middle: 40 minutes in a hot oven (450°F) should be enough.

Place the cooked beef on a long serving dish and surround it with braised cabbage and bacon, small glazed onions and large braised chestnuts.

Make a lightly thickened gravy by adding a small quantity of Brown Stock to the juices from the roasting pan, thickening with *beurre manié* and simmering for a minute or two. Serve the sauce separately.

SERVES 6

Beef Tenderloin Saint-Germain

Filet de Boeuf Saint-Germain

3 lb 6 oz beef tenderloin roast, trimmed
¼ lb slab bacon cut into thin strips approximately 3 inches long

To garnish
Fresh Pea Purée, page 119, made very thick
Glazed Carrots, page 126
Fondant Potatoes (see below)
Béarnaise Sauce, page 13

Lard the beef with the strips of slab bacon and roast it, preferably keeping it slightly rare and pink in the middle: 40 minutes in a hot oven (450°F) should be enough.

Place the cooked beef on a long serving dish and surround with the Fresh Pea Purée, made very thick and molded into small *timbales*, the glazed carrots and the Fondant Potatoes. These are potatoes cut to the shape of large elongated olives, about 3 ounces in weight each, that are then fried slowly in butter and turned frequently until they are soft. Finally they are flattened slightly with a fork without being broken. Drain off the fat, replace with fresh butter, cover and leave on the side of the range until the potatoes have absorbed all the butter. Serve with Béarnaise Sauce.

SERVES 6

Beef Tenderloin Saint-Germain

Beef Tenderloin with Mixed Vegetables

Filet de Boeuf Macédoine

3 lb 6 oz beef tenderloin roast, trimmed
$\frac{1}{4}$ lb slab bacon, cut into thin strips approximately 3 inches long

To garnish
a macédoine of mixed vegetables
Château Potatoes (see below)

Lard the beef with the strips of slab bacon and roast it, preferably keeping it slightly rare and pink in the middle: 40 minutes in a hot oven (450°F) should be enough.

Place the cooked beef on a long serving dish and surround with the *macédoine* of vegetables and the Château Potatoes. These are potatoes trimmed to a smaller olive shape than that of the Fondant Potatoes of the previous recipe, seasoned, cooked slowly in *clarified butter* until soft and golden brown, and sprinkled with parsley. Serve with an unthickened gravy made from the cooking juices.

SERVES 6

Beef Tenderloin Provençale

Filet de Boeuf à la Provençale

3 lb 6 oz beef tenderloin roast, trimmed
$\frac{1}{4}$ lb slab bacon, cut into thin strips approximately 3 inches long
4 tablespoons melted butter

To garnish
Stuffed Tomatoes Provençale, page 147
Stuffed Mushrooms, page 130
Provençale Sauce, page 14

Lard the beef with the strips of slab bacon. Put it in a deep ovenproof casserole, season and cover it with the melted butter. Cover with a lid and *poêlé* in a hot oven (450°F), basting frequently with the butter. To ensure that the tenderloin is kept slightly rare and pink in the middle, cook for about 50 minutes.

When the meat is nearly cooked, remove the lid and allow it to brown. Then place the meat on a long serving dish and surround with the stuffed tomatoes, arranged alternately with the stuffed mushrooms. Serve with Provençale Sauce.

SERVES 6

Beef Tenderloin Montmorency

Filet de Boeuf Montmorency

3 lb 6 oz beef tenderloin roast, trimmed
$\frac{1}{4}$ lb slab bacon, cut into thin strips approximately 3 inches long
salt
pepper
4 tablespoons melted butter

Matignon
1 large carrot, peeled and diced
1 small onion, peeled and diced
1 stalk celery, diced
4 slices bacon, diced
2 tablespoons butter
1 bay leaf
1 sprig thyme
2 tablespoons dry white wine

To finish
$1\frac{1}{4}$ cups Brown Stock, page 8
2 tablespoons dry Madeira

To garnish
6 cooked artichoke bottoms, filled with a macédoine of mixed vegetables
asparagus tips

Lard the beef with the strips of slab bacon. Then prepare the *matignon*: fry the vegetables and bacon gently in the butter and add the herbs. Add the wine and reduce until almost dry.

Place a layer of matignon in a deep heavy ovenproof casserole, just large enough to hold the meat. Put the meat on top of the matignon, season well and coat with melted butter.

Cover with a lid, place in a hot oven (450°F) and *poêlé*, basting frequently with the butter. To ensure that the tenderloin is kept slightly rare and pink in the middle, cook for about 50 minutes. When the meat is nearly cooked, remove the lid and allow it to brown. Place it on a long serving dish, cover and keep warm.

Add the stock to the vegetables, which should not have been allowed to burn. Bring to a boil and simmer for 10 minutes. Strain, remove the fat and reduce by two-thirds. Finally, flavor with Madeira and do not allow to reboil.

Surround the meat with artichoke bottoms filled with a *macédoine* of mixed vegetables arranged alternately with *bouquets* of asparagus tips.

Serve the sauce separately.

SERVES 6

Beef Tenderloin with Mushroom and Madeira Sauce

Filet de Boeuf au Madère et aux Champignons

3 lb 6 oz beef tenderloin roast, trimmed
$\frac{1}{4}$ lb slab bacon cut into thin strips approximately 3 inches long
salt
pepper
4 tablespoons melted butter

Matignon
1 large carrot, peeled and diced
1 small onion, peeled and diced
1 stalk celery, diced
4 slices bacon, diced
1 bay leaf
1 sprig thyme
2 tablespoons butter
2 tablespoons dry white wine
$1\frac{1}{4}$ cups Brown Stock, page 8

Mushroom sauce
$\frac{1}{4}$ lb tiny button mushrooms
2 tablespoons butter
$1\frac{1}{4}$ cups Demi-glace Sauce, page 10
2 tablespoons dry Madeira

To garnish
$\frac{1}{4}$ lb large mushrooms, fried in butter

Lard the beef with the strips of slab bacon. Then prepare the *matignon*: fry the vegetables gently in a pan for a few minutes with the bacon, herbs and butter. Add the white wine and reduce until almost dry.

Place a layer of matignon in a deep heavy ovenproof casserole just large enough to hold the meat. Put the meat on top of the matignon, season well and coat with melted butter.

Cover with a lid, place in a hot oven (450°F) and *poêlé*, basting frequently with the butter. To ensure the tenderloin is kept slightly rare and pink in the middle, cook for about 50 minutes. When the meat is nearly cooked, remove the lid and allow it to brown. Place it on a long dish, cover and keep warm.

Meanwhile, add the stock to the matignon vegetables, which should not have been allowed to burn. Bring to a boil and simmer for 10 minutes. Strain, remove the fat, then reduce the liquid by two-thirds.

Prepare the mushroom sauce by first frying the button mushrooms gently in the butter. Remove the mushrooms, reduce the mushroom cooking juices, then add the Demi-glace Sauce and the reduced juices from the matignon to the reduced mushroom cooking juices and allow all to simmer gently together for a few minutes. Add the Madeira and finish by replacing the fried button mushrooms.

Serve the beef accompanied by this sauce and garnished with large mushrooms fried gently in butter.

SERVES 6

TOURNEDOS

These small steaks, also called filet mignon, are cut from the thinner middle part of the beef tenderloin. They are best when cut approximately $1\frac{1}{4}$–$1\frac{1}{2}$ inches thick, and they weigh about 4–$4\frac{1}{2}$ ounces each when prepared. They should be trimmed of all fat and membrane and the gristly part on one side should be removed. A nice round shape is an essential part of the appearance of the tournedos and this is best achieved by tying around each one with thin string. This helps the meat to keep its shape while cooking.

Tournedos Bréhan

Tournedos Bréhan

4 filet mignon steaks, about $1\frac{1}{2}$ inches thick and weighing $4\frac{1}{2}$ oz each
salt
pepper
1 stick butter
4 artichoke bottoms, fried in butter to a golden brown
$\frac{1}{2}$ cup puréed broad (fava) beans, heated and mixed with a little butter and cream
3 tablespoons dry Madeira
$\frac{1}{2}$ cup Brown Stock, page 8
8 florets cauliflower, boiled and buttered
8 small potatoes, boiled, buttered and sprinkled with chopped fresh parsley

Season the steaks, then fry in 4 tablespoons of the butter for 3–4 minutes on each side if liked rare, 4–5 minutes medium rare, 6–8 minutes for well done. Place on a dish and on top of each steak place an artichoke bottom filled with the purée of broad beans. Keep warm.

Pour off the fat from the pan and deglaze with the Madeira and stock. Reduce until slightly syrupy then blend in the remaining butter. Arrange the cauliflower and potatoes around the steaks. Strain the sauce and serve separately.

SERVES 4

Tournedos with Foie Gras and Truffle

Tournedos Favorite

4 filet mignon steaks, about 1½ inches thick and weighing 4½ oz each
salt
pepper
1 stick butter
3 tablespoons dry Madeira
½ cup Light Gravy, page 9

To garnish

4 slices bread, cut into rounds with a plain pastry cutter
4 tablespoons clarified butter
4 slices foie gras
salt
pepper
flour
2 tablespoons butter
4 slices truffle
buttered asparagus tips
Noisette Potatoes (see below)

Season the steaks and fry in 4 tablespoons butter (see page 65 for timing instructions). Keep warm. Pour off the fat from the pan and deglaze with the Madeira and gravy, then blend in the rest of the butter.

Arrange each steak on a round croûton of bread, fried in *clarified butter*. Season, flour and lightly fry the slices of foie gras in the butter and place these on the steaks, with a slice of truffle on top. Strain the sauce and serve separately.

Serve with buttered asparagus tips and Noisette Potatoes. These are made by cutting out balls of potato the size of large hazelnuts using a melon baller. They are then seasoned and fried in butter until they are soft inside and golden brown on the outside.

Serves 4

Tournedos with Mushrooms

Tournedos aux Champignons

4 filet mignon steaks, about 1½ inches thick and weighing 4½ oz each
salt
pepper
6 tablespoons butter
½ lb small mushrooms
¼ cup mushroom cooking liquid
½ cup Demi-glace Sauce, page 10

Season the steaks and fry in 4 tablespoons of the butter (see page 65 for timing instructions). Fry the mushrooms separately in the remaining butter. Arrange the steaks in a circle and put the mushrooms in the center, placing a handsome mushroom on each steak.

Deglaze the pan with the *mushroom cooking liquid*, add the Demi-glace Sauce and strain. Pour the sauce over the mushrooms in the center of the dish.

Serves 4

Tournedos Catalan-style

Tournedos à la Catalane

1 small onion, peeled and finely chopped
1 small sweet red pepper, skinned, seeded, and cut into short julienne
1 tablespoon oil
½ lb tomatoes, peeled, seeded and roughly chopped
1 pinch chopped fresh parsley
4 filet mignon steaks, about 1½ inches thick and weighing 4½ oz each
salt
pepper
4 tablespoons butter
3 tablespoons dry white wine
1 cup thin Tomato Sauce, page 14

Fry the onion with the sweet pepper gently in the oil and add the prepared tomato. Simmer until the mixture is fairly stiff and finish with the parsley.

Season the steaks and fry in the butter (see page 65 for timing instructions). Pour off the fat from the pan, deglaze with the wine and sauce, strain, and surround the steaks with this sauce. Place a little of the hot tomato, pepper and parsley mixture in the center of each steak.

Serves 4

Tournedos Catalan-style

Tournedos Castilian-style

Tournedos Castillane

4 filet mignon steaks, about 1½ inches thick and weighing 4½ oz each
salt
pepper
1 stick butter
3 tablespoons dry white wine
½ cup Brown Stock, page 8

To garnish
4 slices bread, cut into rounds about the same size as the steaks with a plain pastry cutter
4 tablespoons clarified butter
deep fried onion rings
4 small tartlet cases filled with Tomato Fondue, page 14

Season the steaks and fry in 4 tablespoons of the butter (see page 65 for timing instructions). Keep warm. Pour off the fat from the pan and deglaze with the wine and stock. Reduce until slightly syrupy then blend in the remaining butter; strain and serve this sauce separately.

Arrange each steak on a round croûton of bread fried in *clarified butter*. Surround with deep fried onion rings and serve with a small tartlet case filled with tomato fondue.

SERVES 4

Tournedos Sardinian-style

Tournedos à la Sarde

4 filet mignon steaks, about 1½ inches thick and weighing 4½ oz each
salt
pepper
4 tablespoons butter

To garnish
Stuffed Tomatoes Provençale, page 147
Stuffed Cucumber, page 136
Saffron Rice Croquettes, page 145
thin Tomato Sauce, page 14

Season the steaks and fry in the butter (see page 65 for timing instructions. Arrange on a round dish, surrounded by stuffed tomatoes and cucumber. Fill the center of the dish with rice croquettes and serve with thin tomato sauce.

SERVES 4

Tournedos Provençale

Tournedos à la Provençale

4 filet mignon steaks, about 1½ inches thick and weighing 4½ oz each
salt
pepper
2 tablespoons butter
1 tablespoon olive oil

To garnish
4 slices bread, cut into rounds with a plain pastry cutter
4 tablespoons clarified butter
Stuffed Tomatoes Provençale, page 147
Stuffed Mushrooms, page 130
Provençale Sauce, page 14

Season the steaks and fry in a mixture of butter and oil (see page 65 for timing instructions).

Fry the slices of bread in the *clarified butter*, place a steak on top of each slice, and arrange them neatly on a dish. Place a stuffed half tomato on each steak and surround with stuffed mushrooms.

Serve the Provençale Sauce separately.

SERVES 4

Tournedos with Tarragon

Tournedos à l'Estragon

1 small bunch of tarragon
¼ cup Brown Stock, page 8
4 filet mignon steaks, about 1½ inches thick and weighing 4½ oz each
salt
pepper
4 tablespoons butter
12 blanched fresh tarragon leaves
¾ cup Light Gravy, page 9

Infuse the bunch of tarragon in the stock for 5 minutes, then strain and reduce by half.

Season the steaks and fry in the butter (see page 65 for timing instructions). Place three leaves of tarragon on each steak. Keep warm.

Pour off the fat from the pan and deglaze with the gravy. Add the reduced and flavored stock, then strain and serve separately.

SERVES 4

Tournedos with Tomato and Eggplant

Tournedos Roumanille

4 small filet mignon steaks, about $1\frac{1}{4}$ inches thick and weighing 4 oz each
salt
pepper
2 tablespoons olive oil
2 large tomatoes, cut in half
$1\frac{1}{4}$ cups Mornay Sauce, page 13
1 tablespoon tomato paste

To garnish
4 large black olives, pitted
4 anchovy fillets
1 large eggplant, sliced and fried

Season the steaks and fry in the oil (see page 65 for timing instructions: deduct $\frac{1}{2}$ minute from each, as smaller steaks are used). Broil the tomatoes and place each steak on half a broiled tomato. Color the Mornay Sauce with the tomato paste, coat the prepared steaks with this sauce, and brown quickly under the broiler.

Arrange the prepared steaks on a dish. Put a large olive wrapped in an anchovy fillet on each one, and surround with crisply fried slices of eggplant.

SERVES 4

Cinderella's Tournedos

Tournedos Cendrillon

1 oz truffle, chopped
4 large artichoke bottoms, cooked
4 filet mignon steaks, about $1\frac{1}{2}$ inches thick and weighing $4\frac{1}{2}$ oz each
salt
pepper
1 stick butter
$\frac{1}{2}$ cup Brown Stock, page 8

Onion Purée
1 large onion, peeled and sliced
5 tablespoons butter
$\frac{1}{2}$ cup thick Béchamel Sauce, page 12
salt
pepper
1 pinch sugar
$\frac{1}{4}$ cup heavy cream

First prepare the onion purée. Blanch the sliced onions and drain thoroughly. Stew in 2 tablespoons of the butter, without coloring them, and add the Béchamel Sauce, salt, pepper and sugar. Cover, place in a moderate oven (325°F) and cook gently for about 30 minutes. When the onions are cooked, pass through a fine sieve, reheat and add the remaining butter and the cream.

Mix the onion purée with the chopped truffle. Fill the artichoke bottoms with this mixture and brown them quickly in a hot oven or under the broiler.

Season the steaks and fry in 4 tablespoons of the butter (see page 65 for timing instructions). Place each one on one of the artichoke bottoms and arrange on a serving dish.

Pour off the fat from the pan and deglaze with the stock, reduce until slightly syrupy and blend in the remaining butter. Strain and serve separately.

SERVES 4

Steak Mirabeau

Entrecôte Mirabeau

4 boneless sirloin steaks, weighing about 7 oz each
salt
pepper
2 tablespoons clarified butter
4 oz anchovy fillets (2 cans)
1 stick butter, softened
1 cup black olives, pitted
1 tablespoon fresh tarragon leaves, blanched

Season the steaks, brush with *clarified butter* and broil for 2–3 minutes on each side if liked rare, 4 minutes medium rare, 5–6 minutes for well-done. Meanwhile prepare an anchovy butter by pounding half the anchovy fillets to a paste, mixing with the butter and passing through a fine sieve. Arrange the cooked steaks on a serving dish.

Garnish the steaks with the remaining anchovy fillets, arranged trellis fashion, the black olives and the tarragon. Serve accompanied by the anchovy-flavored butter.

SERVES 4

Forester's Steak

Entrêcote à la Forestière

4 boneless sirloin steaks, weighing about 7 oz each
salt
pepper
1 stick butter
¼ lb mushrooms, preferably morels
1 cup potatoes cut into large dice
4 slices lean bacon
1 tablespoon chopped fresh parsley
2 tablespoons dry white wine
¼ cup Brown Stock, page 8

Season the steaks and fry in 4 tablespoons of the butter for 2–3 minutes on each side if liked rare, 4 minutes medium rare, 5–6 minutes for well done. Arrange them on a serving dish to keep warm. At the same time, fry the mushrooms and the potatoes separately in another 2 tablespoons of butter each. Broil or fry the bacon. Arrange the vegetables and bacon around the steaks and sprinkle with the parsley.

Deglaze the pan with the wine and the stock, pass through a fine strainer and serve the sauce separately.

SERVES 4

Steak Hungarian-style

Entrêcote à la Hongroise

4 boneless sirloin steaks, weighing about 7 oz each
6 tablespoons butter
¼ lb slab bacon, diced and blanched
1 onion, peeled and chopped
1 pinch paprika
½ cup dry white wine
¼ cup Velouté Sauce made with Chicken Stock, pages 9–10

Season and fry the sirloin steaks in 4 tablespoons of the butter (see above for timing instructions). At the same time, fry the bacon in another pan; drain off excess fat. Add the onion and remaining butter and fry together until well colored. Then add the paprika and wine and reduce by two-thirds. Add the Velouté Sauce and cook gently for 7–8 minutes.

Arrange the cooked steaks on a serving dish, cover with the prepared sauce and surround with small boiled potatoes.

SERVES 4

Lyonnaise Steak

Entrecôte à la Lyonnaise

4 boneless sirloin steaks, weighing about ½ lb each
salt
pepper
1 stick butter
1 large onion, peeled and finely sliced
½ tablespoon Meat Glaze, page 9
1 tablespoon chopped fresh parsley
½ cup dry white wine
a few drops white wine vinegar
¼ cup Demi-glace Sauce, page 10

Season the steaks and fry in half the butter (see left for timing instructions). Arrange them on a serving dish to keep warm.

At the same time, fry the onion separately in another 2 tablespoons of the butter. Add the meat glaze and sprinkle with the parsley. Arrange the onion along the sides of the steaks.

Deglaze the pan in which the steak was cooked with the white wine and vinegar. Reduce by two-thirds and add the Demi-glace Sauce. Pass through a fine strainer, swirl in the remaining butter, and pour over the garnished steaks.

SERVES 4

Tyrolean Steak

Entrecôte Tyrolienne

4 boneless sirloin steaks, weighing about ½ lb each
salt
pepper
2 tablespoons clarified butter
1 large onion, peeled and finely sliced
2 tablespoons butter
½ cup Poivrade Sauce, page 10

To garnish
Tomato Fondue, page 14

Season the steaks, brush with *clarified butter* and broil (see page 69 for timing instructions). Meanwhile, fry the onion in the butter and add the Poivrade Sauce. Pour this mixture over the steaks when ready, then surround the steaks with a *cordon* of Tomato Fondue.

SERVES 4

Forester's Steak

Beef Paupiettes Fontanges

Paupiettes de Boeuf Fontanges

2 lb boneless sirloin or top loin steak in one piece
8 thin slices salt pork
2 tablespoons butter
1 large onion, peeled and sliced
1 large carrot, peeled and sliced
1¾ cups Brown Stock, page 8
1 bouquet garni
1 teaspoon arrowroot

Pork forcemeat
1 cup chopped lean boneless pork
1 cup chopped pork fatback
1 pinch fine salt
ground white pepper
1 pinch apple pie spice
1 tablespoon chopped fresh parsley
1 tablespoon brandy
1 egg white

To garnish
8 Potato Croquettes, page 140
purée of white haricot beans

Wipe the steak and cut off any excess fat. Cut the meat into 8 slices, each weighing about ¼ lb, and flatten each to a rectangle about 4 inches long by 2 inches wide. Season the beef slices on one side.

The forcemeat should now be prepared. Pound together the chopped lean pork and the pork fat, then season with salt, pepper, spice and parsley. Moisten with the brandy and add enough egg white to bind the mixture.

Spread the beef slices with the forcemeat on the seasoned side and roll up. Wrap each paupiette in a slice of salt pork, and tie with fine string to keep it in shape.

Fry the paupiettes in a flameproof casserole in the butter until the salt pork is lightly browned, then remove and fry the onion and the carrot in the same fat until just beginning to brown. Place the paupiettes on top of the vegetables and add enough stock to come halfway up the paupiettes. Add the bouquet garni and cover with a tight-fitting lid. Braise in a moderate oven (350°F) for approximately 1½ hours, or until cooked. Twenty minutes before the end of the cooking time, remove the lid and take away the strings and the salt pork slices. Baste frequently with the braising liquid from this point onwards, so as to glaze the surface of the paupiettes.

Place the paupiettes in a circle on a warmed serving dish. To make the sauce, pass the braising liquid through a fine strainer. Dissolve the arrowroot in a little cold water, and use this to thicken the sauce. Place a Potato Croquette on top of each paupiette, fill the centre of the dish with a purée of white haricot beans and surround all with the sauce.

SERVES 8

Hungarian Goulash

Goulash à la Hongroise

½ cup lard or olive oil
2½ lb beef chuck, cut into 12 cubes
1 large onion, peeled and cut into large dice
salt
1 teaspoon paprika
1 lb tomatoes, peeled, quartered and seeded
1½ cups water
1 lb small potatoes, peeled and quartered

Heat the lard or oil in a flameproof casserole and fry the beef and onion over a moderate heat until the onion has become lightly colored. Season with salt and paprika and continue to cook for a few more minutes. Add the tomatoes and ½ cup water. Cover with a lid and cook gently for 1½ hours in a moderate oven (325°F).

Then add the quartered potatoes and the remaining water. Continue cooking in the oven without a lid, basting frequently, until the meat and potatoes are tender.

SERVES 6

Hamburgers with Onions

Beefsteak à la Hambourgeoise

1½ lb beef tenderloin, trimmed
4 egg yolks
1 small onion, peeled and chopped
2 tablespoons butter
salt
pepper
grated nutmeg
flour
clarified butter for frying

To garnish
1 onion, peeled and finely sliced
2 tablespoons butter

Chop the steak finely and mix in the egg yolks. Cook the chopped onion without coloring it in the butter, add to the meat and season with the salt, pepper and grated nutmeg.

Mold into round, flat patties using a little flour, and fry on both sides in the *clarified butter*. They are cooked when little beads of blood appear on the surface. Meanwhile, fry the onion for the garnish to a golden brown in the butter.

Arrange the hamburgers on a serving dish and place the fried onion on top.

SERVES 4

Flemish Beef Carbonnade

Carbonnades de Boeuf à la Flamande

$2\frac{1}{2}$ lb beef chuck or round, cut into small thinnish slices
salt
pepper
2 tablespoons olive oil
$1\frac{1}{4}$ lb onions, peeled and finely sliced
4 tablespoons butter
1 bouquet garni
2 tablespoons flour
3 cups dark beer
3 cups Brown Stock, page 8
$\frac{1}{3}$ cup brown sugar

Season the beef and fry quickly on both sides in the oil. At the same time, fry the onions in the butter.

Put the beef and onions in alternate layers in a shallow ovenproof casserole and add the bouquet garni. Stir the flour into the pan in which the beef was fried and brown lightly. Gradually add the beer and stock, stirring continuously until the mixture thickens. Add the sugar and bring to a boil, still stirring. Strain the sauce over the beef and onions, cover with a lid and cook gently in a moderate oven (325°F) for $2\frac{1}{2}$–3 hours, or until the beef is tender.

SERVES 6

Beef Stew Provençale

Estouffade de Boeuf à la Provençale

3 lb boneless beef for stew (chuck, blade or shank)
$\frac{1}{2}$ lb lean salt pork, diced
1 stick butter
$\frac{1}{2}$ lb small onions, peeled and quartered
salt
pepper
6 tablespoons flour
1 clove garlic, peeled and crushed
1 quart dry white wine
1 quart Brown Stock, page 8
1 lb tomatoes, crushed
1 bouquet garni
$\frac{1}{2}$ lb button mushrooms
2 cups black olives, pitted

Wipe the meat and trim off any excess fat. Cut the meat into about 12 cubes. Fry the diced salt pork in a large flameproof casserole in 5 tablespoons of the butter until brown, then remove and put it to one side. Place the quartered onions and the beef in the same pan, season with salt and pepper, and fry until brown on all sides. Drain off any surplus fat.

Replace the pork, sprinkle with the flour, add the crushed garlic, and continue to cook for a few minutes longer. Add the white wine and brown stock and stir well. Then add the tomatoes and bouquet garni, bring to a boil, cover and cook in a moderate oven (350°F) for $2\frac{1}{2}$–3 hours, or until the beef is tender. Meanwhile, fry the button mushrooms very gently in the remaining butter.

Remove the casserole from the oven when the meat is tender. Place a sieve over a large mixing bowl and tip the stew out into it. Allow to drain for a few minutes, then carefully remove the pieces of beef and pork. Place them in a clean flameproof casserole dish together with the fried mushrooms.

Tip the drained sauce into a pan and allow to rest for a few minutes until all the fat rises to the surface, then skim well. Adjust the consistency of the sauce, either by reducing it if it is too thin or by adding a little more brown stock if it is too thick. Check the seasoning and pass through a fine strainer onto the meat. Add the olives and simmer the stew very gently on top of the stove for 15 minutes before serving.

SERVES 8

Braised Oxtail with Chestnut Purée

Queue de Boeuf Cavour

4 tablespoons butter
3 onions, peeled and sliced
3 carrots, peeled and sliced
1 clove garlic, peeled and crushed
1 bouquet garni
$\frac{1}{4}$ lb fresh pork skin, blanched
2 oxtails, jointed, weighing in total about $5\frac{1}{2}$ lb
salt
pepper
1 quart Brown Stock, page 8
$1\frac{1}{4}$ cups dry white wine
3 tablespoons arrowroot
$\frac{1}{4}$ lb mushrooms, fried in butter
Chestnut Purée, page 139

Butter a flameproof braising pan and cover the bottom with the sliced vegetables, herbs and pork skin. Put the pieces of oxtail on top, season, cover with a lid and braise in a hot oven (475°F) for 15 minutes.

Remove from the oven, moisten with a little stock and reduce this to a glaze on top of the stove. Almost cover with the rest of the stock and the white wine. Cover with the lid, return to the oven and reduce the heat to moderate (325°F). Braise gently for $3\frac{1}{2}$–4 hours, or until the meat is tender.

Drain off the fat from the cooking liquid, then thicken the cooking liquid with the arrowroot, dissolved in a little cold water. Pass this sauce through a fine strainer. Put the pieces of oxtail in a clean pan and cover with the sauce. Add the mushrooms and simmer gently in the oven for another 15 minutes.

Serve the oxtail and its garnish in a deep dish. Serve a dish of chestnut purée separately.

SERVES 8

Tripe and Onions

Tripes à la Lyonnaise

2 lb dressed tripe
salt
1 stick butter
1 large onion, peeled and sliced
pepper
1 tablespoon white wine vinegar
1 tablespoon chopped fresh parsley

Tripe is usually sold as dressed tripe, which in effect means that it is part-cooked. For this recipe the tripe needs to be completely cooked before you start. To cook dressed tripe completely, simmer gently in salted water for about $1\frac{1}{2}$ hours or until the tripe is tender to the knife.

Drain and dry the cooked tripe and cut it into large strips. Heat 6 tablespoons of the butter in a skillet and fry the tripe quickly in the butter until golden brown. Fry the onion separately in the remaining butter until golden brown. Add it to the tripe, season and toss tripe and onions together in the pan until both are well colored.

Transfer the tripe and onions to a deep dish. Deglaze the pan with the vinegar and sprinkle over the tripe. Finally, sprinkle with chopped parsley.

SERVES 8

Veal Chops with Basil

Côtes de Veau au Basilic

1 large bunch basil leaves
1 stick plus 2 tablespoons butter
4 veal chops
salt
pepper
$\frac{1}{4}$ cup dry white wine
$\frac{1}{4}$ cup Meat Glaze, page 9

First prepare some basil-flavored butter. Blanch the basil leaves for 2 minutes, drain, refresh and squeeze dry. Pound finely, then mix in 6 tablespoons of the butter and pass through a fine sieve.

Season the veal chops, shallow fry in the remaining butter and place on a dish. Keep warm. Deglaze the pan with the white wine and add the meat glaze. Take the pan off the heat and shake in the basil-flavored butter.

Coat the chops with this sauce.

SERVES 4

Veal Chops Peasant-style

Côtes de Veau en Cocotte à la Paysanne

4 veal chops
salt
pepper
½ lb slab bacon, cut in lardons
1 stick butter
16 pearl onions
1 lb small potatoes, peeled and thickly sliced
6 tablespoons Brown Stock, page 8

Place the seasoned chops and *lardons* of bacon in a flameproof casserole and brown them in 4 tablespoons of the butter, coloring the chops on both sides.

Fry the pearl onions separately and gently in the remaining butter until lightly browned and add these to the casserole along with the potatoes. Cover with the lid and continue to cook in a moderately hot oven (375°F) for about 30–40 minutes, or until tender. Add the stock a few minutes before removing from the oven.

Serve the chops straight from the casserole dish.

SERVES 4

Farmhouse Veal Chops

Côtes de Veau à la Fermière

4 veal chops
salt
pepper
4 tablespoons butter
6 tablespoons Brown Stock, page 8

Garnish

2 large carrots, peeled and cut into paysanne
2 medium turnips, peeled and cut into paysanne
1 small onion, peeled and cut into large dice
2 stalks celery, cut into paysanne
4 tablespoons butter
salt
1 pinch sugar

Start by preparing the garnish. Fry all of the prepared vegetables gently for a few minutes in the butter with the salt and sugar.

Season the chops and fry gently in the butter in a flameproof casserole. Add the garnish, cover with a lid and continue to cook in a moderately hot oven (375°F) for 30–40 minutes or until the cutlets are tender.

Just before serving, moisten with the stock and serve the chops straight from the casserole.

SERVES 4

Veal Tenderloin with Paprika

Filet de Veau au Paprika

3 lb 6 oz veal tenderloin roast, trimmed
¼ lb slab bacon, cut into thin strips 3 inches long
paprika
salt
4 tablespoons lard or butter
1 large onion, peeled, sliced and blanched
1¼ cups heavy cream

To garnish

Cauliflower au Gratin, page 134, prepared as florets
⅔ cup chopped lean cooked ham
paprika

Lard the veal with the strips of slab bacon, sprinkle generously with paprika, season with salt and fry in hot lard or butter.

Cover the bottom of an ovenproof casserole, just large enough to hold the meat, with a layer of the sliced and blanched onions. Place the meat on top and cover with a lid. *Poêlé* the meat in a hot oven (425°F) basting frequently with the fat, for approximately 1 hour or until just cooked. Place the veal on a serving plate and keep warm.

Meanwhile, prepare the florets of Cauliflower au Gratin, coating them as described with Mornay Sauce; to accompany this particular dish, though, the Mornay Sauce should contain chopped ham and be flavored with paprika. Brown the sauced cauliflower in a hot oven or under the broiler before serving.

Deglaze the meat and onion pan with the cream and pass through a fine strainer. Serve this sauce separately.

SERVES 6

Breast of Veal with Celery

Poitrine de Veau aux Céleris

7 lb breast of veal, boned (about 5½ lb after boning)
6 tablespoons butter
1 quart White Stock, page 9
5–6 bunches of celery, trimmed and blanched

Pork forcemeat
1 tablespoon chopped onion
1 tablespoon chopped shallot
4 tablespoons butter
½ lb mushrooms, finely chopped
salt
pepper
1½ tablespoons chopped fresh parsley
1 tablespoon chopped fresh tarragon
1 lb bulk pork sausage meat
2 cups fresh white bread crumbs
1 egg
1 pinch apple pie spice

First prepare the forcemeat. Fry the onion and shallot gently in the hot butter, and add the mushrooms. Fry gently until all the moisture has evaporated, season and add the chopped herbs. Add the sausage meat, bread crumbs, egg and spice and check the seasoning; mix all these ingredients together, stuff the breast and sew up with butcher's twine.

Heat the butter in a flameproof braising pan, season the veal and color it lightly on both sides. Add the stock and braise the stuffed veal breast slowly, basting frequently, in a moderate oven (350°F) for 2 hours.

The breast should now be about two-thirds cooked. Remove it and place in a clean pan. Surround with the bunches of celery, cover with the strained braising liquid and return to the oven to cook for about 1 hour. Remove the lid just before the end of the cooking time and allow the meat to brown.

Arrange the breast on a serving dish surrounded by the celery, cut into portions. Remove the fat from the braising liquid and reduce to the desired quantity and consistency. Serve this sauce separately.

SERVES 10–12

Veal Sauté Marengo

Sauté de Veau Marengo

3 lb 6 oz veal for stew, cut into small pieces
salt
pepper
½ cup oil
1 onion, peeled and chopped
1 clove garlic, peeled and crushed
1 cup dry white wine
1 quart Brown Stock, page 8
3 lb tomatoes, peeled, seeded and roughly chopped
1 bouquet garni
24 pearl onions
3 tablespoons butter
24 button mushrooms
2 pinches roughly chopped fresh parsley

To garnish
8 slices white bread, cut into heart shapes
clarified butter or oil

Season and fry the pieces of veal in very hot oil until well colored on all sides. Add the onion and garlic and fry until golden brown.

Drain off the oil, add the white wine and reduce a little. Add the stock, tomatoes and bouquet garni and cook gently in a moderate oven (325°F) for 1½ hours.

Meanwhile, fry and color the pearl onions gently in the butter. When the onions are colored, add the button mushrooms and fry lightly. When the veal is cooked, transfer it to a clean pan with the fried pearl onions, the mushrooms and the parsley. Reduce the sauce by one-third and pass it through a fine strainer over the veal and vegetables. Simmer for 15 minutes and remove any fat.

Place in a deep dish and garnish with small heart-shaped croûtons of bread fried in *clarified butter* or oil.

SERVES 8

Veal Sauté Marengo

Veal Blanquette

Blanquette de Veau à l'Ancienne

3 lb 6 oz veal for stew, cut into cubes
enough White Stock to cover the veal, page 9
salt
1 carrot, peeled
1 onion, peeled and stuck with 1 clove
1 leek
1 bouquet garni
5 tablespoons butter
$\frac{1}{2}$ cup flour
$\frac{1}{4}$ lb white mushrooms, chopped, or mushroom trimmings, white pieces only
24 pearl onions, peeled
24 button mushrooms
juice of $\frac{1}{2}$ lemon
5 egg yolks
$\frac{1}{2}$ cup heavy cream
grated nutmeg
2 tablespoons chopped fresh parsley

Cover the veal with stock and add just a little salt. Bring to a boil slowly, stirring frequently, and skim carefully. Add the vegetables and bouquet garni and simmer gently for $1\frac{1}{2}$ hours, or until tender.

Now prepare a velouté. Make a *roux* with the butter and flour and gradually add 5 cups of the cooking liquid from the veal. Add the chopped mushrooms and allow to simmer gently for 15 minutes, skimming the sauce as necessary.

Cook the pearl onions in lightly salted water for 6 minutes. Simmer the button mushrooms separately in water with a few drops of lemon juice for 3 minutes. Drain the pieces of veal and place in a clean pan with the cooked pearl onions and mushrooms.

Finish the sauce at the last moment with a *liaison*, consisting of the egg yolks, cream and a few more drops of lemon juice. Adjust the seasoning and add a little grated nutmeg.

Strain the sauce over the veal, reheat without boiling and place in a deep serving dish. Sprinkle with the chopped parsley.

SERVES 8

Sweetbreads Cévenole

Ris de Veau à la Cévenole

3 pairs veal sweetbreads
1 small onion, peeled and sliced
1 large carrot, peeled and sliced
4 tablespoons butter
1 bouquet garni
salt
pepper
White Stock, page 9
arrowroot

To garnish

6 slices brown bread, cut to the shape of a rooster's comb
4 tablespoons clarified butter
glazed pearl onions
Chestnut Purée, page 139

Soak the sweetbreads under cold running water for 2–3 hours to remove all the blood. Drain and put them in a pan. Cover with cold water, heat and bring to a boil. Pour off the liquid, rinse and cool under cold water. Remove all gristle and connective tissue, then place between two clean cloths, pressed between two plates, until quite cold.

Stew the vegetables gently in the butter for a few minutes in a flameproof casserole. Add the bouquet garni, seasoning and enough stock almost to cover the vegetables, then reduce the stock to a glaze. Place the sweetbreads on top of the vegetables and add more stock, to come halfway up the sweetbreads. Heat to boiling point. Baste the sweetbreads, cover the casserole and cook in a moderate oven (350°F) for 1 hour, basting from time to time. Remove the lid about 10 minutes before the end of the cooking time, baste and allow the sweetbreads to glaze to a light brown.

Fry the shapes of brown bread in the *clarified butter*. Arrange the braised sweetbreads on a dish with glazed pearl onions and the croûtons of fried bread. Serve accompanied by the chestnut purée and the braising liquid, lightly thickened with a little arrowroot.

SERVES 6

Sweetbreads Cévenole with Chestnut Purée

Sweetbreads au Gratin

Ris de Veau au Gratin

3 pairs veal sweetbreads
1 small onion, peeled and sliced
1 large carrot, peeled and sliced
6 tablespoons butter
1 bouquet garni
salt
pepper
White Stock, page 9
1¼ cups reduced Duxelles Sauce, page 12
2 cups sliced button mushrooms
½ cup fresh bread crumbs
4 tablespoons melted butter
a few drops lemon juice
1 tablespoon chopped fresh parsley

Soak the sweetbreads under cold running water for 2–3 hours to remove all the blood. Drain and put them in a pan. Cover with cold water, heat and bring to a boil. Pour off the liquid, rinse and cool under cold water. Remove all gristle and connective tissue then place between two clean cloths, pressed between two plates, and leave until quite cold.

Stew the vegetables gently in 4 tablespoons butter for a few minutes in a flameproof casserole. Add the bouquet garni, seasoning and enough stock to cover the vegetables, then reduce the stock to a glaze. Place the sweetbreads on top of the vegetables, and add more stock to come halfway up the sides of the sweetbreads. Heat to boiling point. Baste the sweetbreads, cover the casserole and cook in a moderate oven (350°F) for 1 hour, basting from time to time. Remove the lid about 10 minutes before the end of the cooking time, baste and allow the sweetbreads to glaze to a light brown.

Cut the braised sweetbreads into slices and reform, in an ovenproof gratin dish, in their original shape, spreading a spoonful of the reduced Duxelles Sauce between each slice.

Fry the button mushrooms gently in the remaining butter. Surround the sweetbreads with the mushrooms, then cover the sweetbreads with some more Duxelles Sauce. Sprinkle the sweetbreads with bread crumbs and melted butter and gratinate quickly in a hot oven (425°F) until the bread crumb mixture is golden brown.

Sprinkle with a few drops of lemon juice and chopped parsley before serving.

SERVES 6

Calf's Liver with Raisins

Foie de Veau aux Raisins

¼ cup golden raisins
¼ cup currants
8 slices calf's liver
salt
pepper
4 tablespoons butter
2 tablespoons red wine vinegar
1 pinch brown sugar
¾ cup Demi-glace Sauce, page 10

Pick over and wash the raisins and currants. Soak them well in advance in warm water to allow them to swell.

Season the liver and fry in the butter, then arrange on a round dish. Keep warm. Deglaze the pan with the vinegar and add the sugar and Demi-glace Sauce. Reduce the sauce to the desired consistency and pass through a fine strainer.

Add the drained raisins and currants to the sauce and simmer for a few more minutes. Pour over the liver and serve.

SERVES 4

Veal Kidneys Robert

Rognons de Veau Robert

3 veal kidneys
salt
pepper
1 stick butter
½ cup brandy
1 teaspoon prepared mustard
½ tablespoon lemon juice
1 pinch chopped fresh parsley

Trim the kidneys, leaving a thin layer of their suet. Season them and fry quickly in 4 tablespoons of the butter in a flameproof *cocotte* to brown slightly on all sides. Cover and cook in a hot oven (425°F) for 20 minutes.

Transfer the kidneys to a warmed dish. Deglaze the cocotte with the brandy and reduce by half. Meanwhile, cut the kidneys into very thin slices, cover and keep warm.

To the reduced brandy add the mustard and the remaining butter. Add the lemon juice and the parsley. Mix together with a fork, then add the prepared slices of kidney along with any juices which have drained from them. Reheat everything together but do not allow to boil, and serve immediately.

SERVES 6

Calf's Liver with Raisins

Veal Kidneys en Cocotte

Rognons de Veau en Cocotte

3 veal kidneys
salt
pepper
6 tablespoons butter
¼ lb slab bacon, diced and blanched
¼ lb mushrooms, quartered
¼ lb small potatoes, peeled, trimmed to the shape of olives and blanched
3 tablespoons Brown Stock, page 8

Trim and season the kidneys, leaving them covered with a thin layer of their suet. Place 4 tablespoons of the butter in a flameproof *cocotte*, heat it, add the seasoned kidneys and fry till slightly brown on all sides.

Meanwhile, fry the blanched bacon separately in the remaining butter, then add the quartered mushrooms and fry together. Surround the kidneys with the fried bacon and mushrooms and the blanched potatoes, cover and complete the cooking in a moderately hot oven (400°F) for 30 minutes.

At the last minute, moisten with the stock and serve straight from the cocotte.

SERVES 6

Brains with Black Butter

Cervelle au Beurre Noir

8 pairs calf's brains
1½ quarts boiling Court-bouillon with Vinegar, page 40
salt
pepper
1½ sticks butter
2 tablespoons chopped fresh parsley
2 tablespoons white wine vinegar

Place the brains under gently running cold water so as to extract as much of the blood as possible, then carefully remove all of the membrane and connective tissue which surrounds them. Place once again under gently running water to soak out any remaining blood.

To cook them, place in the boiling Court-bouillon with Vinegar and allow to poach gently for about 25–30 minutes.

Cut the cooked brains into thick slices and arrange on a dish. Season with salt and pepper. Cook the butter to a dark brown color (or *à la noisette* to a more than usual degree), and then add the parsley to it at the last minute. Pour the butter and parsley mixture over the brains. Swill out the pan in which the butter was cooked with the vinegar and pour this over the buttered brains.

SERVES 8

Lamb Chops Reform

Côtelettes d'Agneau à la Réforme

16 lamb rib chops, well trimmed
salt
pepper
flour
1 stick melted butter
1½ cups dried white bread crumbs
½ cup very finely chopped lean cooked ham
1 stick clarified butter

Reform Sauce

1 cup Poivrade Sauce, page 10
1 cup Demi-glace Sauce, page 10
2 small gherkins, cut into short julienne
1 hard-boiled egg white, cut into short julienne
¼ cup mushrooms, cut into short julienne and cooked in butter
¾ oz truffle, cut into short julienne
1 slice cooked salted beef tongue, cut into short julienne

Lightly flatten the chops to about ¼ inch thick and season. Coat them in flour and dip in the melted butter, then in the bread crumbs mixed with the chopped ham.

Pat carefully with the flat of a knife to ensure that the crumb mixture sticks to the chops, and fry in the *clarified butter* for about 2 minutes on each side or until light golden in color.

Serve accompanied by Reform Sauce. This is made by combining the Poivrade and Demi-glace Sauces and adding the gherkin, hard-boiled egg white, mushroom, truffle and tongue all cut into short *julienne*. Serve the sauce separately.

SERVES 8

Lamb Chops Reform

Lamb Chops Navarraise

Côtelettes d'Agneau à la Navarraise

8 lamb rib chops, well trimmed
salt
pepper
⅔ cup chopped lean cooked ham
¼ lb mushrooms, fried in butter and chopped
1½ tablespoons diced sweet red pepper, cooked
¾ cup very thick Béchamel Sauce, page 12
¼ cup grated Parmesan
4 tablespoons melted butter

To garnish
4 large tomatoes, halved
oil
1 cup Tomato Sauce, page 14

Season and broil the chops on one side only. Coat the cooked sides with a mixture of ham, mushrooms, red pepper and very thick béchamel sauce, arranged in a dome shape.

Place the chops on an ovenproof dish, uncooked sides downwards, and sprinkle with the grated Parmesan and the melted butter. Put in a hot oven (450°F) and cook for about 8–10 minutes, both to complete the cooking and to gratinate the surface of the chops.

When they are ready, arrange in a circle on a dish, placing each chop on half a large tomato, seasoned and fried in oil. Surround with a *cordon* of tomato sauce.

SERVES 4

Shoulder of Lamb Boulangère

Epaule d'Agneau à la Boulangère

1 shoulder of lamb, weighing about 4½ lb, boned
salt
pepper
1 large onion, peeled and sliced
4 tablespoons butter
2½ lb potatoes, peeled and sliced
2 pinches chopped fresh parsley

Season the inside of the shoulder of lamb, then roll and tie it carefully with string. Place it in a roasting pan and cook in a hot oven (425°F) for 30 minutes, until the lamb is brown and partly cooked.

Place the shoulder in an ovenproof dish and surround with the sliced onions, fried in the butter without being colored, and the sliced potatoes. Sprinkle with the fat from the roasting pan and return to the oven. Cook, basting frequently, for another 1½ hours or until the juices that run when the meat is pricked with a trussing needle are colorless.

When the meat is cooked, remove the string and sprinkle with the chopped parsley.

SERVES 8

Shoulder of Lamb with Turnips

Epaule d'Agneau aux Navets

1 shoulder of lamb, weighing about 4½ lb, boned
1 large onion, peeled and sliced
½ lb carrots, peeled and sliced
1 clove garlic, peeled and crushed
1 stick butter
1 bouquet garni
salt
pepper
1 quart Brown Stock, page 8
2 lb turnips, peeled and trimmed to the shape of large olives
1 pinch sugar
20 pearl onions, peeled
½ tablespoon tomato paste
2 tablespoons arrowroot

Pork forcemeat
1 large onion, peeled and chopped
4 tablespoons butter
1 lb bulk pork sausage meat
1 tablespoon chopped fresh parsley
1 pinch powdered thyme
3 cups fresh bread crumbs
1 egg
salt
pepper

First of all prepare the forcemeat. Fry the onion in the butter without allowing it to color, then let it cool. Add the onion to the sausage meat and mix together with the herbs, bread crumbs and egg, and a little seasoning as needed.

Stuff the boned shoulder of lamb with the pork forcemeat, roll and tie carefully with string. Fry the vegetables and garlic in 2 tablespoons of the butter, allowing them to brown slightly, and place with the bouquet garni in the bottom of a flameproof braising pan, just large enough to hold the meat. Season the meat and fry it in another 2 tablespoons of the butter to brown it on all sides. Place on top of the vegetables, moisten with a little stock and cover with the lid. Place over a moderate heat and cook until the stock is reduced to a glaze. Add the rest of the stock, to come about halfway up the meat this time, and bring to a boil. Place the braising pan in a moderate oven (350°F) for about 3 hours, basting frequently.

Meanwhile, fry the turnips gently with the sugar in another 2 tablespoons of the butter, and fry the pearl onions to color lightly in the remainder of the butter.

When the meat is three-quarters cooked (after about 2 hours 10 minutes), remove the shoulder and place it in a shallow pan. Surround with the lightly browned turnips and onions.

Remove the fat from the braising liquid and strain over the meat and vegetables. Cover, return to the oven and complete the cooking. When ready, remove the string and place the shoulder in a deep dish surrounded by its garnish. Keep warm.

Skim the braising liquid of all fat, add the tomato paste and reduce carefully to about 2½ cups. Thicken with the arrowroot dissolved in a little water, season to taste and pass through a fine strainer. Pour some of the sauce over the shoulder of lamb and its garnish and serve the rest separately.

SERVES 8–10

Leg of Lamb Chivry

Gigot d'Agneau Chivry

1 leg of lamb weighing about 4½ lb
salt
pepper
flour

Chivry Sauce

2 good pinches each chopped fresh tarragon, parsley, chervil, chives and shallot, mixed
4 tablespoons butter, softened
½ cup dry white wine
2½ cups Velouté Sauce, pages 9–10, heated to boiling point

Season and flour the leg of lamb and tie it up carefully in a clean piece of cloth. Place in lightly salted boiling water and poach gently, allowing 25 minutes per pound.

Meanwhile, make the Chivry Sauce. First prepare a flavored butter: cover half the herbs and shallot with cold water, bring to a boil quickly, then drain and cool in cold water. Squeeze the herbs to remove as much liquid as possible, then pound to a fine purée and mix with the softened butter. Now bring the wine to a boil in a pan, add the remainder of the herbs and shallot, and allow to infuse for 10 minutes. Strain and add to the Velouté Sauce. Finish, away from the heat, by mixing in the prepared herb butter.

Remove the leg of lamb from the cooking liquid when ready. Place on a dish and serve accompanied by the Chivry Sauce.

SERVES 8

Leg of Lamb Liégeoise

Gigot d'Agneau à la Liégeoise

1 leg of lamb, weighing about 4½ lb
salt
pepper
4 tablespoons melted butter
2 cups Brown Stock, page 8
5 juniper berries, finely crushed
¼ cup gin, flaming

Mirepoix

1 large carrot, peeled and diced
1 small onion, peeled and diced
1 stalk celery, diced
4 slices bacon, diced
1 tablespoon butter
1 bay leaf
1 sprig thyme

Before *poêling* the meat, first prepare the *mirepoix*. Fry the vegetables and bacon gently in the butter and add the herbs.

Place a layer of mirepoix in a deep heavy flameproof *cocotte* just large enough to hold the piece of meat. Put the meat on top of the mirepoix, season well and coat with melted butter.

Cover with a lid and place in a moderately hot oven (400°F). Cook, basting frequently, for about 2 hours. When the meat is cooked, remove it and keep warm. Add the stock to the vegetables, which should not have been allowed to burn. Bring to a boil and simmer for 10 minutes. Strain, remove the fat and reduce by two-thirds. Add the finely crushed juniper berries and the flaming gin. Return the lamb to the cocotte, pour over the sauce and serve.

SERVES 8

Rack of Lamb with Onion Purée

Carré d'Agneau Soubise

1 rack of lamb, weighing about 2½ lb
salt
pepper
1 stick plus 2 tablespoons butter
1 large onion, peeled, finely sliced and blanched
¾ cup boiling Béchamel Sauce, page 12

Season the rack of lamb and fry gently in 4 tablespoons of the butter until golden brown. Fry the onion separately in another 2 tablespoons of the butter without browning.

Transfer the lamb to an ovenproof casserole and surround with the lightly fried onion. Cover with a lid and place in a moderately hot oven (375°F). Cook for 45 minutes.

Transfer the meat to a dish and keep warm. Add the boiling béchamel sauce to the onion, mix together and pass through a fine sieve. Reheat this onion purée and finish with the remaining butter.

Place the meat on a suitable dish and accompany with the onion purée in a sauceboat.

Serves 4

Rack of Lamb Marly

Carré d'Agneau Marly

1 rack of lamb, weighing about 2½ lb
salt
pepper
4 tablespoons butter
1 lb snow peas, broken into small pieces
1 pinch sugar
1 tablespoon water
1½ cups flour
½ cup water

Season the rack of lamb and fry quickly in the butter to a golden brown color. Transfer it to an ovenproof casserole and add the snow peas, sugar, salt and 1 tablespoon water.

Cover with the lid and seal with a band of stiff paste (*repère*) made by mixing together the flour and water. Cook in a moderately hot oven (375°F) for 1 hour.

Serves 4

Rack of Lamb Mireille

Carré d'Agneau Mireille

1 lb unbaked Potatoes Anna, page 142
½ lb raw artichoke bottoms, sliced
1 rack of lamb, weighing about 2½ lb
salt
pepper
4 tablespoons butter

In a shallow oval ovenproof dish large enough to hold the lamb comfortably, prepare a layer of unbaked Potatoes Anna, according to the recipe on page 142, but incorporating the artichoke bottoms as well as the sliced potatoes.

Bake in a hot oven (425°F) for 20 minutes. Meanwhile season the rack of lamb and brown it quickly in the butter.

Place it on top of the potatoes and return to the oven to complete the cooking of potatoes and lamb together. Turn the temperature down to (350°F) and cook for a further 45 minutes, basting frequently. Serve from the dish.

Serves 4

Sauté of Lamb Chasseur

Sauté d'Agneau Chasseur

4½ lb boneless leg and/or shoulder of lamb, trimmed of fat
salt
pepper
4 tablespoons butter
2 tablespoons olive oil
1 cup dry white wine
1¼ cups Chasseur Sauce, page 12
2 tablespoons chopped fresh parsley

Cut the meat into 1-inch cubes, season and fry in the butter and oil on all sides for about 20 minutes, or until completely cooked.

Remove the pieces of lamb and place them on a dish to keep warm. Drain off the fat and deglaze the pan with the white wine. Reduce by half and add the Chasseur Sauce. Replace the pieces of lamb in this sauce and reheat, without boiling, for 5 minutes.

Place in a *timbale* or deep serving dish and sprinkle generously with the chopped parsley.

Serves 8

Lamb Stew with Spring Vegetables

Navarin Printanier

½ cup clean fat, such as strained drippings
5½ lb boneless breast, neck and shoulder of lamb, cut in about 30 pieces
salt
pepper
1 pinch sugar
6 tablespoons flour
1½ quarts Brown Stock, page 8
3 tablespoons tomato paste
1 clove garlic, peeled and crushed
1 large bouquet garni
¾ lb small new carrots, peeled
¾ lb small new turnips, peeled
4 tablespoons butter
20 pearl onions
1 lb small new potatoes
1 cup shelled fresh peas
1 cup green beans, trimmed and cut into diamond shapes

Heat the fat in a flameproof casserole and add the pieces of lamb. Season, add the sugar and fry quickly until brown on all sides. Drain off almost all of the fat, sprinkle with the flour and cook for a few more minutes.

Add the stock and the tomato paste, garlic and bouquet garni. Bring to a boil, stirring continuously, cover with a lid and transfer to a moderate oven (350°F) to cook for about 1 hour, or until almost tender. Meanwhile, fry the carrots and turnips quickly in the butter until lightly browned.

Transfer the meat to a clean ovenproof casserole and add the carrots, turnips, pearl onions, potatoes, peas and beans. Skim off the fat from the sauce and strain over the meat and vegetables. Cover with a lid and return to the oven to cook for approximately 45 minutes more, or until everything is tender, basting frequently with the sauce.

Before serving, remove any remaining fat, place in a deep serving dish and serve very hot.

SERVES 10

Braised Lamb Avignonnaise

Daube à l'Avignonnaise

1½ lb boneless leg of lamb, cut into about 10 cubes
½ lb slab bacon, cut into strips 3 inches long
5 oz thinly sliced bacon
1 large onion, peeled and chopped
2 cloves garlic, peeled and crushed
½ lb slab bacon, diced and blanched
½ lb fresh pork skin, blanched and cut into 1 inch squares
1 pinch dried thyme
1 pinch powdered bay leaf
1 large bouquet of parsley stalks wrapped around a strip of dried orange peel
Brown Stock, page 8
1½ cups flour
½ cup water

Marinade

1 bottle red wine
½ cup olive oil
1 carrot, peeled and sliced
1 onion, peeled and sliced
4 cloves garlic, peeled
1 sprig thyme
1 bay leaf
a few parsley stalks

Lard each piece of lamb with a strip of slab bacon and marinate for 2 hours with all the marinade ingredients. Drain the lamb, reserving the marinade.

Cover the bottom and sides of a flameproof casserole with thin slices of slab bacon, reserving a few for the top. Inside this, arrange the lamb, the chopped onion mixed with the garlic, the diced bacon and the pork skin in alternate layers, lightly seasoning each layer of lamb and finally sprinkling all with dried thyme and powdered bay leaf. Place the *bouquet* of parsley stalks and orange peel in the center.

Strain the marinade and add to the casserole, along with enough stock to cover. Finish with the remaining slices of bacon, replace the lid and seal the casserole with a band of *repère* (see page 86 and Glossary). Bring to a boil, then place in a moderate oven (325°F) to cook for 5 hours.

At the end of the cooking time, discard the bouquet of parsley stalks and orange peel, and skim off any fat from the surface of the cooking liquid. Serve from the casserole.

SERVES 6

Cassoulet

Cassoulet

5 cups dried navy beans, soaked overnight
3 quarts water
1 carrot, peeled
1 onion, peeled and stuck with 1 clove
2 bouquet garnis
3 cloves garlic, peeled
¾ lb fresh pork skin, blanched
¾ lb fresh side pork, blanched
¾ lb whole garlic sausage
1 lb boned shoulder of lamb, cut into about 10 pieces
1 lb boned breast of lamb, cut into about 10 pieces
4 tablespoons lard
1 large onion, peeled and chopped
2 cloves garlic, peeled and crushed
3 tablespoons tomato paste
salt
½ cup fresh bread crumbs

Place the drained beans in a pan with the water and the carrot, onion, 1 bouquet garni, garlic and blanched pork skin. Bring to a boil, skim, cover and simmer gently for 1 hour.

Add the blanched side pork and whole garlic sausage and continue cooking until the beans are cooked but still firm.

Fry the boned shoulder of lamb and the breast of lamb in the lard in a flameproof casserole. Drain off half the fat, add the chopped onion and crushed garlic and continue frying until everything is lightly browned.

Now add enough of the cooking liquid from the beans to cover the meat, plus the tomato paste and the other bouquet garni. Season, cover and place in a cool oven (300°F) to bake very gently, for at least 1½ hours.

Cover the bottom of a deep ovenproof casserole with the pork skin and fill with alternate layers of the lamb and sauce, the beans, the side pork cut into cubes and slices of garlic sausage. Sprinkle with the bread crumbs and gratinate in a moderate oven (350°F) for 1 hour, basting from time to time with a little of the remaining cooking liquid from the beans.

SERVES 10

Kidney Brochettes

Brochettes de Rognons d'Agneau

8 lamb kidneys
salt
pepper
6 tablespoons butter
½ lb large mushrooms, thickly sliced
½ lb sliced bacon, blanched and cut into squares
2 tablespoons melted butter
½ cup fresh white bread crumbs

Skin the kidneys and cut them into round slices about ¼ inch thick. Season with salt and pepper and fry quickly in 4 tablespoons of very hot butter just to set the flesh. Fry the mushrooms gently in the remaining butter.

Thread the slices of kidney on skewers, alternating with squares of blanched bacon and slices of fried mushroom. Brush the skewers with melted butter, sprinkle with the bread crumbs and broil. Serve immediately.

SERVES 4

Broiled Kidneys Vert-Pré

Rognons d'Agneau Vert-Pré

8 lamb kidneys
salt
pepper

To garnish
Straw Potatoes, page 144
a few sprigs watercress

Skin the kidneys and open out by cutting through them from the convex side without actually separating the two halves. Thread them crosswise on a skewer to keep them open, then season and broil.

Arrange on an oval dish with straw potatoes at the sides and sprigs of watercress at either end.

SERVES 4

Cassoulet

Kidneys Turbigo

Rognons Turbigo

4 lamb kidneys
salt
pepper
4 tablespoons butter
½ cup dry white wine
¾ cup Demi-glace Sauce, page 10
½ tablespoon tomato paste
cayenne pepper

To garnish

¼ lb button mushrooms
2 tablespoons butter
8 small cocktail sausages, broiled

Skin the kidneys and cut in half lengthwise. Season and fry quickly in 4 tablespoons of hot butter. Fry the mushrooms for the garnish separately in 2 tablespoons butter.

Drain the kidneys well and arrange in a circle in a deep dish. Place the mushrooms and sausages in the center of the dish.

Deglaze the pan with the white wine and reduce. Flavor the Demi-glace Sauce with the tomato paste and add this to the reduction. Season with a touch of cayenne pepper, and strain this sauce over the kidneys.

SERVES 4

Roast Pork Loin with White Beans

Carré de Porc à la Soissonnaise

4½ lb pork loin roast
salt
pepper
olive oil
3 lb white beans (Great Northern or navy), cooked and drained (about 8 cups)

Season the pork roast, place in a flameproof casserole and sprinkle with a little oil for basting. Roast in a hot oven (425°F) for about 25 minutes per pound.

When the meat is three-quarter cooked (after about 1¼ hours), surround it with the cooked white beans. Finish cooking the meat together with the beans, reducing the temperature if either meat or beans begin to burn, and basting the beans frequently with the fat from the pork. When the meat is cooked, remove from the oven and serve from the casserole.

SERVES 6–8

Roast Pork Loin Peasant-style

Carré de Porc à la Paysanne

4½ lb pork loin roast
salt
pepper
olive oil
1 large onion, peeled and sliced
4 tablespoons butter
2 lb medium-sized potatoes, peeled and quartered
1 tablespoon roughly chopped fresh parsley

Season the pork roast, place in a flameproof casserole and sprinkle with a little oil for basting. Roast in a hot oven (425°F) for about 25 minutes per pound. Fry the onions gently in the butter.

When the meat is half-cooked (after about 50 minutes), surround the pork with the gently fried onions and the quartered potatoes. Lightly season the vegetables and complete the cooking of meat and vegetables together, basting frequently and reducing the temperature if either meat or vegetables begin to burn.

When both meat and vegetables are cooked, remove from the oven, sprinkle with the parsley and serve the dish direct from the casserole.

SERVES 6–8

Braised Ham with Broad Beans

Jambon aux Fèves de Marais

1 small whole smoked country ham, weighing about 10 lb
1¾ cups dry sherry
1½ cups flour
½ cup water
confectioners' sugar

To garnish

broad (fava) beans, cooked, skinned and buttered
1 tablespoon chopped fresh savory

Soak the ham in cold water for 6 hours and remove the aitch (hip) bone. Place it in a large pot with plenty of cold water, but no seasoning or flavoring. Bring to a boil and simmer very gently for 3–3½ hours, allowing 20 minutes per pound.

Remove the ham from the liquid 30 minutes before the end of the cooking time. Remove the skin and trim off excess fat. Place in a braising pan just large enough to hold it and add the dry sherry.

Cover with a tight-fitting lid, seal with a band of *repère* (see page 86 and Glossary) and braise in a cool oven (300°F) for 1 hour, to complete the cooking and to allow the ham to become impregnated with the sherry.

Cover the surface of the cooked ham with confectioners' sugar, using a sugar sifter, and glaze in a very hot oven or under the broiler.

Place on a suitable dish and serve with a dish of very fresh broad beans, boiled, their skins removed and buttered, mixed with a little chopped savory. Serve with the braising sherry from the ham, well skimmed of fat and reduced.

SERVES 10–12

Braised Ham with Lettuce

Jambon aux Laitues

1 small whole smoked country ham, weighing about 10 lb
1¾ cups dry Madeira
1½ cups flour
½ cup water
confectioners' sugar

To garnish
braised lettuce
Demi-glace Sauce, page 10

Soak the ham in cold water for 6 hours and remove the aitch (hip) bone. Place it in a large pot with plenty of cold water, but no seasoning or flavoring. Bring to a boil and simmer very gently for 2½–3 hours, allowing 20 minutes per pound.

Remove the ham from the liquid 30 minutes before the end of the cooking time. Remove the skin and trim off excess fat. Place in a braising pan just large enough to hold it and add the dry Madeira.

Cover with a tight-fitting lid, seal with a band of *repère* (see page 86 and Glossary) and braise in a cool oven (300°F) for 1 hour, to complete the cooking and to allow the ham to become impregnated with the Madeira.

Cover the surface of the cooked ham with confectioners' sugar, using a sugar sifter, and glaze in a very hot oven or under the broiler.

Place on a suitable dish and surround with halves of braised lettuce. Serve accompanied by a light Demi-glace Sauce, page 10, finished with the reduced braising Madeira in place of the final addition of Brown Stock.

SERVES 10–12

Braised Ham with Madeira Sauce

Jambon à la Bayonnaise

1 small whole smoked country ham, weighing about 10 lb
1¾ cups dry Madeira
1½ cups flour
½ cup water
confectioners' sugar

To garnish
Demi-glace Sauce, page 10
2½ cups long-grain rice made into Rice Pilaff, page 145, with ⅔ cup diced tomato flesh, 20 cooked button mushrooms and 20 small cooked cocktail sausages added halfway through the cooking

Soak the ham in cold water for 6 hours and remove the aitch (hip) bone. Place it in a large pot with plenty of cold water, but no seasoning or flavoring. Bring to a boil and simmer very gently for 2½–3 hours, allowing 20 minutes per pound.

Remove the ham from the liquid 30 minutes before the end of the cooking time. Remove the skin and trim off excess fat. Place in a braising pan just large enough to hold it and add the dry Madeira.

Cover with a tight-fitting lid, seal with a band of *repère* (see page 86 and Glossary) and braise in a cool oven (300°F) for 1 hour, to complete the cooking and allow the ham to become impregnated with the Madeira.

Cover the surface of the cooked ham with confectioners' sugar, using a sugar sifter, and glaze in a very hot oven or under the broiler.

Serve accompanied by a light Demi-glace Sauce, page 10, finished with the reduced braising Madeira in place of the final addition of Brown Stock.

Place the ham on a suitable dish and serve with the sauce, handed separately, and a dish of the specially prepared Rice Pilaff.

SERVES 10–12

Ham Mousse

Mousse Froide de Jambon

1 lb lean cooked ham, chopped
1 cup cold Velouté Sauce, pages 9–10
salt
pepper
¾ cup aspic, melted, below
1¾ cups heavy cream, lightly whipped
more aspic, below

Finely pound the chopped ham or work in a food processor, and add the cold Velouté Sauce. Pass through a fine sieve.

Put the resultant purée in a bowl and adjust the seasoning. Gradually add the melted aspic and finally fold in the lightly whipped cream.

Pour the mousse into a suitable mold, containing a set layer of clear aspic in the bottom if the mousse is to be unmolded before serving. Place in the refrigerator to set. If the mousse is to be served from the mold, cover the surface with a layer of aspic and place in the refrigerator to set.

Serves 4–8

Aspic

Gelée Ordinaire

2 quarts cold White Stock, page 9
½ lb lean boneless beef, ground
1 egg white
1 teaspoon chopped fresh chervil
1 teaspoon chopped fresh tarragon
3 envelopes unflavored gelatin

Skim the cold stock and decant, discarding any sediment. Place the ground beef, egg white and herbs in a thick-bottomed pan and add the cold stock, mixing well with a whisk or spatula. Slowly bring to a boil, stirring very gently and occasionally to ensure that the bottom of the pan is kept clean. Allow to simmer gently for 45 minutes without disturbance, then stir in the gelatin until completely dissolved. Strain through cheesecloth.

If wished, the consistency of the aspic may be checked following the addition of the gelatin. This can be done by putting a little on a plate and placing it in the refrigerator until chilled. If, once chilled, the gel is insufficient a little more gelatin may be used.

Makes approximately 1½ quarts

Blood Sausage Normandy-style

Boudins Noirs à la Normande

1 lb blood sausage
6 tablespoons butter
½ lb apples, peeled, cored and thickly sliced

Cut the blood sausage into slices and sauté them in half the butter, tossing frequently. Fry the sliced apples separately in the remaining butter. Combine all the ingredients in the same pan and toss well to mix together, then tip into a deep, warmed earthenware dish for service.

Serves 4

Sausages in White Wine

Saucisses au Vin Blanc

12 fresh pork sausage links
2 sticks butter
½ cup dry white wine
6 slices bread, crusts removed
1 egg yolk
a few drops lemon juice
1 tablespoon Meat Glaze, page 9

Fry the sausages quickly in 4 tablespoons of the butter to color, then poach them gently, covered, in the white wine for about 15 minutes.

Meanwhile, fry the slices of bread in 1 stick of the butter. When the sausages are cooked, arrange them on top of these croûtons.

Reduce the wine by two-thirds, then remove from the heat. When the wine has ceased boiling, add the egg yolk, lemon juice, meat glaze and remaining butter. Stir this sauce well without reheating and pour over the sausages.

Serves 6

Ham Mousse with Salad Aurore

POULTRY & GAME

Chicken Sylvana

Poularde Sylvana

1 large roaster chicken, weighing about 4–5 lb
4 tablespoons butter
$\frac{1}{2}$ lb button mushrooms
$1\frac{1}{2}$ cups flour
$\frac{1}{2}$ cup water

To garnish
$1\frac{2}{3}$ cup shelled peas
10 pearl onions
1 small head lettuce, shredded
1 bouquet garni, comprising fresh parsley stalks, chervil and thyme
1 pinch sugar
1 pinch salt
4 tablespoons butter

Season the chicken inside and out. Cook the butter until it is brown or *à la noisette*, then fry the mushrooms in it. Stuff the chicken with the mushrooms, truss well and roast in a moderately hot oven (400°F) for about 45 minutes, so it is nicely colored but only half-cooked.

Meanwhile, place the peas in a pan with the onions, lettuce, bouquet garni, sugar, salt and the butter. Add 2 tablespoons water, cover with a lid and half-cook, tossing from time to time.

Place the half-cooked chicken in an ovenproof casserole, surround with the garnish, cover with the lid and seal with a band of *repère* (see page 86 and Glossary). Place back in the oven for another 45 minutes or so to finish cooking.

Remove the trussing string and serve the chicken straight from the casserole. If required, it may be accompanied by a good chicken gravy, made using Chicken Stock, page 9.

SERVES 4–6

Tarragon Chicken

Poularde à l'Estragon

1 large roaster chicken, weighing about 4–5 lb
$\frac{1}{4}$ lb salt pork
enough Chicken Stock to cover, page 9
1 bunch of fresh tarragon, separated into stalks and leaves
salt
pepper
2 teaspoons arrowroot
1 tablespoon chopped fresh tarragon

Cover the bird with thin slices of salt pork and tie carefully. Place it in a pan just large enough to hold it and add enough chicken stock to cover. Bring rapidly to a boil, skim, add the tarragon stalks, tied in a bouquet, cover with a lid and allow to poach gently with only a barely discernible movement of the liquid for about $1–1\frac{1}{2}$ hours. The way to tell when the bird is cooked is to pierce the thick part of the leg just above the drumstick with a skewer: the juice should run perfectly clear and white. Meanwhile, blanch the tarragon leaves.

Remove the fat and arrange the cooked chicken on a dish; decorate the breast with a wreath of the blanched tarragon leaves, cover and keep hot. Strain 3 cups of the cooking liquid into a pan and reduce it by half. Blend the arrowroot with a little cold water, then stir it into the hot reduced stock. Bring back to a boil and stir until it thickens and clears. Finish the sauce with the chopped tarragon, season to taste and serve separately.

SERVES 6

Chicken à la Grecque

Poularde à la Grecque

1 large roaster chicken, weighing about 4–5 lb
about 2 cups Rice à la Grecque, page 145, three-quarters cooked only
salt
pepper
2 carrots, peeled and finely sliced
1 small onion, peeled and finely sliced
2 stalks celery, finely sliced
1 clove garlic, crushed
1 bay leaf
1 sprig thyme
4 slices bacon
6 tablespoons butter, melted
1½ cups Brown Stock, page 8
2 teaspoons arrowroot

Stuff the chicken with the Rice à la Grecque and truss. Season well. Layer the vegetables and herbs in the bottom of a deep, heavy ovenproof casserole, then place the chicken on top of these, cover it with the bacon and pour over the melted butter. Cover with the lid and place in a moderately hot oven (375°F). After 45 minutes of cooking time remove the bacon and place at the sides of the chicken. Cook for a further 60 minutes or until the chicken is ready, basting frequently with the butter.

Remove the lid for the last 15 minutes of the cooking time, adding ¼ cup of the stock and use this, together with the butter in the pan, to carry on basting the chicken so as to glaze and color it a light brown.

Remove the chicken when cooked, cover and keep warm.

Add the remaining stock to the pan and simmer gently for 5 minutes, then drain off the liquid and skim off the fat. Lightly thicken the liquid with the arrowroot blended with a little cold water, cook for 1 minute and season as necessary. Pass through a fine strainer.

Remove the trussing string from the chicken and coat with a little of the sauce. Serve the rest of the sauce separately.

Serves 4–6

Braised Chicken from Languedoc

Poularde à la Languedocienne

1 large roaster chicken, weighing about 4–5 lb, trussed
salt
pepper
2 carrots, peeled and finely sliced
1 small onion, peeled and finely sliced
2 stalks celery, finely sliced
1 clove garlic, crushed
1 bay leaf
1 sprig thyme
4 slices bacon
6 tablespoons butter, melted
1½ cups Brown Stock, page 8
2 teaspoons arrowroot
2 tablespoons dry Madeira

To garnish

very small skinned tomatoes lightly cooked in a little olive oil
round slices of eggplant, floured and fried in olive oil
thick slices of ceps or mushrooms fried in olive oil

Season the chicken. Layer a deep heavy ovenproof casserole with the vegetables and herbs, then place the chicken on top of these. Cover with the bacon and pour over the melted butter. Cover with the lid and place in a moderately hot oven (375°F). After 45 minutes of cooking time remove the bacon and place at the sides of the chicken. Cook for a further 60 minutes or until the chicken is ready. Baste frequently.

Remove the lid for the last 15 minutes of the cooking time, adding ¼ cup of the stock and use this, together with the butter in the pan, to carry on basting the chicken so as to glaze and color it a light brown.

Remove the chicken when cooked, cover and keep warm.

Add the remaining stock to the pan and simmer gently for 5 minutes, then drain off the liquid and skim off the fat. Lightly thicken the liquid with the arrowroot blended with a little cold water, cook for 1 minute and season as necessary. Pass through a fine strainer and finish the sauce with the dry Madeira. Do not reboil after the addition of the Madeira.

Remove the trussing string from the chicken and coat with a little of the sauce. Surround with neat *bouquets* of the garnish. Serve the rest of the sauce separately.

Serves 4–6

Springtime Chicken

Poularde Printanière

1 large roaster chicken, weighing about 4–5 lb
salt
pepper
2 carrots, peeled and sliced small
1 small onion, peeled and sliced small
1 clove garlic, crushed
1 bay leaf
1 sprig thyme
4 slices bacon
4 tablespoons butter, melted
½ cup Brown Stock, page 8

Printanier Butter
1 large carrot, peeled and sliced
½ small turnip, peeled and sliced
1 onion, peeled and sliced
White Stock, page 9
1 stick butter
1 pinch chopped fresh parsley
1 pinch chopped fresh tarragon
1 pinch chopped fresh basil
1 pinch fresh thyme

To garnish
4 small new carrots, peeled
4 small new turnips, peeled
⅓ cup shelled peas
½ cup fine green beans, trimmed
10 small new onions, peeled
4 tablespoons butter

First prepare the Printanier Butter. Stew the vegetables in a very little stock with a small pat of butter until tender and dry. When cold, pound the cooked vegetables with the herbs and the rest of the butter and pass through a fine sieve.

Place the Printanier Butter inside the chicken and truss, closing all apertures carefully. Season the chicken well. Layer the vegetables and herbs in a deep heavy ovenproof casserole. Place the chicken on top of the vegetables and herbs, then cover with the bacon and pour over the melted butter. Cover with the lid and cook in a moderately hot oven (375°F) for about 50 minutes or until half-cooked.

Meanwhile prepare the garnish. Blanch the vegetables and drain well. Lightly color the onions in the butter.

Transfer the half-cooked chicken to a clean ovenproof dish and surround with the garnish. Deglaze the casserole with the ½ cup of stock, strain and skim off the fat. Pass this liquid through a fine strainer over the chicken and garnish, then cover. Replace in the oven to complete cooking, for another 50 minutes or so. Remove the trussing string and serve chicken and garnish straight from the casserole.

SERVES 4–6

Chicken Niçoise

Poularde à la Niçoise

1 large roaster chicken, weighing about 4–5 lb, trussed
salt
pepper
2 carrots, peeled and finely sliced
1 small onion, peeled and finely sliced
2 stalks celery, finely sliced
1 clove garlic, crushed
1 bay leaf
1 sprig thyme
4 slices bacon
6 tablespoons butter, melted
1½ cups Brown Stock, page 8
2 teaspoons arrowroot

To garnish
cooked and buttered fine green beans
very small skinned tomatoes, lightly cooked in a little butter
black olives, pitted

Season the chicken. Layer a deep heavy ovenproof casserole with the vegetables and herbs, then place the chicken on top of these. Cover it with the bacon and pour over the melted butter. Cover with the lid and place in a moderately hot oven (375°F). After 45 minutes of cooking time place the bacon at the sides of the chicken. Cook for a further 60 minutes or until the chicken is ready. Baste frequently.

Remove the lid for the last 15 minutes of the cooking time, adding ¼ cup of the stock and use this, together with the butter in the pan, to carry on basting the chicken so as to glaze and color it a light brown.

Remove the chicken when cooked, cover and keep warm.

Add the remaining stock to the pan and simmer gently for 5 minutes, then drain off the liquid and skim off the fat. Lightly thicken the liquid with the arrowroot blended with a little cold water, cook for 1 minute and season as necessary. Strain.

Remove the trussing string from the chicken and coat with a little of the sauce. Surround with the green beans, tomatoes and black olives. Serve the rest of the sauce separately.

SERVES 4–6

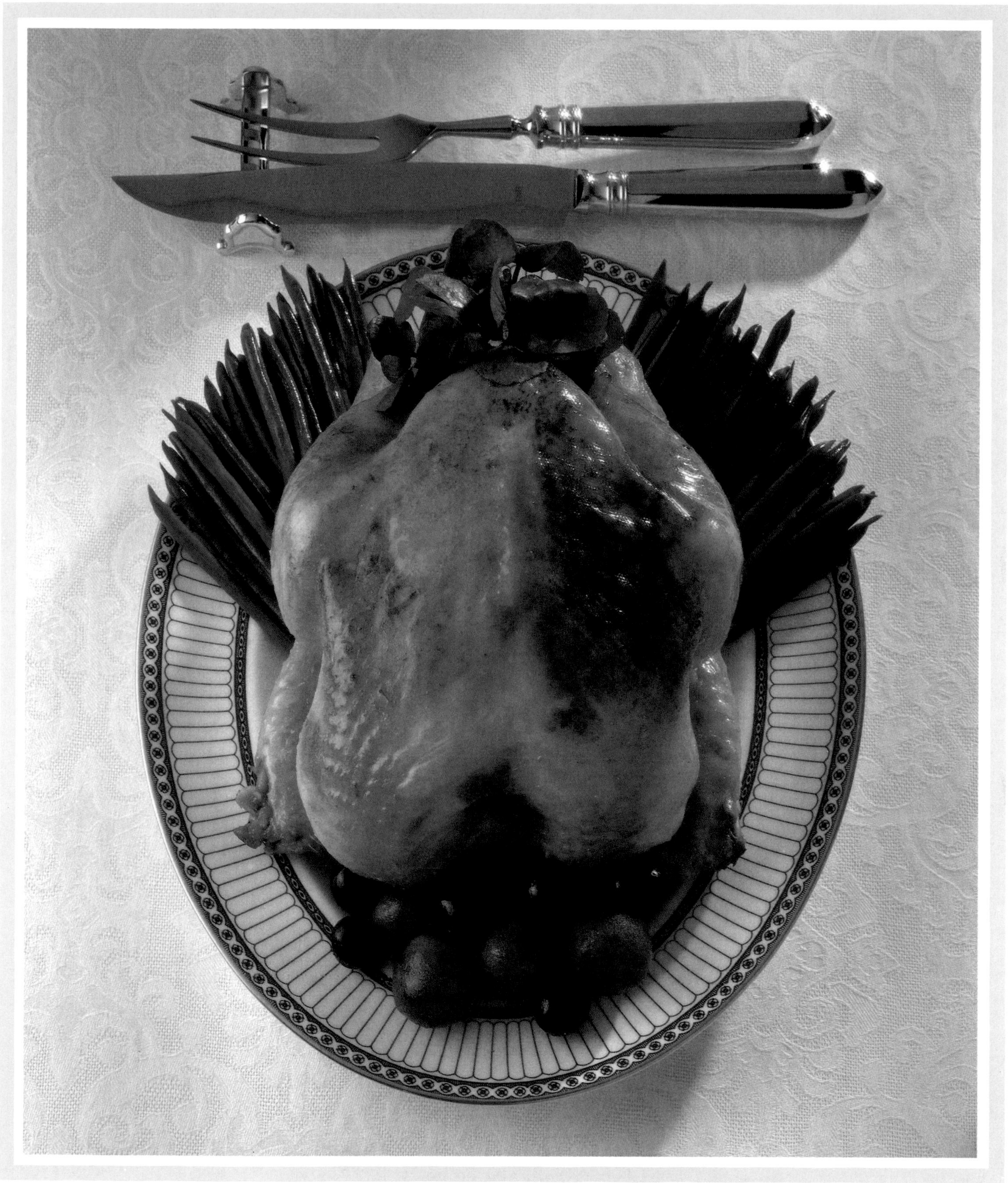

Chicken Niçoise

Chicken Algerian-style

Poulet Sauté Algérienne

1 roaster chicken, weighing about 3 lb 6 oz, cut up
salt
pepper
4 tablespoons butter
½ cup dry white wine
½ clove garlic, peeled and crushed
½ lb tomatoes, peeled, seeded and roughly chopped

To garnish

1 lb orange-fleshed sweet potato, peeled, trimmed to the shape of large olives and gently fried in butter
1 lb chayote, peeled, trimmed to the shape of large olives and gently fried in butter

Season the chicken pieces. Heat the butter in a shallow flameproof casserole, just large enough to hold all the chicken pieces, and fry quickly to brown all over. Cover the casserole with the lid and place in a moderately hot oven (400°F) to finish cooking, removing the most tender pieces after only a few minutes and leaving those that take longer to cook for up to 10–15 minutes.

Remove the chicken pieces and keep warm. Drain off some of the fat and deglaze the pan with the dry white wine. Add the crushed garlic and the roughly chopped tomato flesh. Cook together for a minute or so.

Arrange the chicken in a deep serving dish, coat with the sauce and surround with the prepared garnish.

SERVES 4

Chicken Beaulieu

Poulet Sauté Beaulieu

1 roaster chicken, weighing about 3 lb 6 oz, cut up
1 stick butter
5 oz small new potatoes, or a larger potato cut into small pieces
5 oz small artichoke hearts, quartered
12 black olives, pitted
6 tablespoons dry white wine
a few drops lemon juice
¼ cup White Stock, page 9

Season the chicken pieces, heat half the butter in a shallow flameproof casserole and fry the chicken quickly to brown all over. Meanwhile, fry the potatoes and artichoke hearts gently in the remaining butter until just tender. Add to the chicken, cover the pan and place in a moderately hot oven (400°F) for 10–15 minutes or until just cooked, removing the most tender pieces after a few minutes.

Arrange the chicken, potato and artichoke in the casserole and add the olives. Add the wine, lemon juice and stock.

Cover with the lid and allow to heat in the oven for a further 5 minutes. Serve straight from the casserole.

SERVES 4

Burgundy Chicken

Poulet Sauté à la Bourguignonne

¼ lb slab bacon, diced and blanched
8 pearl onions, peeled
¼ lb mushrooms, cut in quarters
6 tablespoons butter
1 roaster chicken, weighing about 3 lb 6 oz, cut up
salt
pepper
1 clove garlic, peeled and crushed
1 cup good quality red burgundy
1 generous pinch flour

Fry the bacon, onions and mushrooms gently in 4 tablespoons of the butter in a flameproof casserole until golden brown. Remove the bacon and vegetables and keep warm.

Season the pieces of chicken, then fry them in the same casserole until golden brown; return the bacon and vegetables. Cover with a lid and finish cooking in a moderately hot oven (375°F) for about 20 minutes, removing the most tender pieces after a few minutes.

Arrange the chicken and garnish in a deep serving dish and keep warm. Meanwhile, remove the fat from the pan, add the garlic and wine, and reduce by half. Mix the remaining butter with a generous pinch of flour and add this to the sauce to thicken it.

Pour the sauce over the chicken and serve.

SERVES 4

Burgundy Chicken

Chicken Boivin

Poulet Sauté Boivin

1 roaster chicken, weighing about 3 lb 6 oz, cut up
salt
pepper
1 stick butter
12 pearl onions, peeled
3 artichoke hearts, blanched and quartered
24 pieces of potato, cut to the size and shape of hazelnuts
¾ cup White Stock, page 9
a few drops lemon juice
¼ cup Meat Glaze, page 9
½ tablespoon coarsely chopped fresh parsley

Season the chicken pieces and brown quickly in 4 tablespoons of the butter in a flameproof casserole. Meanwhile, brown the pearl onions separately in another 2 tablespoons of butter. Add these to the chicken, along with the blanched and quartered artichoke hearts and the small pieces of potato. Cover with a lid and cook in a moderately hot oven (375°F) for about 20 minutes until just cooked, removing the most tender pieces after a few minutes.

Arrange the cooked chicken and vegetables in a deep dish. Deglaze the pan with the white stock and lemon juice. Add the meat glaze and the remaining butter. Pour this sauce over the chicken and vegetables and sprinkle with the chopped parsley.

SERVES 4

Breton Chicken

Poulet Sauté à la Bretonne

1 roaster chicken, weighing about 3 lb 6 oz, cut up
salt
pepper
6 tablespoons butter
2 leeks, white part only, sliced
½ small onion, peeled and sliced
¼ lb mushrooms, sliced
½ cup heavy cream
½ cup Velouté Sauce, pages 9–10

Season the chicken pieces and fry gently in 2 tablespoons of the butter in a flameproof casserole to stiffen the flesh, but do not allow to brown. At the same time, fry the leek and onion separately in another 2 tablespoons of butter. Add these to the chicken, cover with a lid and place in a moderately hot oven (375°F) to cook for about 20 minutes, removing the most tender pieces after a few minutes. Meanwhile, fry the mushrooms gently in the remaining butter and add these to the chicken about 5 minutes before the end of the cooking time.

When the chicken is cooked, arrange it in a deep serving dish. Add the cream and Velouté Sauce to the vegetables in the pan and reduce by half. Pour this sauce and the vegetables over the chicken and serve.

SERVES 4

Sautéed Chicken Chasseur

Poulet Sauté Chasseur

1 roaster chicken, weighing about 3 lb 6 oz, cut up
salt
pepper
2 tablespoons butter
1 tablespoon olive oil
¼ lb mushrooms, sliced
3 shallots, peeled and finely chopped
½ cup dry white wine
2 tablespoons brandy
½ cup Demi-glace Sauce, page 10
1 tablespoon tomato paste
1 pinch chopped fresh tarragon
1 pinch chopped fresh chervil
1 tablespoon coarsely chopped fresh parsley

Season the chicken pieces and fry in the butter and oil until cooked. Arrange the chicken in a deep serving dish, cover and keep warm.

Quickly fry the mushrooms in the same pan and add the shallots. Cook for another 30 seconds, then add the wine and brandy and reduce by half. Flavor the Demi-glace Sauce with the tomato paste and add this to the pan, together with the tarragon and chervil. Mix all together.

Pour this sauce over the chicken, sprinkle with the parsley and serve.

SERVES 4

Chicken with Fennel

Poulet Sauté au Fenouil

1 roaster chicken, weighing about 3 lb 6 oz, cut up
salt
pepper
3 tablespoons butter
$\frac{1}{4}$ cup heavy cream
2 heads fennel, quartered
$1\frac{1}{4}$ cups Mornay Sauce, page 13

Season the pieces of chicken and fry gently in the butter in a flameproof casserole to stiffen the flesh, but do not allow to brown. Remove the chicken pieces and deglaze the pan with the cream. Replace the chicken.

Trim the fennel quarters into large oval shapes and blanch well in boiling salted water until nearly cooked. Drain and add to the chicken.

Cover with the lid and finish cooking both chicken and fennel in a moderately hot oven (375°F) for about 20 minutes. Remove the most tender pieces of chicken after a few minutes.

Arrange the pieces of fennel around an oval dish, with the pieces of chicken in the center. Flavor the Mornay Sauce with the cooking juices and cream in the pan, and pour this sauce over the chicken and fennel. Brown quickly under the broiler.

Serves 4

Sautéed Chicken Marseillaise

Poulet Sauté à la Marseillaise

$\frac{1}{2}$ cup finely sliced green pepper
3 small tomatoes, peeled and quartered
3 tablespoons olive oil
1 roaster chicken, weighing about 3 lb 6 oz, cut up
salt
pepper
1 clove garlic, peeled and crushed
$\frac{1}{2}$ cup dry white wine
a few drops lemon juice
1 tablespoon coarsely chopped fresh parsley

Fry the green pepper and tomatoes very lightly in half the oil. Season the chicken pieces and fry gently in the remaining oil. When the chicken is half cooked, add the crushed garlic and the lightly fried pepper and tomatoes. Continue to fry all together.

When the chicken is fully cooked, drain off the fat and add the white wine and lemon juice. Reduce until almost dry.

Arrange the chicken in a deep serving dish with the cooking vegetables on top and sprinkle with parsley.

Serves 4

Suprêmes of Chicken

Suprêmes de Volaille

This is the name given to the breast of the chicken with its skin removed, divided into 2 along the breastbone, then removed from the carcass. Suprêmes then only require a little trimming to give a neat and tidy shape. Generally speaking, they are best when cut from a young chicken of $2\frac{3}{4}$ to $3\frac{1}{2}$ lb, giving a weight of between 4 and 5 ounces for each suprême.

Chicken Suprêmes Boitelle

Suprêmes de Volaille Boitelle

6 tablespoons butter
4 boneless chicken breast halves, skinned
$\frac{1}{2}$ lb mushrooms, sliced
salt
pepper
juice of $\frac{1}{4}$ lemon
1 tablespoon chopped fresh parsley

Butter a shallow ovenproof dish, using 2 tablespoons of the butter, and place the chicken breasts and mushrooms in it. Season and sprinkle with a few drops of lemon juice. Cover and cook gently in a moderate oven (375°F) for about 20 minutes.

When they are cooked, transfer the chicken breasts to a serving dish and arrange the mushrooms in the center. Swirl the remaining butter into the cooking liquid and add a few more drops of lemon juice.

Pour this sauce over the breasts and sprinkle with parsley.

Serves 4

Mother Jean's Hare Stew

Civet de Lièvre de la Mère Jean

1 hare, to include blood and liver
5 oz slab bacon, cubed
2 tablespoons olive oil
1½ lb onions, peeled and sliced
4 tablespoons butter
3 tablespoons flour
1 bouquet garni
1 clove garlic, peeled and crushed
½ cup heavy cream

Marinade
salt
pepper
¼ cup Armagnac
1 bottle good red wine

Cut the hare into pieces, reserving the blood and liver. Place the pieces of hare in a bowl with the marinade ingredients. Place in the refrigerator and allow to marinate for 24 hours, turning from time to time.

Fry the bacon in the olive oil in a flameproof casserole. Fry the onions, separately, in the butter and reserve for use later. Sprinkle the flour onto the bacon and cook together for 2 minutes, stirring all the time.

Remove the pieces of hare from the marinade, dry them well and add to the casserole. Stir and allow to cook until they have stiffened and browned. Now add the reserved marinade, bouquet garni, crushed garlic and fried onions.

Cover and simmer very gently for about 2½ hours. When cooked, transfer the pieces of hare to a clean pan. Add the blood and the reserved liver, cut into thick slices, to the sauce. When the liver is cooked, add it to the pieces of hare. Check the seasoning of the sauce.

Strain the sauce over the hare and liver. Reheat without boiling and finish with the cream.

SERVES 6

SADDLE OF HARE

Râble de Lièvre

Correctly speaking, the saddle of hare comprises the whole of the back of the hare from the beginning of the neck to the tail with the bones of the ribs being trimmed back so that the saddle can then sit level in the roasting pan. However, it is more usual these days for the saddle to exclude the ribs (thus corresponding to a saddle, or double loin roast, of lamb) and the following recipes use this shortened version.

Saddle of Hare with Red Currant and Horseradish Sauce

Râble de Lièvre, Sauce Groseilles au Raifort

2 saddles of hare
¼ lb slab bacon, cut into thin strips 2 inches long
salt
pepper

Red Currant and Horseradish Sauce
¼ cup port wine
1 pinch grated nutmeg
1 pinch cinnamon
1 cup melted red currant jelly
2 tablespoons finely grated horseradish

L*ard* the saddles of hare with the slab bacon strips, season and roast them in a very hot oven (475°F) for about 30 minutes.

To prepare the sauce, heat the port in a pan with the nutmeg and cinnamon and reduce by one-third. Add the melted red currant jelly and the finely grated horseradish. Mix well.

Place the saddles on a suitable serving dish and serve, accompanied by the sauce.

SERVES 4

Saddle of Hare Navarraise

Râble de Lièvre à la Navarraise

2 saddles of hare
¼ lb slab bacon, cut into thin strips 2 inches long
salt
pepper
3 onions, peeled and sliced
16 cloves garlic, peeled and crushed
1 stick butter
7 teaspoons flour
1 cup White Stock, page 9
1 pinch chopped fresh thyme
1 bay leaf
8 large mushrooms

Marinade

¼ lb carrots, peeled and sliced
1 onion, peeled and sliced
¼ cup sliced shallot
2 stalks celery, sliced
2 cloves garlic, peeled and crushed
1 sprig thyme
½ bay leaf
6 peppercorns
1½ cups good quality red wine

Lard the saddles with the slab bacon strips and season. Marinate for a few hours with all the marinade ingredients, then drain, reserving the marinade, and dry well. Scatter the vegetables from the marinade on the bottom of a roasting pan, put the hare on top and roast in a very hot oven (475°F) for about 30 minutes.

Meanwhile, fry the sliced onions and garlic gently in 4 tablespoons of the butter until soft. Sprinkle with the flour, cook gently for a few more minutes and add the stock. Add the herbs and simmer gently.

Pass this mixture through a fine sieve or purée in a food processor and reduce over a gentle heat until thick. Broil the mushrooms and fill them with this thick purée.

Arrange the cooked saddles on a dish, surrounded by the prepared mushrooms. Quickly deglaze the roasting pan with the reserved liquid from the marinade and pass it through a fine strainer. Reduce to about ½ cup and finish with the remaining butter.

Serve the saddle accompanied by this sauce.

SERVES 4

Hare Terrine

Terrine de Lièvre

1 hare, prepared according to the instructions given in the method, below
2 oz slab larding bacon, cut into thin strips approximately 2 inches long
salt
apple pie spice
½ cup brandy
½ lb lean cooked ham, cut into thickish strips approximately 4 inches long
½ lb salt pork, cut into thickish strips approximately 4 inches long
11 oz salt pork, cut into very thin slices
1 bay leaf
Aspic, page 92, flavored with the hare trimmings and brandy

Forcemeat

5 oz lean boneless veal
5 oz lean boneless pork
1½ lb fresh pork fatback
salt
pepper
apple pie spice
3 eggs

Bone the saddle and legs of the hare and remove the tendons. *Lard* the tenderloin from the top of the saddle and the best parts only of the hind legs with the strips of slab bacon. Season with salt and spice and place to marinate with the brandy, ham and salt pork strips for 5–6 hours. Turn occasionally to obtain even marination.

Use the rest of the boned hare flesh to make a forcemeat. Chop the hare and other meats and the fat separately, then place them together in a mortar or food processor with the seasonings. Pound or purée finely, adding the eggs one by one and then, finally, the brandy from the marinade. Pass all through a fine sieve.

Line a deep ovenproof terrine with thin salt pork slices, then fill with alternate layers of the forcemeat, the marinated hare and ham and salt pork strips. Finish with a layer of forcemeat. When the terrine is full, fold over any ends of salt pork and cover with any remaining salt pork, plus a pinch more of spice and a bay leaf. Cover the terrine with a lid.

Place the terrine in a shallow roasting pan, pour in enough hot water to half-fill the pan and cook in a moderate oven (350°F) for about 2 hours, or until the fat that rises to the surface is completely clear. A trussing needle may be used to

Saddle of Hare Navarraise

ascertain whether the terrine is cooked: it should come out evenly hot along its entire length when withdrawn after being inserted in the center and left for a moment or two. Add more water to the roasting pan during the cooking as and when necessary.

To serve the terrine from its cooking dish, cover and fill the terrine with flavored aspic a few minutes after taking it out of the oven. Then press it by covering with a chopping board, with a weight positioned on top, while it cools. When cold and set, remove any fat from the surface and trim neatly.

For presenting the terrine as a whole unmolded item, allow to cool, then turn the terrine out of the dish. Trim it neatly. Clean the cooking dish, set a layer of the flavored aspic in the bottom, then replace the unmolded terrine on top and surround with more aspic. When well set, unmold the terrine once again onto a serving dish and surround with cut shapes of the same aspic.

MAKES APPROXIMATELY 4½ LB

Rabbit with Prunes

Lapin aux Pruneaux

1 rabbit
salt
pepper
4 tablespoons butter
1 lb prunes, soaked and pitted
3 tablespoons red currant jelly

Marinade

¼ lb carrots, peeled and sliced
1 onion, peeled and sliced
¼ cup sliced shallot
2 stalks celery, sliced
2 cloves garlic, peeled and crushed
large bunch parsley stalks
1 sprig thyme
½ bay leaf
6 peppercorns
2½ cups dry white wine
¾ cup white wine vinegar
½ cup olive oil

Cut the rabbit into pieces and marinate for 24 hours in all the marinade ingredients.

Drain the pieces of rabbit, reserving the marinade, dry them well and season. Fry in the butter in a flameproof casserole, and brown well on all sides. Meanwhile, strain the marinade into a separate pan and reduce to half its original volume.

Add the reduced marinade together with a little water if necessary to just cover the rabbit, season and add the prunes. Cover and cook gently in a moderate oven (350°F) for about 2 hours.

When the rabbit is cooked, add the red currant jelly to the sauce and transfer to a deep dish to serve.

SERVES 3–4

Rabbit Portuguese-style

Sauté de Lapin Portugaise

2 young rabbits, cut up
salt
pepper
olive oil
1 onion, peeled and chopped
1 clove garlic, peeled and crushed
1 cup dry white wine
1 quart Brown Stock, page 8
4½ lb tomatoes, peeled, seeded and roughly chopped
1 bouquet garni
2 pinches roughly chopped fresh parsley

Season and fry the rabbit pieces in very hot oil in a flameproof casserole until well colored on all sides. Add the onion and garlic and allow to color. Drain off the oil, add the white wine and allow to reduce a little. Then add the stock, half the tomatoes and the bouquet garni. Cook gently in a moderate oven, (350°F) for 1½ hours or until all the rabbit pieces are tender.

Remove the rabbit pieces and transfer to a clean flameproof casserole. Pass the cooking sauce and vegetables through a fine strainer over the rabbit pieces, then add the remaining tomatoes and the parsley. Simmer gently for a further 20 minutes, before serving direct from the casserole.

SERVES 8

Wild Duck with Port

Canard Sauvage au Porto

1 wild duck, preferably a mallard
salt
pepper
melted clean fat, such as lard
$\frac{3}{4}$ cup port wine
2 tablespoons arrowroot

Season the duck, place in a roasting pan and coat with melted fat. Roast in a hot oven (450°F) for 20 minutes, basting frequently. (Wild duck should be served underdone.) Meanwhile, use the trimmings and giblets to make about a cup or so of stock.

At the end of the cooking time, drain off the fat, deglaze the pan with the port and reduce by half. Remove any further fat, add $\frac{3}{4}$ cup of the duck stock prepared from trimmings and giblets, and thicken with the arrowroot, blended with a little cold water. Season, then pass through a fine strainer.

Serve the duck accompanied by this sauce.

SERVES 2 OR 3

Normandy Pheasant

Faisan à la Normande

1 pheasant
salt
pepper
6 tablespoons butter
6 medium apples
$\frac{1}{2}$ cup heavy cream

Season and fry the pheasant in 4 tablespoons of the butter for about 6 minutes, until golden brown on all sides.

Meanwhile, peel the apples, cut them in quarters and slice. Sauté them quickly in the remaining butter. Put a layer of these on the bottom of an ovenproof casserole, place the pheasant on top and surround it with the remaining apple slices. Sprinkle with the cream, season and cover closely with the casserole lid. Cook in a hot oven (425°F) for 30–35 minutes or until just cooked.

Serve the pheasant and apples straight from the casserole.

SERVES 4

Pheasant Titania

Faisan Titania

2 pheasants
salt
pepper
4 tablespoons melted butter
$1\frac{1}{2}$ cups purple grapes, skinned and seeded
2 oranges, peeled and segmented
3 tablespoons Game Stock, page 8
3 tablespoons pomegranate juice

Matignon

1 large carrot, peeled and finely sliced
$\frac{1}{2}$ small onion, peeled and finely sliced
1 stalk celery, finely sliced
4 slices streaky bacon, diced
2 tablespoons butter
1 bay leaf
1 sprig thyme
2 tablespoons dry white wine

Before cooking the pheasant, first prepare the *matignon*. Fry the vegetables and bacon gently in the butter and add the herbs. Then deglaze the pan with the wine.

Place a layer of matignon in a heavy ovenproof *cocotte* just large enough to hold the birds. Put them on top of the matignon, season well and coat with melted butter.

Cover with a lid and braise in a moderately hot oven (400°F) basting frequently, for 1 hour or until the birds are just cooked. Place them in a warmed ovenproof serving dish and surround with the grapes and orange segments.

Add the game stock and pomegranate juice to the juices left from the cooking of the pheasant. Skim off any fat and strain the sauce over the pheasants. Heat all through for about 5 minutes in the same oven, then serve immediately.

SERVES 6–8

Pheasant Georgienne

Faisan à la Georgienne

1 pheasant
30 fresh green walnuts, peeled and halved
2 cups white grape juice
½ cup orange juice
¼ cup sweet Madeira or dessert Muscat wine
¼ cup strong green tea
4 tablespoons butter
salt
pepper
1 cup Espagnole Sauce, page 10

Truss the pheasant and place in an ovenproof casserole with the walnuts, grape juice, orange juice, wine, tea, butter and seasoning. Cover with a lid and place in a moderately hot oven (375°F) to cook for about 35–40 minutes. Remove the lid after this time and allow the bird to brown and finish cooking.

When the pheasant is cooked, cut the trussing string, place on a suitable serving dish and surround with the halved walnuts. Keep warm. Pass the cooking liquid through a fine strainer, add the Espagnole Sauce and reduce by half.

Lightly coat the pheasant and walnuts with this sauce, and serve the rest of the sauce in a sauceboat.

SERVES 4

Pheasant Salmis

Salmis de Faisan

1 pheasant
4 slices bacon
2 tablespoons brandy
2 tablespoons Meat Glaze, page 9, melted
1 cup dry white wine
2½ tablespoons chopped shallot
pepper
¾ cup Espagnole Sauce, page 10
¾ cup Game Stock, page 8
10 button mushrooms
6 tablespoons butter
20 slices truffle

Cover the pheasant with the slices of bacon and roast in a moderately hot oven (375°F) for about 30 minutes, so that it is slightly underdone but not excessively so. Remove from the oven and cut into 6 pieces: 2 legs, 2 wings and the breast cut in 2 lengthwise. Discard the skin from all the pieces and trim these neatly.

Place the pieces of pheasant in a small pan, heat then pour the brandy over the top and flame it by igniting with a match. When the flames have died down, add the melted meat glaze, cover and keep warm.

Pound the carcass and trimmings and place in a pan with the wine, shallot and pepper. Allow to reduce to almost nothing, then add the Espagnole Sauce and game stock and simmer for 10 minutes. Meanwhile, fry the mushrooms gently in 2 tablespoons of the butter and reserve.

Pass the mixture of Espagnole Sauce and game stock through a fine sieve, pressing firmly on the carcass. Reduce by one-third, skimming as necessary, and strain again. Finish with the remaining butter.

Add the fried mushrooms and slices of truffle to the prepared pheasant and cover with the sauce. Place in a deep dish and serve hot.

SERVES 4

Pheasant with Pineapple Juice

Sauté de Faisan au Suc d'Ananas

1 plump pheasant, cut up
salt
pepper
4 tablespoons butter
¼ cup brandy
a few drops lemon juice
2–3 tablespoons fresh pineapple juice

Season the pheasant and heat the butter in a flameproof casserole just large enough to hold all the pieces of pheasant. When it is very hot, put in the pieces of pheasant and brown them quickly on all sides. Cover with a lid and place in a moderately hot oven (375°F) and cook for about 30–40 minutes, or until completely cooked.

Arrange the cooked pheasant in a deep serving dish and keep warm. Deglaze the pan with the brandy and flame by igniting with a match. When the flames have died down, add the lemon juice and, at the last moment, the fresh pineapple juice. Pour this over the pheasant and serve immediately.

SERVES 4

Pheasant Georgienne

Partridge Burgundy-style

Perdreaux à la Bourguignonne

2 young partridges
salt
pepper
6 tablespoons butter
1 large carrot, finely sliced
1 small onion, finely sliced
1 stalk celery, finely sliced
2 slices bacon, finely sliced
1 clove garlic, crushed
1 pinch dried thyme
1 bay leaf
12 pearl onions
1 pinch sugar
12 button mushrooms
1¼ cups red wine
¼ cup Demi-glace Sauce, page 10

Truss and season the partridges. Heat 4 tablespoons of the butter in a deep flameproof casserole and, when it is very hot, add the partridges and brown them quickly on all sides. Add the vegetables, bacon, garlic and herbs. Cover with a lid and place in a hot oven (425°F) to cook for about 30 minutes, until three-quarters cooked.

Meanwhile, fry the pearl onions in 1 tablespoon of the butter and glaze with a pinch of sugar. Fry the mushrooms in another 1 tablespoon of butter.

Transfer the three-quarters cooked partridges to a clean ovenproof casserole with the glazed onions and fried mushrooms. Deglaze the pan in which the partridges were cooked with the red wine, reduce by two-thirds and add the Demi-glace Sauce. Pass through a fine strainer and skim.

Pour this sauce over the partridges, cover with the lid and return to the oven for 10 more minutes to finish cooking. Cut the trussing strings and serve direct from the casserole.

SERVES 2

Braised Partridge

Perdreaux en Estouffade

2 young partridges
salt
pepper
4 tablespoons butter
¼ cup brandy
¼ cup Game Stock, page 8
1½ cups flour
½ cup water

Matignon

1 large carrot, peeled and diced finely
1 small onion, peeled and diced finely
1 stalk celery, chopped finely
4 slices bacon, chopped
½ bay leaf
1 small sprig thyme
1 juniper berry, crushed
2 tablespoons butter
1 tablespoon dry white wine

Season the partridges, dot with half the butter and brown, uncovered, in a hot oven (425°F).

Meanwhile, prepare the *matignon* by frying all the vegetables and flavorings together gently in the butter in a covered pan. Add the white wine and reduce until almost dry.

Place 2 tablespoons of the matignon in a small ovenproof casserole just large enough to hold the partridges. Add the browned partridges and cover with 2 more tablespoonsful of matignon. Add the remaining butter and the brandy. Flame by igniting the contents of the casserole with a match and, when the flames have died down, add the game stock.

Cover with the lid and seal the edges with a band of *repère* (see page 86 and Glossary). Place in the hot oven (425°F) and cook for 25 more minutes, then serve from the casserole.

SERVES 2

Partridge Braised with Cabbage

Perdrix aux Choux

2 old partridges
salt
pepper
6 tablespoons butter
1 small head cabbage, blanched and shredded
4 slices bacon, blanched
4 carrots, peeled
2 small smoked pork sausage links
$\frac{3}{4}$ cup White Stock, page 9

To garnish

$\frac{3}{4}$ cup Demi-glace Sauce, page 10, finished with well-reduced Game Stock in place of Brown Stock
6 cocktail sausages, broiled

Truss the partridges and season. Heat 4 tablespoons of the butter in a deep flameproof casserole and, when it is very hot, add the partridges and brown them quickly on all sides.

Add the cabbage, bacon, carrots, sausages and stock, cover with a lid and place in a moderate oven (350°F) to braise. Remove the bacon, carrots and sausages after about 1 hour, leaving the cabbage and partridges to finish cooking together for another hour or so.

Slice the carrots and sausages and cut the bacon into squares. Butter a clean deep ovenproof casserole using the remaining butter, and line with the slices of sausage and carrot and the squares of bacon. Cover these with a layer of cabbage. Remove the trussing strings from the partridges and place in the center of the casserole. Cover with the remaining cabbage and return to the same oven for 5 minutes or so to reheat.

Turn the casserole upside down onto a round serving dish and allow any liquid to drain and be discarded before removing the casserole dish and "unmolding" the birds and vegetables. Surround with a little game-flavored Demi-glace Sauce and the cocktail sausages.

SERVES 2

Quails Dauphinoise

Cailles à la Dauphinoise

4 tablespoons butter
4 grape leaves
4 quails
4 thin slices bacon
4 thin slices cooked ham

Fresh Pea Purée

1 lb fresh peas, shelled
1 pinch sugar
salt
1 head lettuce, tied together with a few parsley stalks
4 tablespoons butter
salt
pepper

First prepare the purée of peas. Cook the peas in just enough boiling water to cover them, together with the sugar, salt, lettuce and parsley stalks. When they are cooked, drain and pass the peas and lettuce through a sieve; leave the cooking liquid to reduce to a glaze. Add the butter to the puréed peas, season, stir in the glazed cooking liquid, and reduce to a thick consistency.

Butter the grape leaves and wrap each quail in a buttered leaf, then in a slice of bacon. Secure the leaves and bacon by trussing with string. Roast in a very hot oven (475°F) for 10 minutes. Remove the trussing strings.

Cover the bottom of an ovenproof dish with the slices of ham, place the puréed peas on top and smooth over the surface of the purée.

Arrange the quails on top of the purée, pressing them halfway into it. Return to the oven to cook for a further 10 minutes and serve from the dish.

SERVES 2

Quails à la Grecque

Cailles à la Grecque

8 quails
salt
pepper
4 tablespoons butter

To garnish
Rice à la Grecque, page 145
6 tablespoons Game Stock, page 8

Season and place the quails in an ovenproof casserole with the butter, cover and cook in a very hot oven (475°F) for 20 minutes. Half-fill a deep serving dish with Rice à la Grecque and place the quails on top. Deglaze the casserole with the game stock, remove any fat, pour over the quails and serve.

SERVES 4

Squabs with Spring Vegetables

Pigeonneaux à la Printanière

3 plump squabs
salt
pepper
6 tablespoons butter
Brown Stock, page 8
$\frac{3}{4}$ cup Demi-glace Sauce, page 10
1 bouquet garni

To garnish
$\frac{1}{4}$ lb small new carrots, peeled and trimmed
$\frac{1}{4}$ lb small new turnips, peeled and trimmed
20 small new onions, peeled
$\frac{1}{4}$ lb asparagus tips, blanched

Season and fry the squabs gently on all sides in the butter until well browned. Transfer the squabs to an ovenproof casserole. Deglaze the pan with a little stock and add this, the Demi-glace Sauce, bouquet garni and all the garnishing vegetables except the blanched asparagus tips to the casserole containing the squabs.

Finish cooking the squabs with the vegetables in a moderate oven (325°F) for about 1 hour or until the squabs are tender. Add the blanched asparagus tips 5 minutes before the end of cooking time.

Serve the squabs surrounded by the vegetables.

SERVES 6

Squabs in Sauternes

Pigeonneaux au Sauternes

3 plump squabs
salt
pepper
4 tablespoons melted butter
$1\frac{1}{4}$ cups Sauternes
3 tablespoons Meat Glaze, page 9

Matignon
1 large carrot, peeled and finely sliced
$\frac{1}{2}$ small onion, peeled and finely sliced
1 stalk celery, finely sliced
4 slices bacon, diced
2 tablespoons butter
1 bay leaf
1 sprig thyme
2 tablespoons dry white wine

Before cooking the birds, prepare the *matignon*. Fry the vegetables and bacon gently in the butter and add the herbs. Then add the white wine and reduce until almost dry.

Place a layer of matignon in a heavy ovenproof *cocotte* just large enough to hold the birds. Put these on top of the matignon, season well and coat with melted butter.

Cover with a lid and braise in a moderately hot oven, 400°F, basting frequently, for about 1 hour or until the squabs are cooked. When they are cooked, transfer the birds to a serving dish and keep warm.

Deglaze the pan with the Sauternes and reduce by two-thirds. Skim off any fat. Add the meat glaze and pass through a fine strainer. Cover the squabs with the prepared sauce and serve.

SERVES 6

Quails à la Grecque

Vegetable Dishes

Artichokes Cavour

Artichauts Cavour

12 very small, tender globe artichokes
2 quarts White Stock, page 9
6 tablespoons melted butter
½ cup grated Parmesan cheese
½ cup grated Gruyère cheese
2 hard-boiled eggs, chopped
2 tablespoons butter
anchovy paste
1 tablespoon chopped fresh parsley

Trim off any tough or fibrous leaf ends to produce artichokes the shape and size of an egg. Cook them until tender in boiling White Stock, then drain well and squeeze dry.

Dip the artichokes in melted butter, then in a mixture of grated Parmesan and Gruyère. Arrange in a circle on an ovenproof dish and brown in a hot oven (425°F).

Meanwhile, fry the chopped hard-boiled eggs in the butter and, while the butter is still foaming, add a little anchovy paste and parsley. Pour this over the browned artichokes and serve.

Serves 4–6

Artichoke Hearts Clamart

Coeurs d'Artichauts Clamart

4 tablespoons butter
12 small young globe artichokes, trimmed down to the heart and each heart cut into 6
12 small carrots, peeled and quartered
1 lb fresh peas, shelled
1 bouquet garni
1 heaping tablespoon flour

Butter a small ovenproof *cocotte*, using 2 tablespoons of the butter. Arrange the artichoke hearts in the cocotte with the carrots and peas. Add the bouquet garni, a little water and a pinch of salt. Cover and cook slowly in a moderate oven (325°F) for about 50 minutes.

When the artichoke hearts are cooked, remove the bouquet garni and drain off and reserve the cooking liquid. Make a *beurre manié*, using the rest of the butter and the flour, and add this to the cooking liquid. Simmer briefly to thicken. Pour the thickened cooking liquid over the vegetables and serve as they are, direct from the cocotte.

Serves 6–8

Artichoke Purée

Purée d'Artichauts

15 tender young globe artichokes
salt
1 lb medium potatoes, peeled
1½ sticks butter

Trim the artichokes of all fibrous green leaf ends, remove the chokes and parboil in boiling salted water for about 10 minutes. Meanwhile, cook the potatoes in boiling salted water until soft.

Drain the artichokes and finish cooking them in a covered pan in a third of the butter. Drain the potatoes when cooked and mash them thoroughly.

Pass the buttery artichokes through a fine sieve, return to the pan and add the mashed potato. Finish the purée with another third of the butter. Cook the remaining butter until brown (or *à la noisette*) and add this to the purée just before serving. *See photograph on page 129.*

Serves 6–8

Artichokes Cavour

Artichokes Stanley

Fonds d'Artichauts Stanley

1 stick butter
2 large onions, peeled, sliced and blanched
5 oz cooked ham, sliced
16 artichoke bottoms, trimmed
¾ cup dry white wine
¾ cup thin Béchamel Sauce, page 12
1 cup heavy cream
⅔ cup diced lean cooked ham

Butter a shallow saucepan, using 2 tablespoons of the butter, and arrange the onions and sliced ham on the bottom. Place the artichoke bottoms on top, cover the pan closely and allow the artichoke bottoms to cook gently in their own juices for a few minutes.

Add the white wine, allow to reduce, then barely cover with the Béchamel Sauce. Cook until tender, then remove the artichoke bottoms and arrange in a serving dish.

Reduce the sauce and add the cream. Pass all the cooking ingredients firmly through a fine sieve and finish with the remaining butter. Pour this over the artichoke bottoms and sprinkle with the diced ham before serving.

SERVES 8

Artichokes Dietrich

Quartiers d'Artichauts Dietrich

12 very small, tender globe artichokes
½ small onion, peeled and finely chopped
4 tablespoons butter
⅔ cup thin Velouté Sauce, pages 9–10
⅔ cup mushroom cooking liquid
Rice Pilaff, page 145
1 oz raw white Piedmont truffle
¼ cup heavy cream

Trim any fibrous leaf ends from the artichokes, then cut them into quarters lengthwise. Cook them with the onion in the butter for a few minutes, then add the Velouté Sauce and the *mushroom cooking liquid*. Simmer gently until tender.

Put the artichokes in the center of a round serving dish, and surround with a border of Rice Pilaff containing shavings of raw white truffle. Keep warm. Reduce the cooking liquid to a few tablespoons, and finish with the cream. Pour this sauce over the artichokes and serve.

SERVES 4–6

Asparagus au Gratin

Asperges au Gratin

20–30 spears asparagus, trimmed and tied in bundles
salt
1¼ cups Mornay Sauce, page 13
¾ cup grated Parmesan cheese

Cook the asparagus in plenty of boiling salted water, keeping it fairly firm. Drain, and arrange the cooked asparagus in overlapping rows on a serving dish.

Coat the tips of each row with Mornay Sauce. Cover two-thirds of the unsauced stalks of the last row with a band of buttered parchment paper and coat the final uncovered third with thin sauce.

Sprinkle with the grated Parmesan and brown quickly under the broiler. Remove the paper and serve immediately.

SERVES 4–6

Asparagus Polonaise

Asperges à la Polonaise

20–30 spears asparagus, trimmed and tied in bundles
salt
4 hard-boiled egg yolks
2 tablespoons chopped fresh parsley
½ cup fine fresh white bread crumbs
1 stick butter

Cook the asparagus in plenty of boiling salted water. When cooked but still firm, drain and arrange in rows on an oval dish. Sprinkle the tips of each row with a mixture of chopped hard-boiled egg yolks and parsley. Keep warm.

Fry the bread crumbs in the butter until both bread crumbs and butter are golden brown, and coat the tips of asparagus with this just before serving.

SERVES 4–6

Buttered Asparagus Tips

Pointes d'Asperges au Beurre

30–40 spears asparagus, trimmed
salt
4 tablespoons butter

Cut off the asparagus tips about 2 inches from the point and tie in bundles. Cut the remaining tender parts into pieces the size of a pea. Wash all well and cook quickly in boiling salted water so as to keep both tips and cut tender parts very green.

As soon as they are cooked, drain well and place in a pan over a gentle heat to evaporate any remaining moisture. Remove from the heat, add the butter and toss gently to mix.

Place the small pieces in a deep dish, cut the bundles and arrange the tips on top. *See photograph on page 141.*

SERVES 4

Eggplant Egyptian-style

Aubergines à l'Egyptienne

4 eggplants
oil for deep frying
1 onion, peeled and chopped
3 tablespoons olive oil
salt
pepper
8 tomatoes, peeled and cut in thick slices
2 tablespoons butter
2 tablespoons chopped fresh parsley

Cut the eggplants in half lengthwise. Cut around the edges, just inside the skins, and slash the centers, criss-cross fashion, to facilitate their cooking. Deep fry in hot oil (350°F), then drain and scoop out the flesh. Fry the onion in 1 tablespoon of the oil. Season and fry the tomatoes, separately and gently, in another tablespoon of the oil and keep warm. Butter an ovenproof dish and arrange the eggplant skins in it. Chop the flesh of the eggplants and add the fried onion. Season to taste.

Fill the skins with this mixture, sprinkle with the remaining oil and cook in a moderate oven (350°F) for 30 minutes. When you remove them from the oven, place a few overlapping slices of fried tomato along each half eggplant and sprinkle with the chopped parsley.

SERVES 8

Eggplant Serbian-style

Aubergines à la Serbe

4 eggplants
oil for deep frying
1 onion, peeled and chopped
4 tablespoons butter
1 cup peeled, seeded and roughly chopped tomatoes
scant $\frac{1}{2}$ cup long-grain rice
salt
1 heaping cup chopped cooked lamb
pepper
$\frac{1}{4}$ cup dried white bread crumbs

To garnish

$1\frac{1}{4}$ cups Tomato Sauce, page 14
2 tablespoons chopped fresh parsley

Cut the eggplants in half lengthwise. Cut round the edges, just inside the skins, and slash the centers, criss-cross fashion, to facilitate their cooking. Deep fry in hot oil (350°F), then drain and scoop out the flesh.

Fry the onion gently in 3 tablespoons butter until soft, add the tomato flesh and fry for a little longer. Cook the rice in boiling salted water.

Butter an ovenproof dish, using the remaining butter, and arrange the eggplant skins in it. Chop the flesh of the eggplants and add the fried onions, tomatoes, rice and lamb, then season to taste. Fill the eggplant skins with this mixture, sprinkle with the bread crumbs and gratinate in a hot oven (425°F).

Just before serving, surround the stuffed eggplants with a *cordon* of Tomato Sauce and sprinkle with chopped parsley.

SERVES 8

Neapolitan Eggplant

Aubergines à la Napolitaine

4 small eggplants
salt
pepper
flour
oil for deep frying
2 tablespoons tomato paste
$\frac{1}{2}$ cup grated Parmesan cheese
$1\frac{1}{4}$ cups Tomato Sauce, page 14
1 tablespoon olive oil
1 tablespoon melted butter

Peel the eggplants and cut each one into 6 slices lengthwise. Season, coat lightly with flour and deep fry in hot oil (350°F).

Combine the tomato paste with half the Parmesan and spread the slices of eggplant with this. Re-form the eggplants to their original shape and arrange in an ovenproof gratin dish.

Coat with the Tomato Sauce, sprinkle with the remaining Parmesan, then sprinkle with the oil and melted butter, and gratinate in a hot oven (425°F).

SERVES 4

Souffléed Eggplants

Aubergines Soufflées

2 large eggplants
oil for deep frying
$\frac{3}{4}$ cup thick Béchamel Sauce, page 12
$\frac{1}{4}$ cup grated Parmesan cheese
2 eggs, separated, and 1 egg white
2 tablespoons butter

Cut the eggplants in half. Cut around the edges, just inside the skins, and slash the centers, criss-cross fashion. Deep fry in hot oil (350°F), then drain, scoop out the flesh and chop finely.

Flavor the béchamel sauce with the grated Parmesan, thicken with the 2 egg yolks and add the chopped eggplant. Beat the 3 egg whites stiffly and fold into the mixture.

Arrange the skins on a buttered ovenproof dish and fill with this mixture. Cook in a moderate oven (375°F) for 10–15 minutes. Serve immediately.

Broccoli Milanaise

Broccoli à la Milanaise

1 lb broccoli
salt
1 stick butter
1 cup grated cheese

Cook the broccoli in boiling salted water until tender but still firm. Drain well.

Butter an ovenproof gratin dish, using a quarter of the butter, and sprinkle with half the grated cheese. Place the broccoli on top and sprinkle this with the remaining grated cheese. Dot with another 2 tablespoons of the butter cut into small pieces and gratinate in a hot oven (425°F) or under the broiler.

Cook the remaining butter until brown (or *à la noisette*) and coat the broccoli with this as soon as you remove it from the heat. Serve immediately.

SERVES 4–6

Glazed Carrots

Carottes Glacées

1 lb carrots
salt
2 tablespoons sugar
4 tablespoons butter

It is not necessary to blanch new carrots for this recipe: they can be scraped and left whole, or cut into 2 or 4 pieces according to size. Old carrots, on the other hand, should be peeled and trimmed to the shape of elongated olives and blanched before being cooked.

Place the prepared carrots in a pan with just enough water to cover. Add the salt, sugar and butter, and simmer gently without a lid until almost all the moisture has evaporated, leaving a syrupy reduction. Toss the carrots in this to make them glossy.

SERVES 4–6

Souffléed Eggplants

Creamed Carrots

Carottes à la Crème

1 lb carrots
salt
2 tablespoons sugar
4 tablespoons butter
$\frac{3}{4}$ cup heavy cream

Prepare the carrots according to the recipe for Glazed Carrots, page 126, cutting and blanching if necessary. Place the prepared carrots in a pan with just enough water to cover. Add the salt, sugar and butter, and simmer gently until almost all the moisture has evaporated, leaving a syrupy reduction.

Heat the cream until boiling and add to the carrots. Allow to reduce to desired consistency and serve in a deep dish.

SERVES 4–6

Carrots Marianne

Carottes Marianne

1 lb new carrots, scrubbed and cut into coarse julienne
6 tablespoons butter
$\frac{1}{2}$ lb button mushrooms
1 tablespoon Meat Glaze, page 9

Maître d'Hôtel Butter
4 tablespoons butter
1 tablespoon chopped fresh parsley
salt
pepper
a little lemon juice

Cook the *julienne* of carrots in 4 tablespoons of the butter, with the lid on the saucepan. Quickly sauté the mushrooms separately in the remaining butter and, when soft, add these to the carrots.

Prepare the Maître d'Hôtel Butter by beating the butter until soft and smooth, adding all the other ingredients and mixing well together. Shake this into the prepared carrots and mushrooms just before serving, together with the meat glaze.

SERVES 4–6

Braised Celery

Céleri Braisé

2 bunches celery, scrubbed and trimmed to about 6 inches in length
2 tablespoons butter
6 thin slices bacon
1 onion, peeled and sliced
1 carrot, peeled and sliced
1 clove garlic, peeled and crushed
1 bay leaf
1 sprig thyme
salt
pepper
$\frac{3}{4}$ cup White Stock, page 9

Blanch the celery in boiling water for 10 minutes, then refresh and drain. Butter a flameproof braising pan and line with some of the bacon. Place the vegetables and herbs on top, cover with the celery, season lightly and place the remaining bacon on top. Cover and place on top of the stove to stew lightly for a few minutes. Barely cover with the stock, replace the lid and cook in a moderate oven (350°F) for about 50 minutes or until the celery bunches are soft.

Remove the celery and drain. Remove any fat from the braising liquid, strain and reduce. (Discard the cooking vegetables and bacon.) Cut each celery bunch in half, place in a serving dish and moisten with the reduced braising liquid.

SERVES 4–6

Celery Purée

Purée de Céleri

$1\frac{1}{2}$ lb celery, cleaned and sliced
$1\frac{1}{4}$ cups White Stock, page 9
$\frac{1}{2}$ lb potatoes, peeled
6 tablespoons butter

Blanch the celery and drain. Cook in a covered pan in the white stock until tender. Cook the potatoes in boiling salted water, drain and mash.

Drain the celery as soon as it is cooked, reserving the cooking liquid. Pass the celery through a sieve together with a little of the cooking liquid, or process in a food processor, then sieve with a little of the cooking liquid.

Add the mashed potato, mix together and reheat. Finish with the butter, season to taste and serve in a deep dish.

SERVES 4–6

(from left to right, clockwise)
Artichoke Purée, Jerusalem Artichoke Purée, Mushroom Purée

Celeriac Purée

Purée de Céleri-rave

$1\frac{1}{2}$ lb celeriac, peeled and sliced
salt
$\frac{1}{2}$ lb potatoes
1 stick plus 2 tablespoons butter
a little hot milk
white pepper

Cook the celeriac in lightly salted boiling water and drain well. Cook the potatoes in boiling salted water, drain and mash. Pass the celeriac through a sieve and add the mashed potato.

Place the purée in a shallow pan and add 1 stick of the butter. Allow to dry out quickly over a vigorous heat and bring to the desired consistency with a little hot milk. Finish with the remaining butter, season to taste and serve in a deep dish.

SERVES 6–8

Mushroom Tart

Flan Grillé aux Champignons

1 lb button mushrooms
2 tablespoons chopped onion
6 tablespoons butter
$1\frac{1}{4}$ cups Béchamel Sauce, page 12
$\frac{1}{2}$ cup heavy cream
salt
pepper
half-quantity Basic Pie Pastry, page 26
1 egg, beaten

Fry the mushrooms and onion gently in 4 tablespoons of the butter until just golden brown, then add the Béchamel Sauce and cream and allow to cool. Season to taste.

Butter a 7-inch flan ring on a baking sheet, using the remaining butter, and line with the pie pastry. Fill with the mushroom mixture, moisten the edges and cover with thin strips of pastry dough, made from trimmings, arranged trellis-fashion.

Brush the pastry trellis with the beaten egg and bake the tart in a hot oven (425°F) for about 25 minutes. Serve at once.

Small tartlets (*as shown in the photograph opposite*) can be prepared in the same way (reduce cooking time to 10 minutes) and make a particularly good garnish for tournedos.

SERVES 4–6

Stuffed Mushrooms

Champignons Farcis

12 large mushrooms
salt
pepper
2 tablespoons olive oil
$\frac{3}{4}$ cup thick Duxelles Sauce, page 12
2–3 tablespoons fine dried white bread crumbs
4 tablespoons melted butter

Remove the stalks from the mushrooms and use in the preparation of the Duxelles Sauce. Wash and dry the mushrooms well. Arrange them in a gratin dish, season and sprinkle with oil. Place in a moderate oven (350°F) and cook for 5 minutes to extract some of their moisture.

Fill the cavities with the well-reduced Duxelles Sauce, stiffened if necessary with some of the white bread crumbs.

Sprinkle the mushrooms with the remaining bread crumbs and a few drops of melted butter. Gratinate in a hot oven (425°F).

SERVES 6

Mushroom Purée

Purée de Champignons

2 lb mushrooms, coarsely chopped
1 stick plus 2 tablespoons butter
$\frac{1}{2}$ cup heavy cream
$1\frac{1}{4}$ cups Béchamel Sauce, page 12
salt
pepper
grated nutmeg

Pass the chopped mushrooms through a coarse sieve. Melt 4 tablespoons of the butter in a shallow pan, add the sieved mushroom and fry quickly until all the moisture has evaporated.

Add the cream to the Béchamel Sauce and reduce a little. Add this to the mushroom mixture, season with salt, pepper and a little nutmeg, and reduce further over a vigorous heat. Remove from the heat and finish with the remaining butter. Serve in a deep dish. *See photograph on page 129.*

SERVES 4–6

Mushroom Tart

Creamed Ceps

Cèpes à la Crème

2 tablespoons chopped onion
6 tablespoons butter
1 lb fresh ceps or porcini, sliced
salt
pepper
1¼ cups heavy cream

Fry the onion gently in a pat of butter without allowing it to brown. Stew the ceps gently in a covered pan in the remaining butter, add the fried onion and season.

When the ceps are cooked, drain and cover them with 1 cup of the cream, brought to boiling point. Allow to simmer gently until the cream has reduced to virtually nothing. At the last minute, stir in the remaining cream, check the seasoning and serve in a deep dish.

SERVES 6–8

Ceps Provençale

Cèpes à la Provençale

1 lb fresh ceps or porcini
salt
pepper
¼ cup olive oil
2 tablespoons chopped onion
1 clove garlic, peeled and crushed
2 tablespoons fresh white bread crumbs
a few drops lemon juice
1 tablespoon chopped fresh parsley

Remove the stalks from the ceps and reserve them for later use. Slice the caps into fairly thick slices on the slant, season, and fry in hot oil until well-browned. Meanwhile, chop the reserved stalks finely.

When the slices of cep are almost ready, add the chopped reserved stalks, the onion, garlic and bread crumbs to soak up any excess oil. Toss and cook gently for a few minutes.

Arrange in a deep dish and finish with a squeeze of lemon juice. Garnish with the chopped parsley.

SERVES 4–6

Stuffed Morels Forestière

Morilles Farcies à la Forestière

2 lb large fresh morels
4 tablespoons butter
½ cup dried white bread crumbs
2 tablespoons melted butter

For the stuffing
4 tablespoons butter
2 tablespoons olive oil
½ small onion, peeled and chopped
5 tablespoons chopped shallot
salt
pepper
1 tablespoon chopped fresh parsley
¼ cup dry white wine
½ cup tomato-flavored Demi-glace Sauce, page 10
1 clove garlic, peeled and crushed
½ cup fresh white bread crumbs
¼ lb bulk pork sausage meat

Wash the morels and cut off the stalks. Chop the stalks finely and reserve.

Prepare the stuffing by heating the butter and oil, and frying the onion and shallot gently for a few minutes. Add the reserved stalks and continue to cook gently until all the moisture has evaporated. Season with salt and pepper and add the parsley. Moisten with the wine and allow the liquid to reduce to virtually nothing. Add the Demi-glace Sauce, crushed garlic and white bread crumbs. Allow to simmer gently until it acquires a firm consistency. Allow to cool completely then mix in the sausage meat.

Slit the morels through on one side and fill the openings with the prepared stuffing. Use a little of the butter to grease an ovenproof dish and place the stuffed morels in this, cut side down. Sprinkle with the bread crumbs and melted butter and cook in a moderate oven (350°F) for 40 minutes. Serve straight from the dish.

SERVES 8

Creamed Ceps

Creamed Brussels Sprouts

Choux de Bruxelles à la Crème

1 lb Brussels sprouts, trimmed
salt
4 tablespoons butter
$\frac{3}{4}$–1 cup heavy cream

Cook the sprouts in boiling salted water and drain them well without refreshing them. Heat in the butter for a few minutes to dry out any remaining moisture, and chop.

Stir in as much cream as they will absorb and serve.

SERVES 4–6

Chicory Soufflé

Soufflé de Chicorée

$\frac{1}{2}$ lb chicory
3 tablespoons butter
4$\frac{1}{2}$ tablespoons flour
$\frac{3}{4}$ cup White Stock, page 9
salt
1 pinch sugar
3 eggs, separated
$\frac{3}{4}$ cup grated Parmesan cheese

Blanch the chicory in plenty of boiling water for 10 minutes and refresh. Squeeze out all the water, then chop.

Make a brown *roux* by mixing together 2 tablespoons of the butter and the flour in a heavy pan. Cook over a moderate heat, stirring continuously, until you obtain a golden brown color. Gradually stir in the white stock, season with salt and a pinch of sugar, and cook for a few minutes. Add the chicory, cover with a lid and braise in a moderate oven (350°F) for 1 hour until just cooked but still fairly stiff.

Pass the cooked chicory through a sieve. Add the egg yolks and $\frac{1}{2}$ cup grated Parmesan. Beat the egg whites stiffly and fold these in.

Pour the soufflé mixture into a buttered 6-inch soufflé dish and sprinkle with the remaining Parmesan. Return to the oven to bake for 20–25 minutes. Serve immediately.

SERVES 4–6

Creamed Chicory

Chicorée à la Crème

1 lb chicory
3 tablespoons flour
1 stick butter
2 cups White Stock, page 9
salt
1 pinch sugar
$\frac{3}{4}$ cup heavy cream

Blanch the chicory in plenty of boiling water for 10 minutes. Then refresh, squeeze out all the water and chop.

Make a brown *roux* by mixing the flour with 3 tablespoons of the butter in a heavy pan. Cook over a moderate heat, stirring continuously, until you obtain a golden brown color. Gradually stir in the white stock, season with salt and a pinch of sugar and cook for a few minutes. Add the chicory, cover with a lid and braise in a moderate oven (350°F) for 1$\frac{1}{2}$ hours.

When cooked, transfer the chicory to a clean pan and stir in the cream and the remaining butter. Serve in a deep dish.

SERVES 6–8

Cauliflower au Gratin

Chou-fleur au Gratin

1 medium cauliflower, trimmed
2 tablespoons butter
1$\frac{1}{4}$ cups Mornay Sauce, page 13
$\frac{1}{2}$ cup grated Gruyère cheese
$\frac{1}{4}$ cup dried white bread crumbs
2 tablespoons melted butter

Divide the cauliflower into florets and cook in boiling salted water. Drain well and heat in the butter to dry out any remaining moisture.

Arrange the florets upside-down in a closely-fitting round bowl to re-form into the original shape of the cauliflower and fill the center with a few tablespoons of Mornay Sauce.

Coat the bottom of an ovenproof gratin dish with more Mornay Sauce and unmold the cauliflower on top. Cover completely with the remaining sauce and sprinkle with a mixture of grated cheese and bread crumbs. Finally, sprinkle with the melted butter and gratinate in a hot oven (425°F) or under the broiler.

SERVES 4–6

Cauliflower Polonaise

Chou-fleur à la Polonaise

1 medium cauliflower, trimmed
salt
2 tablespoons butter
2 hard-boiled egg yolks
1 tablespoon chopped fresh parsley
1 stick butter
½ cup fine fresh white bread crumbs

Divide the cauliflower into florets and cook in boiling salted water. Drain and place in a buttered dish. Sprinkle with a mixture of chopped hard-boiled egg yolk and chopped parsley. Keep warm.

Cook the butter until brown (or *à la noisette*), then quickly fry the bread crumbs in it until golden brown. Pour over the cauliflower and serve immediately.

SERVES 4–6

Cauliflower Fritters

Fritots de Chou-fleur

1 medium cauliflower
salt
pepper
3 tablespoons olive oil
2 tablespoons lemon juice
Fritter Batter, page 26
oil for deep frying

To garnish
fried parsley
Tomato Sauce, page 14

Divide the cauliflower into florets and cook in boiling salted water for 8–10 minutes or until the cauliflower resists only slightly when pierced. Drain, season and marinate in the oil and lemon juice for 20 minutes.

Dip each floret in frying batter and deep fry in hot oil (350°F) for about 4 minutes until golden brown. Drain well.

Arrange on a napkin on a dish and garnish with fried parsley. Serve accompanied by Tomato Sauce.

SERVES 4–6

Red Cabbage with Chestnuts

Chou Rouge à la Limousine

1 red cabbage, weighing about 2 lb
salt
pepper
⅔ cup White Stock, page 9
3 tablespoons pork drippings or butter
20 chestnuts, shelled and broken

Cut the cabbage into quarters, then discard the outside leaves and core. Slice the rest of the cabbage into fine *julienne*. Season with salt and pepper and place in an ovenproof casserole with the stock, fat and chestnuts.Cover with the lid and cook in a moderate oven (350°F) for about 1–1½ hours or until tender.

SERVES 4–6

Braised Red Cabbage with Apple

Chou Rouge à la Flamande

1 red cabbage, weighing about 2 lb
salt
pepper
grated nutmeg
2 tablespoons wine vinegar
2 tablespoons butter
4 apples, peeled, cored and sliced
1 tablespoon brown sugar

Cut the cabbage into quarters, then discard the outside leaves and core. Slice the rest of the cabbage into fine *julienne*. Season with salt, pepper and grated nutmeg, sprinkle with vinegar and place in a well-buttered ovenproof casserole.

Cover with a lid and cook in a moderate oven (350°F) for 1½ hours. Then add the apple and sugar and continue cooking for another 30 minutes, or until tender.

Serve in a deep dish.

SERVES 4–6

Salad Aïda

Andalusian Salad

Salade à l'Andalouse

$1\frac{1}{4}$ cups long-grain rice
salt
1 small clove garlic, peeled and crushed
1 small onion, peeled and chopped
1 tablespoon chopped fresh parsley
1 lb tomatoes, peeled and quartered
$\frac{1}{2}$ lb sweet peppers, cut into julienne

Dressing
6 tablespoons olive oil
2 tablespoons wine vinegar
salt
pepper

Cook the rice in lightly salted boiling water, cool under running water and drain well. Add the garlic, onion and chopped parsley to the rice, and mix well. Combine the rice mixture with the quartered tomatoes and the *julienne* of sweet peppers.

To make the dressing, combine all the ingredients while stirring briskly. Pour the dressing over the salad and toss gently but thoroughly.

SERVES 8

Salad Aurore

Salade Aurore

3 apples, peeled, cored and sliced
18 fresh green walnuts, skinned and halved
1 head lettuce

Dressing
6 tablespoons heavy cream
1 tablespoon tomato paste
1 teaspoon prepared English mustard
juice of 2 lemons
salt
1 pinch sugar

Arrange the sliced apples and walnuts in a salad bowl and surround with lettuce leaves. Make the dressing by mixing together all the ingredients and pour over the top. *See photograph on page 93.*

SERVES 4–6

Salad Beaucaire

Salade Beaucaire

2 stalks celery, cut into julienne
$\frac{3}{4}$ lb celeriac, peeled and cut into julienne
2 heads Belgian endive, cut into julienne
3 tablespoons olive oil
1 tablespoon wine vinegar
1 teaspoon Dijon mustard
$\frac{1}{4}$ lb lean cooked ham, cut into julienne
1 tart apple, peeled, cored and cut into julienne
$\frac{1}{4}$ lb button mushrooms, cut into julienne
6 tablespoons Mayonnaise, page 13
2 tablespoons chopped fresh parsley, chervil and tarragon, mixed
1 cup cooked, peeled and sliced beets
1 cup cooked, peeled and sliced potatoes

Place the *julienne* of celery, celeriac and endive in a bowl. Mix together the oil, vinegar and mustard, pour onto the salad ingredients, toss and leave for 1 hour.

Then add the julienne of ham, apple and mushrooms and the mayonnaise, and toss everything together. Arrange in a salad bowl and sprinkle with the chopped herbs.

Surround with a border of alternate slices of beet and potato.

SERVES 4–6

Crayfish Salad

Salade Belle de Nuit

20 crayfish, prepared as for Swimming Crayfish, page 60
6 oz black truffle, sliced

Dressing
3 tablespoons olive oil
1 tablespoon wine vinegar
salt
freshly milled black pepper

Remove the tails from the crayfish when cold and arrange, alternating with the sliced truffles, in a serving dish. Combine all the dressing ingredients, seasoning well with the milled pepper, then pour carefully over the salad.

SERVES 6–8

Brazilian Salad

Salade Brésilienne

$1\frac{1}{4}$ cups long-grain rice
salt
1 small pineapple, peeled and diced

Dressing
6 tablespoons light cream
2 tablespoons lemon juice
salt
pepper

Cook the rice in boiling salted water, cool under cold running water, drain and allow to cool. Mix with the diced fresh pineapple.

Combine all the dressing ingredients, pour over the salad and toss well.

SERVES 8

Salad Creole

Salade Créole

6 small ripe melons
salt
1 pinch ground ginger
$2\frac{1}{2}$ cups cold boiled long-grain rice, well drained
6 tablespoons heavy cream
2 tablespoons lemon juice

Slice off the stem ends of the melons and reserve for later use. Scoop out the melon seeds and discard. Carefully scoop out the flesh with a spoon and cut into large dice. Season with salt and ginger, add the rice and mix together.

At the last moment, add the cream and lemon juice and check the seasoning. Refill the hollowed melons with this mixture and replace the reserved tops as lids.

Serve on a bed of finely crushed ice.

SERVES 6

Potato and Watercress Salad

Salade Cressonière

2 lb potatoes, peeled
salt
$1\frac{1}{4}$ cups dry white wine
1 bunch watercress
3 hard-boiled eggs, chopped
1 tablespoon chopped fresh parsley

Dressing
6 tablespoons olive oil
2 tablespoons wine vinegar
salt
pepper

Cook the potatoes in boiling salted water; drain and cut into thin slices while still warm. Place in a bowl and mix in the wine, which the potatoes will absorb.

When you are ready to serve, add the watercress. Mix all the dressing ingredients, pour over the salad and toss gently.

Arrange the salad in a dome shape and sprinkle with chopped hard-boiled egg mixed with chopped parsley.

SERVES 8

Salad Danicheff

Salade Danicheff

$\frac{1}{2}$ lb asparagus tips, lightly boiled and thinly sliced
$\frac{1}{2}$ lb celeriac, peeled, lightly boiled and thinly sliced
$\frac{1}{2}$ lb potatoes, peeled, lightly boiled and thinly sliced
$\frac{1}{2}$ lb tender raw artichoke hearts, sliced
$\frac{1}{2}$ lb mushrooms, sliced

To garnish
16 crayfish tails, cooked
4 hard-boiled eggs, quartered
1 oz truffle, sliced

Dressing
thin Mayonnaise, page 13

Arrange all the salad ingredients in *bouquets* on a serving dish and garnish with the cooked crayfish tails, quartered hard-boiled eggs and slices of truffle.

Dress with thin Mayonnaise.

SERVES 8

Flemish Salad

Salade à la Flamande

2 medium onions
4 heads Belgian endive, thinly sliced
¾ lb potatoes, cooked and cut into julienne
¼ lb salted herring fillet, soaked, drained and diced

Dressing
6 tablespoons olive oil
2 tablespoons wine vinegar
salt
pepper
1 tablespoon chopped fresh parsley
1 tablespoon chopped fresh chervil

Bake the onions in the oven in their skins, then allow to cool, peel and chop finely. Mix this chopped onion with the sliced endive, the *julienne* of potatoes and the diced herring fillet which has been previously soaked to remove excess salt and drained well. Place all these ingredients in a salad bowl.

Mix together the dressing ingredients, pour over the salad and toss gently.

SERVES 6–8

Pineapple, Tomato and Orange Salad

Salade aux Fruits à la Japonaise

1 small pineapple, peeled and cut as required (see below)
juice of 1 lemon
½ lb tomatoes, skinned, seeded and cut as required (see below)
1 pinch sugar
salt
3 oranges, peeled and cut as required (see below)
6 lettuce hearts or 3 hearts romaine lettuce, halved

Dressing
¾ cup heavy cream
a few drops lemon juice
1 pinch salt

If this salad is to be served on hearts of ordinary lettuce, the pineapple, tomato and orange should be cut into small squares; if on half hearts of romaine lettuce, they should be cut into thin slices.

Sprinkle the pineapple with most of the lemon juice. Season the tomato with the sugar, very little salt and a few drops of lemon juice. Do not season the oranges.

Keep the fruit very cold until required, then arrange them on the hearts of lettuce or the half hearts of romaine lettuce.

Acidulate the cream with the lemon juice and season with a pinch of salt. Sprinkle the fruit with a little of this dressing and serve the rest separately.

SERVES 6

Gobelin Salad

Salade des Gobelins

½ lb celeriac, peeled and cooked but still firm
½ lb potatoes, peeled and cooked but still firm
4 tender raw artichoke bottoms, sliced
2 cups sliced mushrooms
5 oz truffles, sliced
¼ lb asparagus tips, cooked

Dressing
¾ cup Mayonnaise, page 13, flavored with 1 teaspoon lemon juice and 1 tablespoon chopped fresh tarragon

Coarsely grate the celeriac and the potatoes. Place in a salad bowl with all the other salad ingredients. Dress with mayonnaise, flavored with lemon juice and tarragon, and toss all together gently.

SERVES 6

Dutch Rice Salad

Salade Hollandaise

2½ cups cold boiled long-grain rice, well drained
1 tart apple, peeled, cored and diced
5 oz smoked herring fillet, diced

Dressing
6 tablespoons olive oil
2 tablespoons white wine vinegar
2 teaspoons Dijon mustard
salt
pepper

Combine all the salad ingredients in a salad bowl. Make the dressing by mixing together all the ingredients, pour over the salad and toss lightly.

SERVES 6–8

Pineapple, Tomato and Orange Salad

Salad Irma

Salade Irma

1 large or 2 small cucumbers, peeled, seeded and diced
½ lb green beans, cut into diamond shapes, cooked
½ lb asparagus tips, cooked
½ lb cauliflower florets, cooked
1 lettuce heart, finely shredded
1 bunch watercress, shredded

Dressing
¾ cup Mayonnaise, page 13
¼ cup heavy cream
1 tablespoon mixed chopped fresh tarragon and chervil

To garnish
4–6 nasturtium flowers
6 radishes, thinly sliced

Mix together the cucumber, beans, asparagus tips and cauliflower florets. Combine the dressing ingredients, pour over the salad and toss. Arrange in a deep salad bowl.

Cover with the finely shredded lettuce and shredded watercress. Garnish with choice nasturtium flowers and thin slices of radish.

SERVES 4–6

Italian Salad

Salade Italienne

1¼ cups long-grain rice
1 lb shelled peas
¾ lb carrots, peeled
1¼ cups White Stock, page 9

Dressing
6 tablespoons olive oil
2 tablespoons wine vinegar
salt
pepper

Cook the rice in lightly salted boiling water, cool under running water and drain well. Cook the peas in lightly salted boiling water, drain and cool. Cut the carrots into dice, cook in the stock, drain and cool.

Combine all the salad ingredients and those for the dressing. Pour the dressing over the salad and toss lightly.

SERVES 8

Vegetable Salad

Salade de Légumes

1⅓ cups small balls of carrot, cut with a spoon cutter
1⅓ cups small balls of turnip, cut with a spoon cutter
6 oz potato, peeled
6 oz green beans, cut into diamond shapes
6 oz shelled peas
6 oz asparagus tips
6 oz cauliflower
salt

Dressing
6 tablespoons olive oil
2 tablespoons wine vinegar
salt
pepper
1 tablespoon chopped fresh parsley
1 tablespoon chopped fresh chervil

Cook all the vegetables separately in lightly salted boiling water until cooked but still firm. Do not refresh after cooking but drain well and allow to cool naturally. Dice the potato and divide the cauliflower into florets.

Arrange the first six vegetables in *bouquets* on a dish, paying particular attention to color contrast. Put a mound of cauliflower florets in the center.

Combine all the dressing ingredients and pour over each bouquet of vegetables.

SERVES 8

Salad Lorette

Salade Lorette

2 stalks celery, cut into julienne
corn salad (lamb's lettuce or mâche)
½ lb cooked beets, peeled and cut into julienne

Dressing
3 tablespoons olive oil
1 tablespoon wine vinegar
salt
pepper

Combine all the salad ingredients and those for the dressing. Pour the dressing over the salad and toss. Arrange in a dome shape in a salad bowl.

SERVES 4–6

Salad Irma

Salad Montfermeil

Salade Montfermeil

½ lb salsify, peeled
4 hard-boiled eggs, separated into yolks and whites
½ lb artichoke bottoms, cooked and thinly sliced
½ lb potatoes, cooked and thinly sliced
2 tablespoons chopped fresh fines herbes*: parsley, chives, chervil and tarragon*

Dressing
6 tablespoons olive oil
2 tablespoons wine vinegar
salt
pepper

Cook the salsify and slice into small *bâtons* while still warm. Cut the hard-boiled egg whites into *julienne*. Mix the salsify with the artichoke bottoms, potatoes and hard-boiled egg whites. Make the dressing by mixing all the ingredients together. Pour over the salad and toss gently.

Arrange the salad in a dome shape in a salad bowl and cover completely with the sieved hard-boiled egg yolks. Sprinkle with the fresh *fines herbes*.

SERVES 6

Salad Niçoise

Salade Niçoise

½ lb green beans, cooked and diced
½ lb potatoes, peeled, cooked and diced
½ lb small tomatoes, peeled, quartered and seeded
3 tablespoons capers
¾ cup black olives, pitted
2-oz can anchovy fillets, drained

Dressing
6 tablespoons olive oil
2 tablespoons wine vinegar
salt
pepper

Mix together the diced green beans, diced potatoes and prepared tomatoes in a salad bowl. Combine the dressing ingredients, pour over the salad and toss gently. Arrange in a dome shape in a salad bowl.

Decorate with the capers, olives and anchovy fillets.

SERVES 6

Orange Salad

Salade d'Oranges

3 ripe oranges, peeled

Dressing
a few drops Kirsch

Cut the oranges in half vertically, remove the seeds and cut the flesh into thin, evenly sized pieces. Sprinkle with a little Kirsch.

SERVES 6 AS ACCOMPANIMENT TO RICH ROAST MEATS

Oriental Rice Salad

Salade Orientale

½ lb small tomatoes, skinned, halved and seeded
4 cloves garlic, peeled and crushed
2 tablespoons olive oil
1 large sweet red pepper
1 large green pepper
½ lb green beans
1¼ cups long-grain rice
salt

Dressing
6 tablespoons olive oil
2 tablespoons wine vinegar
salt
pepper
2-oz can anchovy fillets, drained and diced

Fry the tomato halves very gently with the crushed garlic in the olive oil. Broil the peppers, remove their skins, seed and dice. Cook the green beans and slice into small *bâtons*. Boil the rice in salted water until cooked and drain well.

Mix all these ingredients together. Combine all the dressing ingredients, pour over the salad while still warm and allow to cool. Arrange in a dome shape in a salad bowl.

SERVES 8

Russian Salad

Salade Russe

⅔ cup diced cooked carrots
⅔ cup diced cooked turnips
⅔ cup diced cooked potatoes
4 oz truffles, diced
¾ cup diced cooked green beans
1½ cups diced mushrooms, cooked with a little lemon juice and butter
⅔ cup diced salted beef tongue or lean cooked ham
⅔ cup diced cooked lobster
⅔ cup diced gherkins
¼ lb smoked sausage, diced
4 oz anchovy fillets, drained and diced (2 cans)
⅔ cup cooked peas
6 tablespoons capers

Dressing
1¼ cups Mayonnaise, page 13

To garnish
⅔ cup cooked, peeled and sliced beets
3 tablespoons caviar

Mix together all the salad ingredients and combine with the mayonnaise. Arrange in a salad bowl, and garnish with the beets and caviar.

SERVES 6–8

Salad Tourangelle

Salade Tourangelle

½ lb green beans, cooked and cut into diamond shapes
½ lb flageolet or lima beans, cooked
½ lb waxy potatoes, cooked and cut into thick julienne

Dressing
½ cup Mayonnaise, page 13
2 tablespoons cream
1 tablespoon chopped fresh tarragon

Combine all the ingredients for the salad and all those for the dressing. Pour the dressing over the salad vegetables and toss gently.

SERVES 6

Salad Trédern

Salade Trédern

24 live crayfish (see below)
24 shucked oysters
a few drops lemon juice
3 tablespoons asparagus tips
2 oz truffles, very thinly sliced
2 tablespoons heavy cream

Dressing
¾ cup Mayonnaise, page 13

Prepare and cook the crayfish according to the recipe for Swimming Crayfish, page 60. Drain and shell, reserving the shells for later use. Poach the oysters with the lemon juice and their own juices and remove their beards. Cook the asparagus until just tender. Place all these ingredients, while still lukewarm, in a bowl and add the sliced truffles.

Pound the crayfish shells finely with the cream and pass through a fine sieve. Add the pink, crayfish-flavored cream to the mayonnaise and use to dress the salad.

SERVES 4–6

Waldorf Salad

Salade Waldorf

¾ lb apples, peeled and diced
¾ lb celeriac, peeled and diced
½ lb fresh walnuts, shelled and halved

Dressing
⅔ cup thin Mayonnaise, page 13

Place all the salad ingredients in a salad bowl, dress with the mayonnaise and toss gently.

SERVES 6–8

DESSERTS & ICES

Egg Custard Sauce

Crème à l'Anglaise

scant 1 cup sugar
6 egg yolks
$\frac{1}{2}$ teaspoon arrowroot
$2\frac{1}{2}$ cups scalded milk

Place the sugar, egg yolks and arrowroot in a bowl and beat until the mixture thickens and forms a slowly dissolving ribbon when the beater is lifted out of the bowl.

Add the hot milk, a little at a time, place over the heat and stir with a wooden spoon until the yolks thicken the mixture and it sticks to the back of the spoon. Do not allow the custard to come to a boil, as this will cause it to separate.

As soon as it is cooked, pass the custard through a fine strainer and keep it warm in a *bain-marie*. When required as a sauce this egg custard may be flavored as desired with, for example, vanilla, orange or lemon rind infused in the milk, or with $\frac{1}{4}$ cup of a liqueur, added at the last moment. When flavored, the Egg Custard Sauce takes the name of the flavoring. For example, if flavored with rum, the Custard becomes Rum Sauce, and so on.

MAKES $2\frac{1}{2}$ CUPS

Frangipane Custard

Crème Frangipane

3 cups milk
1 vanilla bean
$\frac{1}{2}$ cup sugar
$\frac{1}{2}$ cup flour
2 eggs
4 egg yolks
salt
6 tablespoons butter
$\frac{1}{4}$ cup crushed macaroons

Bring the milk to a boil and infuse with the vanilla bean for 30 minutes. Place the sugar, flour, eggs, egg yolks and salt in a pan and stir with a wooden spoon. Slowly stir in the hot milk and bring to a boil, stirring continuously. Allow to boil for 2 minutes, then transfer to a bowl.

Add 4 tablespoons of the butter and the crushed macaroons and stir. Smooth the surface with the remaining butter on the point of a knife to prevent a skin from forming.

MAKES 3 CUPS

Chantilly Cream

Crème Chantilly

1 quart heavy cream
$\frac{1}{2}$ cup sugar
1 teaspoon vanilla extract

Whip the cream until it becomes stiff enough to stand in peaks on the beater. Add the sugar and vanilla extract: mix well. This cream should be prepared at the last moment.

MAKES 1 QUART

Sugar Syrup

Sirop

$2\frac{1}{4}$ cups sugar
$2\frac{1}{2}$ cups water

Place the sugar and water in a pan, bring to a boil and skim. Allow to cool and use as required.

This syrup may be flavored where necessary by the addition of an appropriate extract such as vanilla, or it may be flavored by infusing with vanilla bean, orange or lemon rind and so on.

MAKES APPROXIMATELY 1 QUART

Chocolate Sauce

Sauce au Chocolat

8 oz semisweet chocolate
$1\frac{1}{4}$ cups cold water
1 tablespoon vanilla sugar
3 tablespoons heavy cream
pat of butter

Put the chocolate in the cold water, then heat very gently until it is fully melted. Add the vanilla sugar and simmer gently for 25 minutes. Finish with the cream and butter.

MAKES $1\frac{1}{4}$ CUPS

Rich Pie Pastry

Pâte à Foncer Fine

$1\frac{3}{4}$ cups flour, sifted
1 pinch salt
2 tablespoons sugar
1 egg, beaten
1 stick plus 2 tablespoons butter, softened
2 tablespoons water

Make a well in the flour and place the salt, sugar, egg, butter and water in the center. Mix the flour gradually into the other ingredients until it is incorporated and forms a paste. Roll the paste into a ball, then push small pieces away from the ball with the heel of the hand, thus assuring the complete blending of all the ingredients. Do this twice.

Form into a ball then wrap in a cloth and place in the refrigerator to chill, preferably for a few hours, before use.

MAKES APPROXIMATELY 1 LB

Orange Finger Cookies

Biscuits à la Cuiller

8 eggs
$1\frac{1}{3}$ cups sugar
1 tablespoon orange flower water
$1\frac{1}{3}$ cups flour, sifted
butter

Separate the eggs and beat the whites stiffly. Beat $1\frac{1}{4}$ cups of the sugar and the egg yolks in a bowl until thick and pale. Add the orange flower water, fold in half the stiffly beaten egg whites, then rain in the flour followed by the rest of the whites, folding and cutting all the ingredients together with a spoon so as to keep the mixture light.

Place the mixture in a pastry bag with a plain $\frac{1}{2}$ inch diameter tube and pipe in $3\frac{1}{2}$ inch lengths on sheets of buttered parchment paper. Sprinkle all over with the remaining sugar, then shake off the surplus by holding the paper at both ends and agitating it slightly.

Spray a few fine drops of water over the cookies to help them become pearly, then bake in a moderate oven (335°F) for 12–15 minutes, or until lightly browned.

MAKES APPROXIMATELY 40 COOKIES

Apricot Macaroon Tart

Abricots Bourdaloue

1 lb apricots, halved and pitted
$\frac{3}{4}$ cup vanilla-flavored Sugar Syrup, above left
1 large cooked tart case made with Rich Pie Pastry, left
$1\frac{1}{4}$ cups Frangipane Custard, page 158
1 cup crushed macaroons
2 tablespoons melted butter

Poach the halved apricots in the vanilla-flavored syrup and allow to cool thoroughly. Cover the bottom of the tart case with a layer of frangipane custard containing half the crushed macaroons. Arrange the drained apricot halves on top of this and cover with more frangipane custard.

Sprinkle the surface with the remaining crushed macaroons and the melted butter and glaze quickly in a hot oven or under the broiler.

SERVES 6–8

Apricot Meringue

Abricots Meringués

1 lb apricots, halved and pitted
$\frac{3}{4}$ cup vanilla-flavored Sugar Syrup, page 159
$\frac{1}{2}$ recipe quantity Rice Pudding, page 176
confectioners' sugar

Meringue
4 egg whites
1 cup superfine sugar

To garnish
red currant jam
apricot jam

Poach the halved apricots in the vanilla-flavored syrup and allow to cool thoroughly. Place a layer of the rice pudding on a dish and arrange the halves of poached apricot on top.

Make the meringue by beating the egg whites stiffly and sprinkling in the sugar, mixing lightly with a spoon so that the egg whites do not lose their lightness.

Cover the apricots with meringue, piled in a dome shape, and decorate with more meringue, using a pastry bag and tube.

Dredge with confectioners' sugar and place in a warm oven (325°F) for approximately 45 minutes to cook and color the meringue.

On removing the dish from the oven, decorate the meringue by piping red currant and apricot jam on it using fine plain tubes.

Serves 6

Pineapple Royale

Ananas à la Royale

1 large pineapple, with leaves
fresh fruit salad (see below)
6–8 large strawberries, halved
Kirsch
4 peaches, peeled and halved
$1\frac{1}{4}$ cups vanilla-flavored Sugar Syrup, page 159

Cut the top off the pineapple leaving its leaves intact, and put this to one side for use later. Scoop out the inside of the pineapple, leaving a case about $\frac{1}{2}$ inch thick.

Make a fresh fruit salad using fruit of your choice, but including the inside of the pineapple. Macerate both the fruit salad and the halved strawberries in Kirsch for at least 30 minutes. Meanwhile, poach the peaches in the vanilla-flavored syrup until just tender and allow to cool.

Fill the pineapple case with the fruit salad and place the filled pineapple in the middle of a large glass bowl. Surround the base of the pineapple with the poached peaches and decorate the peaches with the strawberries. Replace the top of the pineapple before serving.

Serves 8

Pineapple Fritters

Beignets d'Ananas Favorite

1 pineapple
6 tablespoons sugar
3 tablespoons Kirsch
2 tablespoons shelled, skinned and chopped pistachios
$2\frac{1}{2}$ cups thick Frangipane Custard, page 158, almost cold
oil for deep frying
confectioners' sugar

Light frying batter
$\frac{3}{4}$ cup flour, sifted
1 tablespoon melted butter
1 pinch salt
1 pinch sugar
1 egg
$\frac{1}{4}$ cup beer

First, prepare a light frying batter. Mix all the ingredients together with a little lukewarm water, using a spoon. Do not overmix, and leave in a warm place for an hour.

Meanwhile, cut the pineapple into round slices, $\frac{3}{8}$ inch thick. Cut each slice in half and remove both the outer skin and the inner core. Sprinkle with the sugar and Kirsch and allow to macerate for 30 minutes.

Add the pistachios to the thick, almost cold frangipane custard. Dry the pieces of pineapple and dip into the prepared frangipane custard. Place the coated slices of pineapple on a tray and allow to become quite cold.

Stir the light frying batter. Remove the pineapple slices from the tray and dip carefully into this batter. Deep fry in the hot oil (350°F), drain and dredge with confectioners' sugar. Glaze quickly in a hot oven (425°F) or under the broiler.

Arrange the pineapple fritters slightly overlapping each other on a folded napkin on a suitable dish.

Serves 6–8

Strawberry Bavarian Cream

Flambéed Bananas

Bananes Flambées

6 bananas, peeled and cut in half lengthwise
$\frac{1}{2}$ cup sugar
flour
1 egg, beaten
4 tablespoons clarified butter
2 tablespoons Kirsch, warmed

Sprinkle the bananas with 6 tablespoons of the sugar. Dip in the flour, then in the beaten egg, and then in the flour again. Fry in *clarified butter*.

Arrange the fried bananas side by side on an oval dish and sprinkle with the remaining sugar. Pour over the warmed Kirsch and set it alight just as you bring it to the table.

SERVES 6

Banana Salad

Bananes en Salade

6 bananas
$\frac{1}{4}$ cup orange rind, cut into very fine julienne
$\frac{1}{4}$ cup Sugar Syrup, page 159
6 tablespoons sugar
2 tablespoons Kirsch

Choose bananas that are just ripe but still fairly firm. Blanch the *julienne* of orange rind, cook it in the sugar syrup for a few minutes and drain.

Peel the bananas and cut into round slices. Place these on a dish, sprinkle with the sugar and orange rind, and allow to macerate for 15 minutes.

Arrange the slices of banana and the rind in a serving bowl, sprinkle with Kirsch and toss lightly, taking care not to break the slices.

SERVES 6

Cherry Tart Dubarry

Cerises Dubarry

Rich Pie Pastry, page 159
2 tablespoons sugar
1 lb cherries, pitted
2 cups Chantilly Cream, page 158
$\frac{3}{4}$ cup crushed macaroons

Line an 8-inch flan ring on a baking sheet with pastry and prick the bottom to prevent it from rising during cooking. Sprinkle it with the sugar, then fill it with the cherries, packing them tightly.

Bake in a moderately hot oven (400°F) for 20 minutes. Then reduce the temperature to 350°F and bake for another 15 minutes or until the pastry edges have baked to a golden brown.

Allow to cool. When the tart is completely cold, cover the cherries with most of the Chantilly Cream mixed with half the crushed macaroons. Smooth the top and sides of the cream and coat with the remaining crushed macaroons. Finish by piping rosettes of Chantilly Cream around the tart to decorate.

SERVES 6

Cherries Jubilée

Cerises Jubilée

1 lb large cherries, pitted (about $3\frac{1}{2}$ cups)
$1\frac{1}{4}$ cups Sugar Syrup, page 159
$\frac{1}{2}$ tablespoon arrowroot
2 tablespoons Kirsch, warmed

Poach the cherries in sugar syrup, then remove and place them in 4 deep individual serving dishes. Reduce the syrup and thicken with the arrowroot, dissolved in a little water.

Coat the cherries with the thickened syrup, pour $\frac{1}{2}$ tablespoon warmed Kirsch into each dish and set it alight just as you bring them to the table.

SERVES 4

Peaches Cardinal

Cherries in Red Wine

Cerises au Claret

1 lb cherries
2 cups red wine
$\frac{1}{3}$ cup sugar
1 cinnamon stick
2 tablespoons red currant jelly

To serve
Orange Finger Cookies, page 159

Remove the cherry stalks and place the cherries in a flameproof *timbale*. Cover with the wine and add the sugar and cinnamon stick. Cover with a lid and poach over a low heat for 15 minutes.

Allow the cherries to cool in the red wine syrup, then drain this off and reduce by a third. Add the red currant jelly to thicken it and sweeten it slightly.

Pour the syrup back over the cherries and serve very cold, accompanied by Orange Finger Cookies.

SERVES 4–6

Figs Carlton

Figues à la Carlton

9 fresh figs
1 lb raspberries (about $3\frac{1}{2}$ cups)
sugar to taste
$2\frac{1}{2}$ cups Chantilly Cream, page 158

Peel the figs, cut them in half and place in the refrigerator. Prepare a raspberry purée by passing the raspberries through a sieve and adding sugar to taste.

Stir the Chantilly Cream into the raspberry purée and pour over the figs to cover completely.

SERVES 6

Strawberries Romanoff

Fraises Romanoff

$\frac{1}{4}$ cup orange juice
3 tablespoons Curaçao
1 lb strawberries
$1\frac{1}{4}$ cups Chantilly Cream, page 158

Pour the orange juice and Curaçao over the strawberries and leave to macerate in the refrigerator for at least 30 minutes.

Arrange the macerated strawberries, orange juice and liquor in a chilled dish and cover the fruit with most of the Chantilly Cream. Decorate with the remaining Chantilly Cream, using a pastry bag and tube.

SERVES 4

Strawberries Femina

Fraises Fémina

1 lb strawberries (3 cups)
$\frac{1}{4}$ cup sugar
$\frac{1}{4}$ cup Grand Marnier
1 pint Orange Ice, page 186

Sprinkle the strawberries with the sugar, then mix with the Grand Marnier and macerate in the refrigerator for 1 hour.

Drain the strawberries and mix the liquid from the maceration into the orange ice. When you are ready to serve, cover the bottom of a chilled glass bowl with a layer of the Grand Marnier-flavored orange ice and arrange the strawberries neatly on top.

SERVES 4–6

Strawberry Bavarian Cream

Bavarois aux Fraises

14 oz strawberries (about 3 cups), cleaned and hulled
$1\frac{1}{4}$ cups sugar
1 cup water
$2\frac{1}{2}$ envelopes unflavored gelatin
juice of 1 lemon
$1\frac{1}{2}$ cups heavy cream, lightly whipped
almond oil

To serve
Chantilly Cream, page 158

Figs Carlton

Pass the strawberries through a fine sieve to give approximately 1½ cups purée, free of seeds.

Place the sugar and water in a pan, heat gently until the sugar has dissolved then bring to a boil, skim and simmer for 5 minutes. Remove from the heat and stir in the gelatin until completely dissolved, then cool but not so much as to set.

Add this syrup to the fruit purée together with the lemon juice and mix thoroughly. Fold in the lightly whipped cream when the mixture becomes more viscous but just before it starts setting.

Pour into a lightly oiled 5-cup capacity mold, cover with a round of wax paper and leave to set in the refrigerator for at least 2 hours. When required for serving, the mold should be plunged quickly into warm water, dried and unmolded onto a serving dish. Decorate with a little Chantilly Cream. *See photograph on page 161.*

SERVES 6–8

Chestnut Mont Blanc

Mont Blanc aux Marrons

1 lb chestnuts (about 4 cups)
2 cups milk
¼ cup sugar
1 vanilla bean
1¼ cups Chantilly Cream, page 158

To shell the chestnuts, make a shallow incision in the round side of the shell and place in an ovenproof dish with a little water. Place in a hot oven (425°F) for 7–8 minutes, then remove both the outer shells and the inner skins without breaking the chestnuts.

Heat the milk, sweeten with the sugar and infuse with the vanilla bean. Simmer the chestnuts gently in the flavored milk for 35–40 minutes.

When they are cooked, drain well and pass through a coarse sieve into a ring mold and refrigerate. Unmold before serving and fill the center with Chantilly Cream, forming it into a rugged, irregular shape.

SERVES 4–6

Strawberry-filled Melon

Melon à l'Orientale

4 small ripe melons
confectioners' sugar to taste
1 lb wild (alpine) strawberries (about 4 cups)
¼ cup Kirsch
softened butter

To serve
wafer cookies

Cut a round incision in the top of each melon. Remove this lid and reserve. Discard the seeds, scoop out the flesh and cut into cubes. Sprinkle the inside of each melon skin with confectioners' sugar and fill with alternate layers of strawberries and diced melon, sprinkling each layer with sugar.

Pour a tablespoonful of Kirsch into each melon, close with the reserved lid and seal the join with softened butter. Refrigerate for 2 hours. Serve accompanied by wafer cookies.

SERVES 4

Surprise Oranges

Oranges en Surprise

6 large oranges
1 pint Orange Ice, page 186
6 leaves of lemon geranium or mint

Meringue
¾ cup superfine sugar
3 egg whites

Cut off the top quarters of the oranges and reserve. Remove the flesh, place the skins in the freezer to set firm, then fill with orange ice. Replace in the freezer.

To prepare the meringue, place the sugar and egg whites in a bowl and mix together. Place in a *bain-marie* over a gentle heat and beat continuously until the mixture is thick enough to hold its shape between the wires of the beater. Remove from the heat and beat until cold.

Take the filled oranges from the freezer and, using a pastry bag and star tube, cover the ices with meringue. Place in a very hot oven (475°F) to bake for just 2–3 minutes so that the heat colors the meringue but does not melt the ice inside.

On removing the oranges from the oven, replace the reserved lids and decorate with lemon geranium or mint.

SERVES 6

Surprise Oranges

Empress Peaches

Pêches Impératrice

4 peaches, peeled, halved and pitted
1¼ cups vanilla-flavoured Sugar Syrup, page 159
1 recipe quantity Rice Pudding, page 176
1 tablespoon Kirsch
1 tablespoon Maraschino
½ cup crushed macaroons

Apricot Sauce

½ cup very ripe or slightly stewed apricots, pitted
½ cup Sugar Syrup, page 159
1–2 tablespoons Kirsch

Poach the peaches in the vanilla-flavored syrup and allow to cool thoroughly. Flavor the rice pudding with Kirsch and Maraschino and cover the bottom of an ovenproof serving dish with it. Arrange the poached halves of peach on the rice and cover them with another layer of rice.

Prepare the apricot sauce by passing the apricots through a fine sieve or puréeing them in a food processor and diluting with a little sugar syrup. Bring to a boil, skimming carefully, and simmer. The sauce is ready when it coats the back of a spoon. Flavor to taste with a little Kirsch.

Spread a layer of apricot sauce over the rice and sprinkle with the crushed macaroons. Place in a moderate oven (325°F) and cook for 10–12 minutes or until warmed through fully. Do not allow the surface to brown.

SERVES 8

Cardinal Peaches

Pêches Cardinal

6 peaches, peeled, halved and pitted
1¼ cups vanilla-flavored Sugar Syrup, page 159
½ lb raspberries (about 2 cups)
sugar to taste
1 tablespoon Kirsch
1 pint Vanilla Ice Cream, page 184
⅔ cup shelled almonds, blanched and cut into fine strips

Poach the peaches in the vanilla-flavored syrup and allow to cool thoroughly. Meanwhile, prepare a raspberry purée by passing the raspberries through a sieve and flavoring to taste with the sugar and Kirsch.

Arrange the peaches in a serving dish on a bed of vanilla ice cream and coat with raspberry purée. Sprinkle the surface with the fine strips of almonds. *See photograph on page 163.*

SERVES 6

Pears Hélène

Poires Hélène

4 large pears, peeled and cored from the bottom
2½ cups vanilla-flavored Sugar Syrup, page 159
1¼ cups Chocolate Sauce, page 159
1 pint Vanilla Ice Cream, page 184
2 oz crystallized violets

Poach the pears in the vanilla-flavored sugar syrup and allow to cool thoroughly. Meanwhile, prepare the chocolate sauce. Keep warm.

Arrange the pears on a bed of vanilla ice cream and sprinkle with crystallized violets. Serve with the hot chocolate sauce.

SERVES 4

Pears Condé

Poires Condé

1 lb small pears, peeled and cored from the bottom
1¼ cups vanilla-flavored Sugar Syrup, page 159
⅔ cup diced candied fruits
2 tablespoons Kirsch
½ recipe quantity Rice Pudding, page 176
½ tablespoon arrowroot

Poach the pears in the syrup and drain, reserving the syrup. Soak the candied fruits in half the Kirsch and add most of these to the rice pudding, reserving a few for decoration. Arrange a border of this rice around a serving dish and arrange the poached pears in the center. Decorate with the reserved candied fruits.

Reduce the reserved pear syrup, thicken with a little arrowroot and flavor with the remaining Kirsch. Pour this over the top of the pears.

SERVES 6–8

Pears Condé

Pears with Praline

Poires Pralinées

4 large pears, peeled, halved and cored
2½ cups vanilla-flavored Sugar Syrup, page 159
1¼ cups Frangipane Custard, page 158
½ cup heavy cream
¾ cup Chantilly Cream, page 158
1¼ cups Chocolate Sauce, page 159

Almond Praline
1 cup sugar
1½ cups shelled almonds

Poach the pears in the vanilla-flavored sugar syrup and allow to cool thoroughly. Meanwhile, prepare the almond praline. Melt the sugar very slowly with a small quantity of cold water and cook to a light caramel color. Mix in the almonds, pour onto an oiled marble slab and allow to cool completely. Crush coarsely in a mortar.

Arrange the pears in a dish and coat with Frangipane Custard, softened by the addition of the cream. Place a nicely molded tablespoon of Chantilly Cream between each pear half, and sprinkle the whole with the coarsely crushed almond praline.

Serve accompanied by hot or cold chocolate sauce.

SERVES 4

Baked Apples in Pastry

Douillons Normande

4 large apples, peeled
Rich Pie Pastry, page 159
¼ cup sugar
1 egg, beaten
butter

Remove the core of the apples using an apple corer. Place each apple on a square piece of pastry dough, fill the centers of the apples with sugar and fold the pastry over to enclose the apples. Place a fancy round of the same pastry on top and brush with beaten egg. Score with the point of a knife and seal the edges.

Grease a baking sheet, place the apples on this and bake in a hot oven (425°F) for 5 minutes to set and lightly color the pastry, then lower the temperature to 350°F and continue cooking the apples for a further 25–30 minutes.

SERVES 4

Apple Charlotte

Charlotte de Pommes

4 tablespoons butter
1 loaf white bread
6 tablespoons melted butter
12 large, firm, tart-sweet apples, peeled, cored and sliced
2 tablespoons sugar
grated rind of ½ lemon
1 pinch ground cinnamon
3 tablespoons good apricot jam

Apricot Sauce
½ cup very ripe or lightly stewed apricots
¾ cup Sugar Syrup, page 159
1–2 tablespoons Kirsch

Butter a 1-quart charlotte mold, using 2 tablespoons of the butter. Cut the bread into slices about ¼ inch thick and brush with the melted butter; reserve a thin round piece of bread and more melted butter for the top of the mold (see below). Line the bottom and sides of the mold with slightly overlapping slices of bread.

Meanwhile, gently fry the slices of apple in a shallow pan with the remaining butter, the sugar, lemon rind and ground cinnamon. When the apples are cooked and reduced to a very thick purée, add the apricot jam.

Place this mixture in the prepared mold, bringing it just above the top of the mold so as to allow for shrinkage. Cover with the reserved piece of bread, dipped in melted butter, and cook in a moderately hot oven (400°F) for 35–40 minutes.

Prepare the apricot sauce by passing the apricots through a fine sieve or puréeing them in a food processor and diluting with a little sugar syrup. Bring to a boil, skimming carefully, and simmer. The sauce is ready when it coats the back of the spoon. Flavor to taste with a little Kirsch.

Remove the cooked charlotte from the oven, turn it upside down on a serving dish, and allow it to rest for a few minutes before removing the mold. Serve with the apricot sauce.

SERVES 8

Apple Charlotte

Layered Apple Custard

Crème Villageoise aux Pommes

5 oz ladyfingers (13–15)
1 tablespoon Kirsch
1 tablespoon Maraschino
$1\frac{1}{2}$ lb apples, peeled, cored and sliced
1 cup sugar
4 egg yolks
8 whole eggs
1 quart hot milk

Sprinkle the ladyfingers with the Kirsch and Maraschino. Stew the apples with 2 tablespoons of the sugar and a little water to a thick purée. Arrange the ladyfingers in a deep ovenproof dish in layers, alternating with layers of apple purée.

Mix the remaining sugar with the egg yolks, eggs and hot milk. Pour this mixture over the cookies and apple purée, and cook in a *bain-marie* in a moderate oven (350°F) for about 35 minutes or until set.

SERVES 8

Apples Châtelaine

Pommes Châtelaine

6 medium apples, peeled
6 tablespoons sugar
1 stick butter, softened
$\frac{1}{2}$ cup diced glacé cherries
6 tablespoons fresh apricot purée
$1\frac{1}{4}$ cups thin Frangipane Custard, page 158
$\frac{3}{4}$ cups finely crushed macaroons
2 tablespoons melted butter

Core the apples, using an apple corer. Arrange them in an ovenproof dish and fill the centers with a mixture of sugar and softened butter, using all the sugar and 6 tablespoons of the butter. Pour a little water around them and bake in a moderate oven (350°F) for about 1 hour or until the apples are soft.

Use the remaining butter to grease an ovenproof dish and arrange the cooked apples on it. Mix the glacé cherries with the apricot purée and fill the apple centers with this mixture.

Cover with thin frangipane custard and sprinkle with the finely crushed macaroons and melted butter. Glaze quickly under a hot broiler.

SERVES 6

Baked Apples with Brandy

Pommes au Beurre

6 medium apples, peeled
3 tablespoons lemon juice
1 stick plus 2 tablespoons butter
6 tablespoons vanilla-flavored Sugar Syrup, page 159
3 brioches, cut into rounds
confectioners' sugar
$\frac{1}{2}$ cup granulated sugar
1 tablespoon brandy
$\frac{1}{2}$ cup fresh apricot purée

Core the apples, using an apple corer, and blanch in boiling water, containing a little lemon juice, for 2 minutes. Butter a shallow ovenproof dish, using 2 tablespoons of the butter, and arrange the apples in it. Add the vanilla-flavored syrup, cover with a lid and bake in a moderate oven (350°F) for 1 hour or until the apples are soft.

Dredge the slices of brioche with confectioners' sugar and brown slightly under the broiler. When the apples are cooked, arrange each apple on a slice of brioche. Reserve the cooking syrup.

Mix together the remaining butter and the granulated sugar, flavor with brandy and fill the center of each apple with this brandy butter.

Lightly thicken the vanilla-flavored cooking syrup with the apricot purée and pour this over the apples.

SERVES 6

Caramel Cream

Crème Moulée au Caramel

$2\frac{1}{2}$ cups milk
1 cup sugar
1 vanilla bean
4 egg yolks
3 whole eggs

Bring the milk to a boil and dissolve half of the sugar in it. Add the vanilla bean and allow to infuse for 20 minutes, then remove the bean.

Meanwhile, cook the remaining sugar with a little water to a light caramel color. Line the bottom and sides of a 1-quart charlotte or other suitable mold with this caramel.

Beat the egg yolks and whole eggs together in a bowl then pour in the milk little by little, whisking well, as you do so. Pass through a fine strainer and allow to rest for a few minutes. Then

Baked Apples with Brandy

remove any froth which has formed on the surface. Pour into the prepared mold.

Cover the mixture and cook in a *bain-marie* in a moderate oven (325°F) for 40–45 minutes, or until set. The water in the bain-marie must not be allowed to boil at any time during the cooking. (If this is allowed to happen, the high temperature will cause the air mixed in with the mixture to expand and form a mass of tiny bubbles; when the cream has cooled it will consequently be riddled with little holes which will spoil its appearance.)

As soon as the cream is cooked, remove it from the bain-marie and allow to become completely cold over at least 2–3 hours, to ensure an adequate set for unmolding. To unmold the cream, turn the mold over carefully onto a serving dish and leave for a few minutes before removing.

SERVES 4–6

Omelette Célestine

Omelette Célestine

5 eggs
4 tablespoons butter
2 tablespoons apple purée, prepared as for Apple Charlotte, page 170
3 tablespoons apricot jam
confectioners' sugar

Beat 2 of the eggs until the whites and yolks are thoroughly blended. Heat half the butter in an omelette pan until it begins to brown. Pour in the beaten eggs, shake the pan and stir briskly with a fork to ensure even cooking. (See the instructions for omelette-making on page 36.) Cover the center of the omelette with the apple purée and fold as usual.

Make a second, slightly larger omelette using the remaining 3 eggs, and cover its center with the apricot jam.

Now place the first, folded omelette on top of the second larger one and fold the larger omelette over the smaller. Dredge with confectioners' sugar and glaze for a few minutes in a hot oven (425°F).

SERVES 2 OR 3

Crêpes Suzette

Crêpes Suzette

scant 1 cup flour, sifted
3 tablespoons sugar
1 tablespoon vanilla sugar
1 pinch fine salt
3 eggs
about 1½ cups milk
butter

To flavor
1 stick butter, softened
½ cup sugar
3 tablespoons Curaçao
a few drops tangerine or orange juice

Place the flour, sugars and salt in a bowl and beating gradually add the eggs and milk, whisking well to form a smooth batter.

Prepare the flavoring by mixing the softened butter with the sugar and adding the Curaçao and tangerine or orange juice.

Pour a little crêpe batter into a hot pan containing a little butter. Cook to a light brown color then toss the crêpe to cook the other side.

Spread the crêpes with the flavored butter, fold into four, and arrange, overlapping, on a hot dish for serving.

SERVES 4–6

Pear Crêpes

Crêpes du Couvent

scant 1 cup flour, sifted
3 tablespoons sugar
1 tablespoon vanilla sugar
1 pinch fine salt
3 eggs
1¼ cups milk
butter
4 medium pears, peeled and finely diced

Place the flour, sugars and salt in a bowl. Gradually add the eggs and milk, whisking well to form a smooth batter.

Pour a little crêpe batter into a hot pan containing a little butter. Sprinkle with a little diced pear and cover with more of the crêpe batter. Toss to cook on both sides, arrange on a napkin and serve very hot.

SERVES 4–6

Crêpes Suzette

Norwegian Omelette

Omelette Norvégienne

2 tablespoons butter
flour
Orange Ice, page 186, or other fruit ice or ice cream

Genoise sponge cake
1 cup sugar
6 eggs
grated rind of ½ orange
1⅓ cups flour, sifted
7 tablespoons melted butter
butter
flour

Meringue
6 egg whites
1¾ cups superfine sugar

To prepare the genoise sponge cake, mix the sugar and eggs in a bowl and place over a gentle heat in a *bain-marie* so that the mixture becomes slightly warm. Beat until it thickens and forms a ribbon when you lift the beater from the bowl. Remove from the heat and continue to beat until it is cold. Now add the orange rind, fold in the flour and add the melted butter in a thin stream. Spread on a buttered and floured baking pan measuring 12 by 6 inches and bake in a moderately hot oven (375°F) for 20–25 minutes or until golden brown and firm to the touch. Allow to cool, then cut out an oval shape of genoise to fit neatly on the serving dish (see below).

To make the meringue, beat the egg whites stiffly and sprinkle in the sugar, mixing lightly with a spoon so that the egg whites do not lose their lightness.

Place the oval-shaped base of genoise on an ovenproof oval serving dish. Place an oval pyramid of ice cream on top of the genoise, and cover with a layer of meringue. Smooth over with a palette knife so as to give an even coating of meringue about ¾ inch thick.

Decorate quickly with some more meringue, using a pastry bag and tube, and place in a very hot oven (475°F) to bake for 2–3 minutes so that the meringue cooks and browns rapidly but the heat does not penetrate to the ice cream inside. Serve immediately.

SERVES 8

French-style Bread Pudding

Pouding au Pain à la Française

1 quart milk
1 vanilla bean
1¼ cups sugar
7 cups fine fresh white bread crumbs
6 egg yolks
4 whole eggs
4 egg whites, stiffly beaten
butter

To serve
Egg Custard Sauce, page 158

Bring the milk to a boil with the vanilla bean and sugar. Soak 6 cups of the bread crumbs in it and pass through a sieve. Stir in the egg yolks and whole eggs, and then fold in the stiffly beaten egg whites.

Butter a deep 2-quart capacity mold and sprinkle with the remaining bread crumbs. Pour the mixture into the prepared mold and cook in a *bain-marie* in a moderate oven (350°F) for about 45–50 minutes. Allow to settle for a few minutes before unmolding onto a serving dish.

Serve accompanied by Egg Custard Sauce.

SERVES 8–10

Rice Pudding

Riz pour Entremets

1 cup short-grain rice
3 cups milk
½ cup sugar
1 pinch salt
1 vanilla bean
3 tablespoons butter
6 egg yolks

Wash the rice and bring to a boil in a pan of water. Drain, wash again in warm water, and drain again. Bring the milk to a boil with the sugar, salt, vanilla bean and butter. Strain and add the rice. Put in a flameproof casserole, bring back to a boil, cover with a lid and cook gently in a moderate oven (350°F) for 25–30 minutes without stirring.

When the rice is cooked, remove from the oven and add the egg yolks, mixing them in quickly and carefully with a fork so as not to break up the grains of rice which should remain whole.

SERVES 6–8

Norwegian Omelette

Empress Rice Mold

Riz à l'Impératrice

1 recipe quantity Rice Pudding, page 176
3 tablespoons red currant jelly, warmed
2 cups Egg Custard Sauce, page 158
2 envelopes unflavored gelatin
$\frac{2}{3}$ cup finely diced candied fruit
$\frac{1}{4}$ cup fresh apricot purée
2 cups heavy cream, whipped

Make the Rice Pudding and allow to cool. Meanwhile, prepare a large ring mold by coating the bottom with the warmed red currant jelly and allow to set in the refrigerator. Prepare the Egg Custard Sauce and, when it is almost cooked, add the gelatin. Pass through a fine strainer into a bowl and stir until cool but not set.

Stir the candied fruit and apricot purée into the rice. Add the Egg Custard Sauce and the whipped cream.

Pour the mixture into the prepared mold and place to set in the refrigerator. Unmold just before serving.

SERVES 8–10

Saxon Pudding

Pouding Saxon

1 stick plus 2 tablespoons butter
$\frac{3}{4}$ cup sugar
1 heaping cup flour, sifted
$1\frac{1}{4}$ cups boiling milk
5 egg yolks
5 egg whites, stiffly beaten

To serve
Egg Custard Sauce, page 158

Stir the stick of butter over a gentle heat until soft and smooth. Mix in the sugar and flour, then add the boiling milk. Bring to a boil, stirring continuously, and continue to stir until the paste leaves the spoon clean and small beads of moisture appear on the surface.

Take off the heat, carefully mix in the yolks, one at a time, and then gently fold in the beaten whites. Butter 8 or 10 individual ovenproof molds, using the rest of the butter. Divide the mixture between the molds and cook in a *bain-marie* in a moderately hot oven (400°F) for 15–20 minutes. Serve accompanied by Egg Custard Sauce, flavored if so desired.

SERVES 8–10

Souffléed Rice Pudding

Pouding au Riz

6 egg whites, stiffly beaten
1 recipe quantity Rice Pudding, page 176
2 tablespoons butter
flour

To serve
Egg Custard Sauce, page 158

Fold the stiffly beaten egg whites into the rice pudding. Butter a suitable ovenproof mold and sprinkle with flour. Pour in the rice and cook in a *bain-marie* in a moderately hot oven (375°F) for 25 minutes or until set and firm to the touch. Allow to rest for 7–8 minutes, then unmold onto a dish and serve. Serve accompanied by Egg Custard Sauce, flavored if so desired.

SERVES 6–8

Snow Eggs

Oeufs à la Neige

$2\frac{1}{2}$ cups milk
1 vanilla bean
scant 1 cup sugar
6 egg yolks
$\frac{1}{2}$ teaspoon arrowroot

Meringue
6 egg whites
$1\frac{3}{4}$ cups superfine sugar

First prepare the meringue by beating the egg whites stiffly and sprinkling in the sugar. Mix lightly with a spoon. Meanwhile, bring the milk to a boil, infuse with the vanilla bean and sweeten with the sugar. Mold the meringue into egg shapes, using two spoons, and drop into the sweetened simmering milk. Turn them over when half-cooked, so they poach evenly. When firm, remove from the pan, drain, and strain the milk.

Make a custard sauce by beating the egg yolks and arrowroot together in a bowl and adding the hot, strained milk, a little at a time. Place over the heat and stir with a wooden spoon until the yolks thicken the mixture slightly. Do not allow the custard to boil as this will cause it to separate. Cool.

Arrange the cooked meringues in a bowl and coat with the cold custard. Serve very cold.

SERVES 6–8

Empress Rice Mold

Floating Island

Ile Flottante

1 Savoy Sponge Cake (see below)
$\frac{1}{4}$ cup Kirsch
$\frac{1}{4}$ cup Maraschino
6 tablespoons apricot jam, slightly thinned with lemon juice
$\frac{1}{3}$ cup currants, soaked in Kirsch to swell, then drained and dried
$\frac{1}{2}$ cup flaked almonds
$2\frac{1}{2}$ cups Chantilly Cream, page 158
$2\frac{1}{2}$ tablespoons finely shredded pistachio nuts

To serve
$2\frac{1}{2}$ cups Egg Custard Sauce, page 158

Cut a dry Savoy Sponge Cake horizontally into slices approximately $\frac{1}{2}$ inch thick. Sprinkle each slice with the Kirsch and Maraschino, spread with apricot jam and sprinkle with half the soaked currants and the flaked almonds.

Reform the cake, placing the slices on top of one another, and coat the whole neatly with Chantilly Cream. Sprinkle the cream with the finely shredded pistachio nuts, then with the remaining currants. Place in a deep glass dish and surround with the Egg Custard Sauce.

SERVES 8

Savoy Sponge Cake

Biscuit de Savoie

7 eggs
$1\frac{1}{4}$ cups sugar
1 tablespoon vanilla sugar
$\frac{1}{2}$ cup plus 1 tablespoon flour and $\frac{2}{3}$ cup cornstarch, sifted together
2 tablespoons butter
cornstarch for dredging

Separate the eggs and beat the egg whites stiffly. Beat the sugar and egg yolks together until the mixture becomes thick and pale. Add the vanilla sugar and the sifted flour and cornstarch mixture, then fold in the stiffly beaten egg whites.

Butter a deep round cake pan 6 inches in diameter and dredge with cornstarch. Pour the batter into this, filling it no more than two-thirds full. Bake in a moderate oven (350°F) for about 30 minutes, then lower the temperature to (325°F) for a further 30 minutes, until the sponge is cooked and dry.

MAKES A DEEP 6-INCH CAKE

Charlotte Malakoff

Pouding Malakoff

$2\frac{1}{2}$ cups Egg Custard Sauce, page 158
2 envelopes unflavored gelatin
$1\frac{1}{4}$ cups heavy cream
$\frac{1}{4}$ lb ladyfingers (9–10)
1 tablespoon Kirsch
$\frac{1}{2}$ cup purée of apples and pears, prepared as for Apple Charlotte, page 170
almond oil
$\frac{2}{3}$ cup currants and golden raisins, mixed and soaked
$\frac{1}{3}$ cup shelled almonds, blanched and cut into strips
2 tablespoons diced candied orange peel

Sabayon
$\frac{1}{2}$ cup sugar
2 egg yolks
$\frac{1}{2}$ cup dry white wine
1 tablespoon Kirsch

Prepare the Egg Custard Sauce and, when it is almost cooked, add the gelatin. Pass through a fine strainer into a bowl and stir continuously until cool but not set. Add the heavy cream.

Sprinkle the ladyfingers with the Kirsch and spread them liberally with the apple and pear purée.

Lightly oil a $1\frac{1}{2}$-quart capacity charlotte mold with almond oil and pour in a $\frac{1}{2}$-inch layer of the Egg Custard Sauce. On top of this, place a layer of the prepared ladyfingers. Sprinkle with the currants and raisins, almonds and orange peel. Cover with another layer of Egg Custard Sauce, another layer of cookies and so on until the mold is full. Place in the refrigerator and allow the charlotte to set.

Meanwhile, prepare a Kirsch-flavored sabayon. Place the sugar and egg yolks in a bowl and beat until the mixture thickens and forms a ribbon when the beater is lifted from the bowl. Mix in the dry white wine, then place the bowl in a pan of very hot water over a gentle heat, and beat until the mixture becomes thick and frothy. Flavor to taste with the Kirsch, then allow the sabayon to cool.

Unmold the charlotte just before serving and coat with the Kirsch-flavored sabayon.

SERVES 8

Sweet Farina Cakes

Subrics de Semoule

2 cups milk
½ cup sugar
1 vanilla bean
⅔ cup farina
6 tablespoons butter
6 egg yolks
4 tablespoons clarified butter

To decorate
firm red currant or quince jelly

Place the milk, sugar and vanilla bean in a saucepan, bring to a boil and infuse for a few minutes. Remove the vanilla bean and transfer the milk to an ovenproof dish. Rain in the farina and mix well. Add 4 tablespoons of the butter and a few grains of salt and stir well. Cover with a lid and cook in a moderate oven (350°F) for 25 minutes.

Remove the dish from the oven, then stir the egg yolks into the mixture and spread the mixture out in a layer about ¾ inch thick on a buttered baking sheet. Coat the surface with the remaining butter to prevent a skin forming and allow to cool.

Cut the mixture into circles about 2½ inches in diameter. Heat the *clarified butter* in a frying pan and fry the farina cakes until golden. Arrange on a dish and place a spoonful of jelly on the center of each cake.

MAKES 6–8

Hazelnut Praline Soufflé

Soufflé aux Avelines

½ cup milk
¼ cup sugar
1 tablespoon flour, sifted
2 tablespoons butter
2 egg yolks
3 egg whites, stiffly beaten
confectioners' sugar

Hazelnut Praline
2 tablespoons sugar
2 tablespoons hazelnuts
almond oil

First make the hazelnut praline: melt the sugar slowly with a little water and cook to a light caramel color. Mix in the hazelnuts thoroughly, pour onto an oiled marble slab or tray and allow to become cold. Crush in a mortar or with a rolling pin.

Bring most of the milk to a boil, reserving just a little cold milk for later, and infuse with the hazelnut praline. Then add 3 tablespoons of the sugar and stir until dissolved. Mix the flour with the reserved cold milk and add to the mixture. Stir over the heat for 2 minutes. Remove from the heat and mix in half the butter and both egg yolks. Carefully fold in the stiffly beaten egg whites.

Use the remaining butter and sugar to prepare a 6-inch soufflé dish and pour the soufflé mixture into this. Cook in a moderately hot oven (400°F) for 25–30 minutes until well risen and just firm to the touch.

About 2 minutes before removing the soufflé from the oven, dredge the surface with confectioners' sugar (this will caramelize and form a glaze). Serve immediately.

SERVES 4

Violet Soufflé

Soufflé aux Violettes

½ cup milk
1 vanilla bean
¼ cup sugar
1 tablespoon flour
2 oz crystallized violets
2 tablespoons butter
2 egg yolks
3 egg whites, stiffly beaten
confectioners' sugar

Bring most of the milk to a boil, reserving just a little cold milk for later, and infuse with the vanilla bean for 30 minutes. Remove the bean. Then add 3 tablespoons of the sugar and stir until dissolved. Mix the flour with the reserved cold milk and add to the mixture. Stir over the heat for 2 minutes. Crush half the crystallized violets and add to the mixture. Take off the heat and add half the butter and both egg yolks. Fold in the stiffly beaten egg whites.

Use the remaining butter and sugar to prepare a 6-inch soufflé dish and pour the soufflé mixture into this. Arrange a circle of whole crystallized violets on top.

Cook in a moderately hot oven (400°F) for 25–30 minutes until well risen and just firm to the touch.

About 2 minutes before removing the soufflé from the oven, dredge the surface with the confectioners' sugar (this will caramelize and form a glaze). Serve immediately.

SERVES 4

Chocolate Soufflé

Soufflé au Chocolat

$\frac{1}{2}$ cup milk
1 vanilla bean
2 oz semisweet chocolate
$\frac{1}{4}$ cup sugar
1 tablespoon flour
2 tablespoons butter
2 egg yolks
3 egg whites, stiffly beaten
confectioners' sugar

Bring most of the milk to a boil, reserving just a little cold milk for later, and infuse with the vanilla bean for 30 minutes. Then melt the chocolate in the hot milk and add 3 tablespoons of the sugar. Mix the flour with the reserved cold milk and add this to the pan. Stir over the heat for 2 minutes. Take off the heat and add scant 1 tablespoon of the butter and the egg yolks. Fold in the stiffly beaten egg whites.

Use the remaining butter and sugar to prepare a 6-inch soufflé dish and pour the soufflé mixture in this. Cook in a moderately hot oven (400°F) for 35–40 minutes until well risen and just firm to the touch.

About 2 minutes before removing the soufflé from the oven, dredge the surface with confectioners' sugar (this will caramelize and form a glaze). Serve immediately.

SERVES 4

Meringues Germaine

Meringues Germaine

$\frac{1}{4}$ lb Petit Suisses or other unsalted cream cheese
$\frac{3}{4}$ cup heavy cream
3 tablespoons sugar
$\frac{1}{2}$ lb strawberries ($1\frac{1}{2}$ cups)
red food coloring (optional)
a few drops vanilla extract or Kirsch
8 dry meringue shells

Mash the cream cheese in a bowl with a wooden spoon and add the cream and sugar. Make a strawberry purée by passing the strawberries through a sieve, and add this purée to the cream cheese mixture. (If the color is not sufficiently pink, you may add a few drops of red coloring.)

Flavor to taste with the vanilla extract or Kirsch as desired, and sandwich between meringue shells.

SERVES 4

Meringue Layer Cake Monte-Carlo

Biscuit Monte-Carlo

12 egg whites
$3\frac{1}{4}$ cups sugar
$2\frac{1}{2}$ cups Chantilly Cream, page 158
2 oz semisweet chocolate, grated
3 oz semisweet chocolate, melted
1 oz crystallized violets

Cover several slightly moistened baking sheets with sheets of parchment paper. Position 4 or 5 6-inch flan rings on these baking sheets.

Beat the egg whites until stiff and sprinkle in the sugar, mixing lightly with a spoon so that the egg whites do not lose their stiffness.

Half-fill each flan ring with the meringue and bake in a very cool oven (225°F) for 7–8 hours until the meringue is completely dry.

Put the rounds of meringue on top of one another with Chantilly Cream between, sprinkling each layer with grated chocolate. Glaze the top layer of meringue with melted chocolate and decorate the sides with more Chantilly Cream using a pastry bag. Pipe small rosettes of Chantilly Cream on top of the Layer Cake Monte-Carlo, and place a crystallized violet on top of each rosette.

SERVES 8

Asparagus Ice Cream

Glace aux Asperges

6 oz asparagus tips
1 quart milk
$1\frac{1}{2}$ cups sugar
10 egg yolks

Blanch the asparagus tips for 2 minutes and drain. Pound quickly while adding a few tablespoons of the milk. Bring the remaining milk to a boil and put the asparagus mixture into the boiling milk to infuse for 20 minutes or so.

Beat the sugar and egg yolks together in a bowl until the mixture becomes thick and white. Gradually mix in the boiling milk and asparagus mixture, place over a gentle heat and cook until the mixture coats the back of the spoon. Stir continuously and do not allow to boil, or the mixture will curdle.

Pass through a strainer into a bowl and stir occasionally until cold. Pour into an ice-cream maker and freeze.

MAKES 1 QUART

Meringues Germaine

Hazelnut Ice Cream

Glace aux Avelines

¾ cup shelled hazelnuts
1 quart milk
1½ cups sugar
10 egg yolks

Lightly toast the hazelnuts then pound finely, adding a few tablespoons of the milk. Stir the resulting mixture into the remaining milk and heat to boiling point. Allow to infuse for 20 minutes or so.

Beat the sugar and egg yolks together in a bowl until the mixture becomes thick and white. Gradually mix in the boiling milk and hazelnut mixture, place over a gentle heat and cook until the mixture coats the back of the spoon. Stir continuously and do not allow to boil, or the mixture will curdle.

Pass the mixture through a strainer into a bowl and stir occasionally until cold. Pour into an ice-cream maker and freeze.

MAKES 1 QUART

Vanilla Ice Cream

Glace à la Vanille

1 quart milk
1 vanilla bean
1½ cups cups sugar
10 egg yolks

Bring the milk to a boil, add the vanilla bean and allow to infuse for 20 minutes. Remove the vanilla bean.

Beat the sugar and egg yolks together in a bowl until the mixture becomes thick and white. Gradually add the boiling milk, place over a gentle heat and cook until the mixture coats the back of the spoon. Stir continuously and do not allow to boil, or the mixture will curdle.

Pass through a strainer into a bowl and stir occasionally until cold. Pour into an ice-cream maker and freeze.

MAKES 1 QUART

Sundae Adelina Patti

Coupe Adelina Patti

1 pint Vanilla Ice Cream, opposite
24 brandied cherries
¼ cup sugar
1¼ cups Chantilly Cream, page 158

Place the vanilla ice cream in 4 sundae glasses or bowls. Drain the brandied cherries, roll in sugar and arrange in a circle on top of each portion. Decorate each glass with a generous whirl of Chantilly Cream.

SERVES 4

Sundae Hélène

Coupe Hélène

1 pint Vanilla Ice Cream, opposite
2 oz crystallized violets
1¼ cups Chantilly Cream, page 158
1½ oz semisweet chocolate, grated

Place the vanilla ice cream in 4 sundae glasses or bowls. Decorate with a circle of crystallized violets, place a dome of Chantilly Cream in the center, and decorate the cream with grated chocolate.

SERVES 4

Chestnut Sundae

Coupe Germaine

⅓ cup glacé cherries
2 tablespoons Kirsch
1 pint Vanilla Ice Cream, opposite
¼ lb marrons glacés (candied chestnuts)
1¼ cups Chantilly Cream, page 158

Macerate the glacé cherries in the Kirsch for at least half an hour. Place the vanilla ice cream in 4 sundae glasses or bowls and arrange the macerated glacé cherries in a group on top of each coupe.

Pass the candied chestnuts through a coarse sieve, which will produce a purée that looks rather like vermicelli, and place this on top of the glacé cherries. Surround with a decorative border of Chantilly Cream.

SERVES 4

Sundae Hélène (left), Sundae Adelina Patti (right)

Peach and Red Currant Sundae

Coupe Gressac

1 pint Vanilla Ice Cream, page 184
12 small macaroons
3 tablespoons Kirsch
2 peaches, poached, peeled, halved and pitted
½ cup fine sweet red currants
1¼ cups Chantilly Cream, page 158

Place the vanilla ice cream in 4 sundae glasses or bowls. Soak the macaroons in the Kirsch and arrange these on top. Cut the peaches in half and fill the centers with red currants. Arrange these on top of the macaroons and decorate with a border of Chantilly Cream.

SERVES 4

FRUIT ICES

Glaces aux Fruits

The basis of these ices is a syrup, made of sugar and water, to which some fruit purée or juice is then added.

The following recipes for fruit ices give excellent results as they stand but if thought desirable the density of the final cold mixture can be checked on a *saccharometer* and adjusted before freezing. If too dense add cold water, if too light add a little syrup made from 6 parts of sugar to 5 parts of water.

Orange Ice

Glace à l'Orange

5–6 medium oranges, to give 2 cups juice
2¼ cups sugar
1¾ cups water
juice of 1 lemon

Remove the rind from the oranges and reserve. Place the sugar and water in a pan, bring to a boil, skim and boil gently for 2 minutes. Add the orange rind, reboil then allow to cool. Squeeze the oranges to give 2 cups juice.

When cold add the juice from the oranges and the lemon to the syrup. Pass through a fine strainer then pour into an ice-cream maker. (The density of the cold mixture before freezing should be 20°–22° Baumé, measured on a saccharometer.)

MAKES APPROXIMATELY 1 QUART

Red Currant Ice

Glace à la Groseille

2¼ cups sugar
1¾ cups water
2 lb ripe red currants, to give 2 cups juice
lemon juice, if necessary

Place the sugar and water in a pan, bring to a boil while stirring, skim and boil gently for 2 minutes. Remove from the heat and allow to cool.

Meanwhile, wash and crush the red currants then pass through a fine strainer to give 2 cups juice. Add to the cold syrup. Add a little lemon juice if thought necessary, then pass again carefully through a very fine strainer. Pour into an ice-cream maker and freeze. (The density of the cold mixture before freezing should be 19°–21° Baumé, measured on a saccharometer.)

MAKES APPROXIMATELY 1 QUART

Pineapple Ice

Glace à l'Ananas

2¼ cups sugar
1¾ cups water
1 medium size, ripe pineapple, to give 2 cups pulp
juice of 2 lemons
2 tablespoons Kirsch

Place the sugar and water in a pan, bring to a boil while stirring, skim and boil gently for 2 minutes then allow to cool. Meanwhile, carefully remove the outer skin of the pineapple, cut in half and discard the fibrous central core.

Grate or finely crush the pineapple flesh to give 2 cups pulp and add to the cold syrup together with the lemon juice and Kirsch. Allow to macerate for 2 hours. Pass through a fine strainer then pour into an ice-cream maker and freeze. (The density of the cold mixture before freezing should be 18°–20° Baumé, measured on a saccharometer.)

MAKES APPROXIMATELY 1 QUART

Bombe Formosa

Bombe Formosa

1 pint Vanilla Ice Cream, page 184
½ cup sugar
½ cup water
4 egg yolks
½ lb strawberries (1½ cups), puréed
1¼ cups heavy cream, whipped
little extra sugar
vanilla extract
½ lb strawberries (1½ cups), to decorate

Thoroughly chill a 1-quart bombe mold, then line with vanilla ice cream and replace in the freezer.

Meanwhile, place the sugar and water in a pan, heat to dissolve and allow to cool. Beat this cool syrup together with the egg yolks in the top of a double boiler or *bain-marie* over a low heat until the mixture becomes thick and white.

Remove from the heat and continue beating until cold. Add the puréed strawberries and fold in half of the whipped cream.

Fill the center of the prepared mold with the strawberry bombe mixture and cover, first with a circle of wax paper and then with the lid. Freeze for at least 2 hours.

Unmold the bombe onto a chilled, round dish and decorate with the remaining whipped cream, lightly sweetened with sugar and flavored with vanilla extract. Place a circle of strawberries around the bombe.

SERVES 6–8

Bombe Frou-Frou

Bombe Frou-Frou

1 pint Vanilla Ice Cream, page 184
½ cup finely diced candied fruits
2 tablespoons rum
½ cup sugar
½ cup water
4 egg yolks
1¼ cups heavy cream, whipped
little extra sugar
vanilla extract

Thoroughly chill a 1-quart bombe mold, then line with vanilla ice cream and replace in the freezer to set well. Macerate the candied fruits in the rum.

Meanwhile, place the sugar and water in a pan, heat to dissolve and allow to cool. Beat this cool syrup together with the egg yolks in the top of a double boiler or *bain-marie* over a low heat until the mixture becomes thick and white. Remove from the heat and continue beating until cold. Add the candied fruits and rum and fold in half the whipped cream.

Fill the center of the prepared mold with the fruit mixture and cover, first with a circle of wax paper and then with the lid. Freeze for at least 2 hours.

Unmold the bombe onto a chilled, round dish and decorate with the remaining whipped cream, lightly sweetened with sugar and flavored with a little vanilla extract.

SERVES 6–8

Bombe Hilda

Bombe Hilda

1 pint Hazelnut Ice Cream, page 184
½ cup sugar
½ cup water
4 egg yolks
2 tablespoons Chartreuse
1¼ cups heavy cream, whipped
little extra sugar

Hazelnut Praline

¾ cup sugar
1⅓ cups skinned hazelnuts

First make the hazelnut praline: melt the sugar slowly with a little water and cook to a light caramel color. Mix in the hazelnuts, pour onto an oiled marble slab and allow to become cold. Crush in a mortar then pass through a fine sieve.

Thoroughly chill a 1-quart bombe mold, then line with the hazelnut ice cream and replace in the freezer to set well.

Meanwhile, place the sugar and water in a pan, heat to dissolve and allow to cool. Beat this cool syrup together with the egg yolks in the top of a double boiler or *bain-marie* over a low heat until the mixture becomes thick and white. Remove from the heat and continue beating until cold. Add the Chartreuse and praline and fold in half the whipped cream.

Fill the center of the prepared mold with the praline mixture and cover, first with a circle of wax paper and then with the lid. Freeze for at least 2 hours.

Unmold the bombe onto a chilled, round dish and decorate with the remaining whipped cream, lightly sweetened with sugar.

SERVES 6–8

Accolades for *Paramount Cooking . . .*

Paramount Cooking *reeks of strong flavours, with no pretty garnishes and no false modesty. It is bold, imaginative and uncompromising, like the author and her restaurant.*

jill dupleix
The Sydney Morning Herald

This is a book for the passionate cook. It is, in a sense, a manifesto of modern Australian cooking. But it is also Christine Manfield's own manifesto: it shows innovation, passion, intensity, pride, breadth of experience.

rita erlich
The Age

Paramount Cooking *reaffirms Australia's culinary sophistication. This is the most stylish-looking cookbook ever to have come out of this country – perhaps anywhere.*

cherry ripe
The Weekend Australian

Christine Manfield has a simple philosophy: 'Life is too short to eat bad food'. This inventive Sydney chef might like to add: life is too short to read bad cookbooks, because . . . Paramount Cooking *sets exciting new standards.*

simon plant
The Herald Sun

This is the first book to show truly modern eclectic Australian food, food stolen – dare I say plagiarised – from so many cultures (as we are ourselves), and put together with a freshness that is at long last giving us our own recognisably Australian culinary style.

ann oliver
The Advertiser, Adelaide

PARA
MOUNT

CHRISTINE MANFIELD

COOK
ING

VIKING

Viking
Penguin Books Australia Ltd
487 Maroondah Highway, PO Box 257
Ringwood, Victoria 3134, Australia
Penguin Books Ltd
Harmondsworth, Middlesex, England
Viking Penguin, A Division of Penguin Books USA Inc.
375 Hudson Street, New York, New York 10014, USA
Penguin Books Canada Limited
10 Alcorn Avenue, Toronto, Ontario, Canada M4V 3B2
Penguin Books (N.Z.) Ltd
Cnr Rosedale and Airborne Roads, Albany
Auckland, New Zealand

First published by Penguin Books Australia Ltd 1995

10 9 8 7 6 5 4

Designed by Guy Mirabella
Photography by Ashley Barber
Restaurant and Store photos by Sharrin Rees
Typeset by Bookset, Melbourne
Printed and bound through Bookbuilders Limited
Hong Kong

National Library of Australia
Cataloguing-in-Publication data

Manfield, Christine.

Paramount Cooking.

Includes index.
ISBN 0 670 86372 6.

1. Paramount Restaurant. 2. Cookery, Australian.
I. Title.

641.5994

FRONT COVER PHOTOGRAPH: Eggplant, Goat's Cheese and Pesto Sandwich (see page 16)
TITLE PAGE: Chocolate Mocha Tart with Espresso Ice-cream (see page 131)

Contents

This book is a tribute to my partner, Margie Harris, who has been part of the vision from the beginning and has given me her unquestioned support and devotion to an ideal. She is my greatest critic and my greatest fan and has made the entire process memorable, possible and endurable.

Introducing the Paramount

MY PHILOSOPHY of life and work is based on the premise that life is too short to eat bad food. I am motivated by passion, care and integrity, not by profit at the expense of those qualities. My driving ambition has always been the pursuit of excellence and that is what guides me in my work and my life. Attention to detail is of utmost importance. Mediocrity has no place in my world; it smacks of sloppiness, slackness, indifference and many weaknesses. Strength of character, the ability to learn through criticism and the obsessiveness that forces me to push myself to the limits physically, mentally and emotionally affect the way I work and how I expect those around me to work. It breeds a toughness and it is a quality I seek in others.

I enjoy cooking for and being with people who celebrate the richness and diversity that food offers us in our daily lives, and who understand how it affects our wellbeing and its important role in the social process. People should not be afraid of food or cooking. It is an act of offering and it sustains the soul; it is an act of generosity and it comes from the heart. I enjoy being cooked for as much as cooking for other people. The strongest advice I can give anyone is never to be intimidated by the act of cooking. If you like it, it does not matter a bit who you are cooking for, just relax and get on with it. It is thoroughly pretentious to change your *modus operandi* according to the *who*; the *what* and the *how* are the essence of a good cook.

My professional cooking life has been comparatively short. In 1985, at the age of 33, I abandoned the safe haven of a teaching career to pursue an ambition of perfecting the art and science of cooking in the professional arena with an obsessiveness that has sometimes bordered on madness, at least that's how it has felt. The opportunities that were offered to me early on were fortuitous and allowed me to progress at a rapid rate. I felt I had to absorb and learn so very quickly to achieve what I had set out to do – there was no time to waste. I approached everything with a sense of urgency and this has been absorbed into the way I think and act. In the process, I have been most fortunate to have worked for and with some wonderful, like-minded and talented people.

My first opportunity was given to me by Marianne Harris, my partner's sister, who operated Greymasts, a seaside guest-house in Robe, South Australia, that was granted a restaurant licence in 1986. Robe is a busy summer holiday spot as well as a crayfish port, so our menu was based around what the fishing boats brought in each day, and the cellar was stocked with the local wines from the Coonawarra district. It provided a solid and exciting beginning and we learned much.

Within six months, the new Petaluma Restaurant had opened at Bridgewater in the Adelaide Hills, a showcase for Petaluma wines under the guidance and direction of Catherine Kerry, the catering queen of Adelaide. Her faith in my abilities provided great confidence and stimulation, and her intelligence, style and wit are gifts I treasure and still carry with me.

Restaurant life became a consuming passion and in 1988 it led to Sydney and a lifetime of experiences packed into two years working for Phillip Searle at the now-defunct Oasis Seros. He is the vanguard of the industry: a supreme artist and skilled craftsman who instilled in me a sense of purpose, a focus, a discipline, an intensity, a thorough attention to detail and a steely determination to be successful for the right reasons. The essence of his work is that he redefines the boundaries constantly and I feel most privileged to have had a small glimpse of the process, to have been involved along the way. He has been a major influence over the way I cook, think and operate in the kitchen.

Institutional education pales into insignificance when compared to the working relationships and opportunities I have been fortunate enough to have experienced. There are many others in the industry whom I hold in the highest regard, who demand respect and who provide inspiration. Our culinary world and intellectual life are all the richer for their presence.

The Paramount Restaurant represents a collection of life experiences; our ambitions, tastes, desires and style are reflected in our professional attitudes and management. The road that led to the Paramount has been varied, interesting, diverse and, of course, sometimes difficult.

The mellow interior of the Paramount Restaurant features a fibreglass wall

The Paramount Restaurant in Potts Point viewed from the outside

When the Paramount Restaurant opened in July 1993, Margie Harris and I realised our dream of having a space that we could call our own and the luxury of being in control of the entire package for the first time since we had gone into business together. Our working partnership began in June 1990 when we opened our first restaurant, the Paragon, in the Paragon Hotel at Circular Quay, Sydney. This was followed a year later by our second venue at the Phoenix Hotel in Woollahra. Both restaurants were dining rooms within the hotels and while we operated them concurrently as independent businesses to the hotels, we were restricted by the ambience, the adopted style and the very nature of 'pub life'. The advantage was that we were able to establish businesses with little capital outlay while developing a strong profile within the restaurant scene.

With the advent of the Paramount Restaurant, we have been able to concentrate solely on one place – a place that is our own, where we make all the rules and decisions, which is reflected in every aspect of the restaurant. We control the cooking, the presentation, the wines, the feel, the look, the ambience, the attitude – all the components that make up a restaurant. The decision to invest money, time and energy in opening a restaurant is never an easy one. It's a bit like coming to the edge of a cliff and jumping – you either fall or fly. The very nature of the business is precarious in that it is purely subjective. After all, eating is a personal and subliminal act. It relies on many senses and experiences. What and how we eat is based on knowledge, understanding, attitude, availability and acceptance. Any opinion is coloured by all these facts, so pure objectivity is an illusion; the bottom line is that we must trust our own perceptions and desires. Critical analysis is an important and viable aspect of the entire eating procedure but it must be seen within these parameters. Restaurateurs must accept the fact that it is impossible to please all people all the time, just as customers must realise that owning and running restaurants does not endow us with infallibility or that we can satisfy every demand, whim or desire.

The premise for this book came about with the opening of the Paramount Store, which took the concept of the Restaurant into the retail area of the market. The Store opened in December 1993 and is situated three doors down from the Restaurant. Macleay Street has taken on the feel of a village more recently, with its interesting make-up of residents and the expanding services that are on offer. We see our position as one of enhancement to the area as we are also local residents.

Our intention with the Paramount Store is to offer a variety of services to people who wish to cook or entertain at home. It is possible to purchase preparations that form the basis of cooking, thereby removing some of the time-consuming processes and allowing the cook to produce food that is interesting and tasty but not factory processed. Also on offer at the Store are ready-made items, such as breads, pies, salads, tarts, cakes, dinners, desserts, pasta, sauces, ice-creams, sorbets and biscuits – many things of indulgence. We make everything we sell with the exception of the cheese, olive oil and coffee (which we have blended for us exclusively). Our ambition for the Store is to maintain tight control and to limit the supply of produce to on-site. The food for sale has to measure up to the same exacting standards as the Restaurant, to live up to the Paramount philosophy of providing well-crafted food with assertive flavours. As a consequence, the two establishments bear a direct relationship to each other and ultimately give consumers greater diversity in their eating habits and lifestyles. The future direction of food in Australia is dependent on us maintaining an honesty about our produce and the ensuing processes and not succumbing to the dominant, inferior mass-produced food.

The Paramount Store viewed from the outside

Cooking involves all the senses, such is its diversity, and once you understand the fundamental principles a recipe book should be seen as merely a guide to help you. Feel free, then, to interpret the information as you see fit, to use what is helpful to you. Don't treat a cookbook as a blueprint – you'll be doing the book and yourself a disservice. Recipes are a means of documenting work as it happens at the time, in a particular instance with specific ingredients, and by their very nature are open to change and interpretation. Cooking is self-expression, so make what you do your own, in your own way. That doesn't mean you should plagiarise or take credit for something that is not yours; it is important to give acknowledgement where it is deserved. After all, recipes are about the sharing and passing on of information and are a vital part of our documented history, reflecting our social, cultural and economic development.

To make this book user-friendly, I have often used prepared items that we make and sell in the Store as the starting points for each chapter. I explain their place in culinary history, and how they can be made and used. I then give you an insight into some of the ways I use these items in the Restaurant through the recipes that are documented within these covers. The recipes vary in their complexity, so start with what you feel is achievable.

As you read through the recipes, you will note that I have given very precise quantities of measurement. This is to reduce the element of error, making the process more exacting so as to eliminate any vagueness that may change the outcome. For example, the juice of one lemon can vary according to the variety you use; a woody lemon will yield much less juice than one picked at its peak, particularly if it has a thinner skin. All these factors can alter and sometimes mess up a recipe, so I have given exact weights and measurements to reduce confusion and error.

The recipes in this collection generally serve six, but sometimes you may come across one part of a recipe that will yield more. Do not worry! I tend to always err on the side of generosity. The extra can always be used later to cover your tracks if something goes wrong or can be incorporated into another dish, whatever! That is how I cook and I can only encourage you to do the same. As you become more comfortable with the recipes, you will find it easier to adjust and amend where you may feel it is necessary. Cooking is about adaptation, refining and change, I do not see it as an absolute.

Throughout this book you may come across terms or ingredients that may be unfamiliar to you. For the purpose of demystification, I have included an extensive glossary at the back of the book for reference. Some simple terms used in a recipe (for example, '60 ml tamarind juice', '2 teaspoons cummin seeds, roasted and ground' or 'smoke the eggplant') may in fact involve a recipe or process that is explained to make the procedure easier to comprehend. I have tried not to leave too much to assumption. I advise that you familiarise yourself early on with the ingredients and processes described in the Glossary.

An important tip I can offer, and one that has been mentioned elsewhere many, many times, is that when you are reading a recipe for the first time, it is essential to read it *right* through, especially the method, to familiarise yourself with the idea and the process, to reduce the potential for mistakes and to give you a sense of confidence when you undertake it. Reading and acting on new information should enrich and expand the creative spirit. A sense of accomplishment and success can be gained by thinking laterally as well as literally. Bear this in mind when browsing through the recipes in this book; don't be daunted by their length or perceived complexity. The purpose of *Paramount Cooking* is to give you, the reader, an insight into my approach to cooking, it is a vehicle for me to translate my restaurant life into the domestic arena. Cooking well does demand time, organisation, reading and thinking, but the subsequent sense of achievement is satisfying and unparalleled.

ACKNOWLEDGEMENTS Behind anyone in a position of prominence are the faceless slaves, the team that makes it all happen, and credit is often denied them. One person cannot do it all alone; he or she sets the standards and ensures they are maintained and, with luck, provides a working environment that is thought-provoking, challenging and creative. I extend a big hand of thanks to our staff, past and present, who have been major players in the success we enjoy, have assumed responsibility and given genuine commitment to our vision, and without whose contribution I could not have survived. The Paramount is about being a team player and it's a strong team that keeps the ball rolling and maintains the rage! I salute you all and you are part of our glory.

Customers – where would we be without you? The rapport we have built up with and the support we have had from our customers is testament, I think, to our hard work, dedication and hospitality. Some have been travelling along the road with us for quite a while now and there is always plenty of room for new ones to jump on board. Mutual understanding allows the relationship between restaurateur and customer to blossom and flourish and both parties are necessary for survival. I thank you for your loyalty, trust and support.

Part of my job is transforming available produce into an edible art form and this is made easier by the tireless efforts of some of the best suppliers available in the market place (most of these are Sydney-based, given our location). I would like to make particular mention of some of the suppliers with whom I have had close working relationships over the years, who have provided me with inspiration, who constantly inform, who seek out what is best and who give me a starting point. *Every* supplier plays a vital part; to those not mentioned here, your time and efforts are most valued and appreciated.

The Flying Squid Brothers have set new standards for the use of fish and seafood in restaurants. As brokers, they go directly to the source to get the best produce, and they promote Australia's food image in the most positive way. They have helped give a broader and fresher scope to menu planning and diners are at the beneficial receiving end of the bargain.

Simon Johnson, Purveyor of Quality Foods, supplies boutique Australian and imported cheeses, oils and many other edible delicacies and luxuries that make our choices diverse, indulgent and exciting. His devotion and belief in what he does is exemplary, his background knowledge unparalleled.

Fruit and vegetables are a staple and major part of our daily purchasing. As with everything else, there is the excellent, the good and the bad. Buying quality demands attention to detail, liaising closely with growers and keeping a finger on the pulse. Supplying fruit and vegetables means keeping anti-social hours, working when we sleep, so things are at the ready when we start work. Barry McDonald of B. J. Lizard and Connie Simon of Eastside Providores are two of the best in the business. They are in tune with what's happening in the food business, look out for the interesting items and advise how we might use them and keep us abreast of what's at its best, economical and coming up.

The quality and availability of premium meats and poultry is a direct result of the hard work put in by the likes of Glenloth Game in Victoria and Courier Cuts in Sydney, both of which provide us with some of the best meat a restaurateur can lay his or her hands on. Such delicacies as hand-raised squab, corn-fed chickens and ducks, milk-fed veal and lamb, premium beef and velvety-textured prime venison reveal a dedication to quality not at all common in our general butcheries and give us the opportunity to work with and taste fabulous produce.

There are many in the wine industry who have been most generous with their time and product and who have helped us develop a strong wine knowledge and portfolio. I thank those people who see the important relationship between food and wine and, as a consequence, have worked with us in developing that relationship. The education of the palate is a multi-faceted process and the better we all are at being ambassadors for our collective product, at providing guidelines, the more informed and knowledgeable the customers will be in making their decisions.

The masterminds behind the style and ambience of both the Restaurant and the Store are Iain Halliday and David Katon, of Burley Katon Halliday, who produced an environment that reflects our personal and professional outlook and taste. Design affects mood and is as subjective as food and it is important that the two work in harmony. Iain and David understand the big picture, the whole package, and have proved they are brilliant conceptual artists. I certainly acknowledge their genius.

Finally, my gratitude goes to my publisher, Julie Gibbs, for her vision and persistence in guiding me down the sometimes exhilarating and sometimes difficult road that produced this piece of work. Her tenacity and discipline have proved contagious and rewarding.

Pesto

Pesto is commonly known as the wonderfully pungent basil sauce that hailed originally from Genoa, Italy. When freshly made, its fragrance and taste is powerful and intoxicating, hence its popularity and widespread use in everyday cooking. The word 'pesto' refers to the method of preparation, where the ingredients are pounded together by hand in a mortar and pestle to make a paste. This time-consuming but rewarding process has been largely replaced by the mechanical food processor, making it a quick and simple task.

By adapting the literal meaning of the word, I use various forms of pesto in my cooking to give added depth and complexity to a particular dish. Basil Pine Nut Pesto, Coriander Peanut Pesto and Sun-dried Tomato Pesto are my staples and I always have them on hand at the Restaurant and at home for a ready-to-go snack or for more intricate use, as illustrated by the recipes that follow.

Pesto is at its best uncooked as its flavour changes when heated; it is tastiest when added at the last moment. The classic Basil Pine Nut Pesto can be served simply with ripe tomatoes, grilled meats or fish, pasta and hot potatoes or spooned over baked ricotta, added to roasted capsicum salad or spread onto bruschetta. The magic of basil pesto lies in its freshness and its direct association with the flavours of summer.

Coriander Peanut Pesto is made with Asian ingredients such as holy basil, coriander and mint spiked with a touch of chilli. Holy basil (also referred to as Thai or Asian basil) has a strong aniseed flavour and, used in this pesto preparation, its fresh and zesty flavour tantalises the tastebuds with the essence of the Orient. It is as versatile as its Mediterranean counterpart – simply spoon it over hot noodles or deep-fried seafood wontons or stir it into a light soup or broth. Try it out and expand your repertoire in the kitchen.

Sun-dried Tomato Pesto is another tasty addition to the larder. A recent phenomenon gives the popular use of sun-dried tomatoes with its origins in the Mediterranean. Its pungency gives a lift to an antipasto plate, pasta, grilled seafood or charcuterie items for a picnic.

Having these preparations on hand allows for a greater scope in producing something fabulous in a short amount of time. They are available for purchase at the Paramount Store ready to be eaten or used according to the whim of the buyer. However, should you feel inclined to start from scratch, these recipes are offered as a guide.

basil pine nut pesto

This is the universally well-known and original pesto that hails from Genoa in the Ligurian region of northern Italy. It keeps well for a month, refrigerated.

200 g basil leaves, washed
½ teaspoon sea salt
150 ml virgin olive oil
125 g pine nuts, lightly roasted
4 cloves garlic, minced
½ teaspoon black peppercorns, freshly ground
150 g parmesan cheese, freshly grated

1 In a food processor, blend the basil leaves with the salt and 50 ml of the olive oil until a paste has formed. Add the pine nuts, garlic and pepper and pulse to a paste.

2 Drizzle in the remaining olive oil with the motor running and process until smooth. Remove the paste from the processor bowl and gently stir in the parmesan cheese. Check the seasoning and adjust if necessary.

3 To store, spoon the pesto into a container, cover with a film of oil and seal. Keep refrigerated until ready to use.

coriander peanut pesto

This recipe uses the same method of preparation as that for the Basil Pine Nut Pesto but the Mediterranean flavours have been replaced by Asian ones; cheese, which is not part of the Asian repertoire, has been omitted. The pesto keeps well for a month, refrigerated.

200 ml peanut oil
40 g raw blanched peanuts
2 green bird's-eye chillies, minced
1 tablespoon freshly minced ginger
8 cloves garlic, minced
100 g holy basil leaves
25 g Vietnamese mint leaves
100 g coriander leaves
1 teaspoon shaved palm sugar
2 teaspoons fish sauce
20 ml fresh lime juice, strained

1 Heat the oil and roast the peanuts over medium heat until golden. Strain the peanuts from the oil and cool. Reserve both.

2 Blend the peanuts in a food processor with the chilli, ginger and garlic. Add the herbs and half the reserved oil and blend to form a smooth paste.

3 Add the sugar, fish sauce and lime juice and blend until the herbs are finely minced. Gradually pour in the remaining oil to make a smooth paste.

4 To store, spoon the pesto into a container, cover with a film of oil and seal. Keep refrigerated until ready to use.

sun-dried tomato pesto

For this recipe, I use sun-dried tomatoes that are packed in oil, so they need to be strained before being used. Alternatively, you can use tomatoes that you have oven-dried yourself. This is a very rich paste that has strong garlic overtones, so it is best used in moderation. The pesto keeps well for a month, refrigerated.

150 g ripe roma tomatoes, peeled and seeded
200 g sun-dried tomatoes
5 large cloves garlic
50 g sun-dried tomato paste
100 ml virgin olive oil
15 ml balsamic vinegar
15 ml red wine vinegar
½ teaspoon sea salt
½ teaspoon black peppercorns, freshly ground

1 Roughly chop the tomatoes, sun-dried tomatoes and garlic and blend with the sun-dried tomato paste in a food processor until smooth.

2 With the motor running, gradually add the olive oil in a thin stream. Add the vinegars and season to taste with the salt and pepper.

3 To store, spoon the pesto into a container, cover with a film of oil and seal. Keep refrigerated until ready to use.

chargrilled baby octopus with roasted capsicum, oven-dried tomatoes, olives and sun-dried tomato pesto

This dish celebrates the rich flavours of seafood, olive oil, garlic and tomatoes. The combination is a heady one and reminds us of the cuisines and cultures of other lands that have been brought to our doorstep. It is easy to execute as long as the basic preparations have been made beforehand and you have a good hot chargrill or barbecue at your disposal. The secret with the octopus lies in careful buying – be sure to look out for baby octopus, preferably from Port Lincoln, South Australia. Avoid the small, fully grown variety pummelled in cement mixers and often sold at fish markets as they do not become tender regardless of how carefully they have been cooked. Alternatively, braise a large octopus until just tender and toss it on the barbecue briefly before slicing it into bite-sized strips.

1 kg baby octopus, cleaned and head (and beak) removed
100 ml olive oil
a little freshly ground black pepper
6 tablespoons roasted red capsicum strips
3 tablespoons thinly sliced oven-dried tomatoes
2 tablespoons finely sliced red onion
18 kalamata olives, pitted and sliced lengthwise
2 tablespoons basil leaves, shredded
mizuna leaves, washed
6 teaspoons Sun-dried Tomato Pesto (see page 12)

Tomato Dressing
1 tablespoon sun-dried tomato paste
40 ml balsamic vinegar
120 ml virgin olive oil
1/2 teaspoon sea salt
1/2 teaspoon black peppercorns, freshly ground

1 Cut the octopus tentacles in half and marinate in the olive oil until ready to use. Season with black pepper.

2 To make the Tomato Dressing, whisk together the sun-dried tomato paste, balsamic vinegar, virgin olive oil, salt and pepper in a bowl until well incorporated.

3 In a large stainless steel bowl, mix together the roasted capsicum, oven-dried tomato, red onion, olives and basil. Pour on the dressing and mix well with a large spoon. Allow the bowl to warm gently at the edge of the chargrill or barbecue while the octopus is cooking.

4 Heat a chargrill or barbecue grill until very hot and then toss on the octopus. Distribute it evenly and cook quickly – the cooking will take only a couple of minutes. Use tongs to toss the octopus continuously to ensure even cooking without burning. The octopus will be cooked when the tentacles start to curl and the meat feels soft and tender to the touch – don't allow it to become firm or the meat will be overcooked.

5 Add the cooked octopus and mizuna leaves to the bowl, mix well and divide evenly between six plates Spoon a teaspoon of Sun-dried Tomato Pesto on top of each and serve immediately. Alternatively, this dish can be served in one large bowl as part of a centre-table offering where guests can help themselves.

Serves 6

yamba prawn and saffron risotto with pesto

Risotto, one of my all-time favourites, is cooked regularly for our staff meals and at home as the ideal one-pot meal. It makes an appearance at the Restaurant as a special addition to the menu or as part of a set menu for a group. It is a dish that requires time, patience and constant attention to elevate it to its correct place. To cook and reheat it only results in a stodgy, sticky mess that dissatisfies the palate.

The basic rules for perfect risotto include using arborio rice, not a cheap substitute; frying the aromatic base and the rice first so that the rice is coated with fat, which allows the rice to swell and the hot liquid to be absorbed more readily; bringing the stock to simmering point and adding it gradually to the rice so that the cooking temperature remains even; careful and constant cooking, and serving the risotto as soon as it has been cooked. Making risotto is one of the most satisfying cooking and consuming processes in a culinary repertoire, so go ahead and experiment, keeping in mind the basic rules.

The Yamba prawns I recommend using here are caught along the coastline of northern New South Wales and sent directly to the Flying Squid Brothers in Sydney, avoiding the chemical and freezing treatment that usually occurs on the large prawn trawlers that may be at sea for up to a week or ten days. The freshness of these prawns shows in their taste and texture. When looking for prawns to cook, always choose green (uncooked) prawns that smell fresh and show no sign of blackening in the head.

900 ml fish stock
18 green Yamba king prawns
100 ml olive oil
2 tablespoons finely diced brown onion
2 teaspoons minced garlic
2 red bird's-eye chillies, minced
350 g arborio rice, rinsed
150 ml sauvignon blanc
1 teaspoon saffron threads
20 basil leaves, shredded
75 g unsalted butter
3 tablespoons Basil Pine Nut Pesto (see page 10)
1 teaspoon sea salt
1 teaspoon black peppercorns, freshly ground

1 Bring the fish stock to a boil in a saucepan and allow to maintain a gentle simmer.

2 Peel and clean the prawns then split each one in two.

3 Heat a wide-based braising pan and add the olive oil. Sauté the onion, garlic and chilli until the onion has softened and is golden. Add the rice and, stirring continuously, cook until it is coated with the oil.

4 Pour in the sauvignon blanc. As the wine is absorbed by the rice, add the saffron and start to ladle on the simmering fish stock, 150 ml at a time. Maintaining a fairly high heat, allow the rice to absorb the liquid before adding the next quantity and stir frequently to prevent the mixture from sticking. With each addition of stock, the rice will steam and swell to absorb the liquid. As you near the end of the stock the rice should still have a bit of bite in it; it will have become creamy but the grains will remain separate.

5 When the last ladle of stock has been absorbed, add the prawn meat and basil leaves, stirring constantly. Cook just until the prawns are translucent, then stir in the butter and pesto and season to taste with the salt and pepper.

6 Serve the risotto immediately with some chilled sauvignon blanc to accompany it.

Serves 6

deep-fried eggplant stuffed with coffin bay scallops, ginger and coriander with pesto dressing

This dish, a regular feature on the Paramount menu, is deceptively simple in appearance but a little time-consuming to make. It works beautifully as a dish because its texture, balance of flavours, method of cooking and its presentation make a great 'package'. For me, this dish epitomises the skill and craft of a professional cook in a technical and creative sense.

7 eggplants (8 cm in diameter)
18 large Coffin Bay scallops
1 egg white
1 teaspoon strained lemon juice
pinch of sea salt
pinch of freshly ground white pepper
20 ml single (35%) cream
2 egg yolks, beaten
1 tablespoon dried prawns, roasted and ground
vegetable oil for deep-frying

Smoked Eggplant Stuffing

3½ eggplants
vegetable oil
2 spring onions, finely sliced
2 coriander roots, finely sliced
2 teaspoons coriander leaves, chopped
1 teaspoon freshly minced ginger
½ teaspoon black peppercorns, freshly ground
1 teaspoon strained fresh lime juice
1 teaspoon fish sauce
½ teaspoon sesame oil

Pesto Dressing

50 ml fresh lime juice, strained
25 ml coconut vinegar
50 ml reduced tomato essence
25 ml fish sauce
1 teaspoon castor sugar
10 ml sesame oil
15 ml olive oil
3 tablespoons Basil Pine Nut Pesto (see page 10)

1 To make the Smoked Eggplant Stuffing, smoke and peel 3 of the eggplants. Squeeze out the excess juices and chop roughly.

2 Finely dice the remaining ½ eggplant. Deep-fry the diced eggplant until golden, then drain on paper towels. Combine the smoked and fried eggplant in a bowl. Add the remaining ingredients and mix well. Taste and adjust if necessary.

3 To prepare the 7 eggplants, cut 12 thin rounds from one of the eggplants. Brush with a little vegetable oil and chargrill on each side.

4 Cut the tops and bottoms off the remaining 6 eggplants to leave a trunk on each one that is 8 cm high. Cut a 3 mm slice off the top end of each eggplant and reserve for later use as lids.

5 Take an eggplant and sit it upright. Use a 5 cm round pastry cutter to press down through the centre of the eggplant trunk until 1 cm from the bottom. Using a small paring knife, make a 2 cm long horizontal incision into the side of the eggplant 1 cm up from the base. Move the knife from side to side to loosen the 'core'. Be careful not to pierce the other side of the eggplant. Remove the core to form a well in the centre of the eggplant trunk. Repeat with the remaining eggplants.

6 Blend 6 of the scallops in the chilled bowl of a food processor with the egg white, lemon juice, salt and white pepper until smooth. Add the cream and pulse until just incorporated. Do not overwork this paste or it will separate – it must hold together to act as a 'glue'. Slice each of the remaining scallops into 3 discs, leaving the coral intact.

7 To make the Pesto Dressing, mix together all the ingredients except the pesto and stir well. Taste and adjust, if necessary, and set aside.

8 To assemble, rub a small amount of the scallop paste around the inside of the eggplant's cavity, especially over the small incision that was made with the paring knife. Position a slice of grilled eggplant on the bottom of the cavity and spoon in Smoked Eggplant Stuffing until a little over half full. Cover the stuffing with 6 fanned-out scallop discs. Top the scallops with another grilled eggplant slice and seal with the scallop paste. Brush with the beaten egg yolk and press on the reserved lid. Brush the top of the lid with egg yolk and sprinkle on a little of the ground prawns.

9 Repeat this process with the other 5 eggplant trunks. Allow the stuffed eggplants to set in the refrigerator for 3 hours before cooking.

10 To cook the prepared eggplants, heat a deep-fryer or 5 litre stockpot with enough vegetable oil to cover the eggplants. When the oil reaches 180°C, cook the eggplants for 8 minutes, ensuring they remain submerged in the oil. I use wooden skewers threaded across the deep-fryer's wire basket to keep them in place. (It may be necessary to cook the eggplants 2 or 3 at a time, depending on the size of the pot.) Carefully remove the eggplants from the oil with a flat slide or spatula and drain on paper towels momentarily before plating.

11 Mix together the dressing and pesto, and spoon over and around each eggplant. Serve immediately.

Serves 6

eggplant, goat's cheese and pesto sandwich

This dish was born in the early days of the Paragon kitchen, when we were new kids on the block, and still makes regular appearances on the Paramount menu. Its success lies in the combination of flavours and its last-minute cooking and assembly. Its construction is a play on the concept of a sandwich, where the eggplant takes on the role of bread and simply transforms a classic idea into a more theatrical presentation. The underlying intention is that when you cut through the sandwich from top to bottom your mouth is assaulted with all the flavours and textures at once. Another endearing feature of this dish is that it's as easy to put together as a regular sandwich and the mini version, using Japanese eggplants, makes an interesting appetiser or canapé.

3 eggplants
sea salt
vegetable oil for deep-frying
30 ml balsamic vinegar
90 ml virgin olive oil
extra pinch of sea salt
pinch of freshly ground black pepper
300 g Kervella or Milawa fresh goat's cheese, at room temperature
2 roasted red capsicums, cut into strips lengthwise
9 teaspoons Basil Pine Nut Pesto (see page 10)
3 tablespoons finely shredded rocket leaves

1 Cut the eggplants into 12 × 2 cm thick slices, sprinkle with salt and leave to sweat on a dry tray for 1 hour. Dry with paper towels to remove any excess moisture and salt.

2 Heat the vegetable oil in a deep-fryer or large saucepan to 180°C and fry the eggplant slices until golden brown on both sides. Drain, then pat dry with paper towels.

3 Make a vinaigrette by whisking together the balsamic vinegar, virgin olive oil and the extra salt and the pepper.

4 To assemble the sandwiches, cut the goat's cheese into 6 × 1 cm thick slices. Put a slice of eggplant on a plate and top with a slice of goat's cheese. Cover the cheese with a few strips of the roasted capsicum and then add 1 teaspoon of the pesto. Drizzle over some vinaigrette and then sprinkle on some of the finely shredded rocket leaves. Cover with another slice of eggplant and top this with a little extra pesto, vinaigrette and shredded rocket. Repeat this process using the remaining ingredients to make 6 sandwiches.

5 Serve immediately, while the eggplant is hot.

Serves 6

Eggplant, Goat's Cheese and Pesto Sandwich

stir-fried pacific oysters and seaweed noodles with bok choy and coriander peanut pesto

Here's a fabulous way to present oysters that have been literally just warmed through by a fast application of heat. The combined flavours have a strong association with the iodine headiness of the sea. Its size, fresh, salty sea flavour and ability to take a quick show of heat without shrinking away to nothing make the large Pacific oyster ideal for this preparation. The only trick with this dish is to cook each serve separately as the small quantities ensure that ingredients heat through quickly without lowering the temperature of the wok and the oysters do not overcook. You will need 12 bowls to prepare this dish; the secret to cooking this dish successfully lies in quick cooking. Cook two or three serves at a time and rest the cooked serves briefly while cooking the next batch. Small Teflon woks, which make cooking this dish a breeze, are available from Asian food stores.

36 large Pacific oysters, unshucked
12 bok choy hearts
2 large green chillies
3 teaspoons Pickled Ginger, finely sliced (see page 52)
3 tablespoons coriander leaves
6 spring onions, cut into 1 cm rounds
125 g snow pea sprouts
6 teaspoons Coriander Peanut Pesto (see page 11)

Seaweed Noodles
250 g bread flour
½ teaspoon sea salt
2 nori seaweed sheets, toasted, chopped and ground
3 large (61 g) eggs
2 teaspoons virgin olive oil
rice flour

Oyster Dressing
200 ml reserved oyster juices
160 ml fish stock
20 ml fish sauce
10 ml light soy sauce
20 ml mirin
60 ml tamarind juice
30 ml fresh lime juice, strained

1 To make the Seaweed Noodles, mix together the flour, salt and ground seaweed in a food processor. With the motor running, add the eggs and the oil and process until the dough comes together to form a ball. Wrap the dough in plastic foodwrap and refrigerate for 1 hour.

2 Cut the chilled dough into 4 portions to make it easier to handle and roll out each piece on a cool, flat surface sprinkled with fine rice flour. (The rice flour makes the dough pass through the rollers on the pasta machine easily without tearing. The gluten-free rice flour is used so that no extra gluten, which would toughen the dough, is introduced.) Pass each piece of dough through the rollers on a pasta machine, starting at the thickest setting and working through to the thinnest setting. Dust the sheets of dough each time with rice flour so they do not become sticky and unmanageable. Pass the thin sheets of pasta through the spaghetti cutters on the machine.

3 Bring a large saucepan of water to a rolling boil. Cook the noodles for 2 minutes. Remove the noodles from the boiling water and refresh under cold, running water. Drain and dress with a little olive oil to prevent them from sticking together.

4 Shuck the oysters and reserve all the strained juices for the dressing. Refrigerate the oysters and their juices until ready to use.

5 To make the Oyster Dressing, mix together all the ingredients in a bowl (if necessary, top up the oyster juices with fish stock to make 200 ml). Taste and adjust if necessary. Keep refrigerated until ready to use.

6 Trim the bok choy hearts of any limp or broken outer leaves, leaving the stem and leaves intact so they do not separate during cooking. Rinse under cold water. Steam the bok choy hearts for 3 minutes in the tray of a metal Chinese steamer or a bamboo basket until softened. Refresh immediately in a bowl of iced water.

7 Remove the seeds and membrane from the chillies and cut the flesh into fine julienne.

8 To assemble, divide the noodles, bok choy and dressing between six bowls and the remaining ingredients between another six bowls.

9 Heat the woks over a high heat and add the first preparation of noodles, dressing and bok choy to each. Toss over the heat until warmed, being careful that the noodles don't stick. Add a bowl of the second preparation, which includes the oysters, to each wok, stir with tongs to combine quickly and toss over the heat until warmed through, about 1 minute. Pile the noodles onto serving plates and repeat the cooking process. Serve immediately.

Serves 6

crispy duck and scallop rice-paper rolls with coriander peanut pesto

This recipe takes its lead from the Vietnamese-style spring roll, cha giò, *and gives it a refreshing lift with the addition of the Coriander Peanut Pesto. You can prepare the duck according to the recipe for Five-spice Duck and Shiitake Mushroom Pies with Ginger Glaze (see page 98) or simply buy a roast duck from an Asian food store.*

50 g cellophane noodles
9 tablespoons Coriander Peanut Pesto (see page 11)
3 large eggs
25 ml fish sauce
½ teaspoon finely ground black pepper
125 g cooked duck meat, finely chopped
125 g scallop meat, minced
50 g water chestnuts
1 small carrot, peeled and finely shredded
3 spring onions, sliced into fine rounds
½ small cucumber, peeled, seeded and finely shredded
2 teaspoons Vietnamese mint leaves, shredded
2 teaspoons coriander leaves
24 round rice-paper wrappers
egg wash
oil for deep-frying

1 Blanch the cellophane noodles in boiling water for 1 minute. Refresh under cold water and strain. Slice the noodles into 2 cm lengths and mix in a bowl with 3 tablespoons of the Coriander Peanut Pesto.

2 Whisk the eggs, fish sauce and pepper together. Add to the noodles with all the other ingredients except the rice-paper wrappers. Mix thoroughly.

3 Soak a rice-paper wrapper in a large bowl of warm water until it softens and becomes pliable. Lay the softened wrappers on a clean cloth. Fold over the bottom edge of the wrapper towards the centre and place 2 tablespoons of filling on the folded portion. Roll over once, fold in the edges and roll over again. Brush the edges with egg wash to secure. Rest the roll on its seam on a tray lined with absorbent paper until ready to cook. Repeat until all the wrappers are used.

4 Heat the oil in a deep-fryer or a deep saucepan until it reaches 160°C. Fry the rolls, 6 at a time (to avoid lowering the temperature), for 8 minutes until pale golden. Remove from the oil and drain on paper towels. Keep the rolls warm in the oven while you cook the remaining rolls. Don't have the frying oil too hot or the rolls will burn and split; rice paper is more fragile than regular spring roll pastry.

5 Serve the rice-paper rolls with the remaining Coriander Peanut Pesto.

Serves 6

Preserved Lemons

The versatile lemon plays an integral role in the culinary process – the skin, seeds, juice and flesh all contribute in their own right and collectively to the chemistry of food. The lemon activates change – it is the revolutionary of the food world. The lemon has a major role as a flavour enhancer and it doesn't come out of a bottle! As a fresh ingredient, the lemon has great longevity or shelf life but, of course, it is best when freshly picked and ripe. Many cuisines of the world use the lemon to balance richness, to preserve food or to add a necessary zest or lift to a dish. In addition, the lemon is a wonderful source of vitamin C, a most necessary part of our diet.

Maximise resources during times of abundance and preserve lemons when they are at their best, and enjoy their special characters through to the next season. Often used in conjunction with aromatic spices and herbs, preserved lemons provide an antidote to the richness of meat and the oiliness of fish and olives, at the same time as transforming an acceptable dish into a taste sensation.

Historically linked with the cuisine of Morocco, preserved lemons are part of the staple diet of that country and give a unique perfume and pickled taste to the foods with which they are cooked. Their yellowness and firm shape is retained as they rest glistening in their salty preserving liquid, dispelling their potent acidity and changing the taste we most usually associate with this member of the citrus family to a more mellow, musky and syrupy flavour.

We preserve lemons at the Restaurant twice a year – during autumn and spring when the fruit is plentiful, juicy and cheap. We stock Preserved Lemons at our Store so that last-minute decisions can be made by the home cook who can use them in a variety of ways: to spike a lamb stew, as part of a garlic and onion stuffing for a barbecued fish, to flavour a rice pilaf, to add to a sizzling plate of garlic prawns or mushrooms or to give a lift to a seafood salad.

Spices symbolise luxury and, as good cooking is luxurious, I adopt the principle that spices should be used generously and wholeheartedly. This philosophy is particularly evident in the recipes of this chapter as the combination of preserved lemons with rich and varied spices seems a natural one. Don't look to these recipes when trying to whip together a last-minute dinner without preserved lemons to hand, however, as there is no substitute. Lemon juice or zest will not suffice.

preserved lemons

Important tips to remember when preserving lemons include choosing ripe, fragrant fruit, ensuring the lemons are washed thoroughly before salting, covering the lemons completely with liquid during storage and keeping them refrigerated once opened. Once preserved, the lemons need to be stored for 6 weeks before use and keep for 12 months.

10 ripe thin-skinned lemons
150 g fine table salt
1 litre lemon juice (about 20 lemons)

1 Wash the lemons thoroughly, scrubbing the skins if necessary. Cut the lemons into quarters lengthwise to within 1 cm of the base. Pack each lemon with salt and reshape the fruit by pressing the quarters back together.

2 Place the lemons into a 2 litre preserving jar and sprinkle with a little extra salt. Pour in the lemon juice until the lemons are covered. Seal the jar and store the lemons for 6 weeks in a cool place away from direct light.

3 When the lemons are ready to use, remove from the jar as needed and rinse with water. Discard the flesh and use the preserved lemon as required. Refrigerate the opened jar.

hot pot of slow-braised beef brisket with preserved lemons and waxy potatoes

This is a perfect heart-warming, cold-weather dish that requires a time-honoured, slow-cooking process to extract maximum flavour from all the ingredients. We serve it during the winter months presented in a clay pot with couscous dressed with Preserved Lemon Gremolata on the plate so that the diner can make a real feast of it. The richness is ambrosial.

2 kg beef brisket
200 ml olive oil
2 brown onions, finely diced
6 cloves garlic, minced
1 tablespoon freshly minced ginger
1 red bird's-eye chilli, minced
2 teaspoons ras el hanout (see page 162)
1 teaspoon cummin seeds, roasted and ground
2 teaspoons coriander seeds, roasted and ground
2 dried large red chillies, roasted and ground
1 teaspoon hot paprika
2 teaspoons black peppercorns, freshly ground
3 litres light beef or veal stock
1 Preserved Lemon, finely chopped (see page 24)
1 teaspoon sea salt
9 waxy potatoes (patronne or pink fir apple), parboiled
750 ml chicken stock
50 g unsalted butter
500 g couscous grains
extra sea salt
extra freshly ground black pepper

Preserved Lemon Gremolata

½ cup flat parsley leaves, chopped
1 tablespoon finely diced red onion
2 cloves garlic, minced
2 teaspoons finely diced Preserved Lemon (see page 24)

1 Put a roasting pan in the oven and preheat to 140°C. Brush the beef brisket with some of the olive oil and sprinkle with a little black pepper. Seal the meat in the hot roasting pan in the oven (this will take about 10 minutes on each side to allow it to brown).

2 Remove the meat (but leave the oven on) and, in the same pan, add the rest of the olive oil. Sauté the onion, garlic, ginger and chilli on the stove top until fragrant. Add the spices and cook for a few minutes. Pour in the beef stock and bring it to a boil. Reduce to a simmer, add the browned beef brisket and cover with foil.

3 Return the meat to the oven for 3 hours, or until the meat is very tender. Turn the meat in the stock during the cooking process. After 2 hours of cooking, stir half the Preserved Lemon into the stock. When the meat is ready, remove the pan from the oven and take the meat out of the stock. Rest the meat until it is cool enough to handle.

4 Pass the stock through a fine-mesh sieve, saving the onion and lemon mixture to add later to the reduced stock. Bring the strained stock to a boil in a saucepan and allow to reduce by half until the sauce thickens and becomes unctuous but not sticky. Add the reserved onion and lemon mixture, the remaining lemon and the salt to the sauce. Taste for seasoning and adjust if necessary. (The lemon usually provides enough salt to balance and enhance the meat but a little extra pepper may be required.)

5 Carefully prepare the brisket by removing any fat, bones, tendons and muscle tissue and cut the meat into large chunks so it doesn't fall apart when it is reheated in the sauce. Bring the finished sauce to a boil with the parboiled potatoes, reduce the heat and add the meat. Simmer very gently for 10 minutes.

6 Prepare the couscous by bringing the chicken stock to a boil and adding it with the butter to the couscous grains in a large bowl. Season with salt and pepper and stir. Allow the grains to absorb the liquid. Put the bowl in a steamer and steam for 5 minutes.

7 Just before serving, finely mince the Gremolata ingredients together with a cleaver.

8 To serve, spoon some couscous onto each plate and add the meat, potatoes and sauce and sprinkle with gremolata. Alternatively, the couscous can be placed in a large bowl in the middle of the table with the meat in another bowl and everyone can help themselves to give the meal a more informal tone.

Serves 6

rare roasted squab with saffron, green olives and preserved lemon

Squabs are delectable birds and their meat holds up very well to rich, spicy flavours. Squab meat is at its best when cooked rare, when it is at its juiciest and tastiest. I am quite adamant that particular meats should never be overcooked. I would rather people choose something else if they are turned off by the relaxed nature of rare meat than have them disappointed by the texture of overcooked meat and laying that responsibility with the cook. The generic steak house can play that role but we, as restaurateurs, have a greater responsibility in the education and understanding of the palate.
The squabs can be served with either couscous or a crisp potato galette. Individual finger bowls provide a finishing touch.

2 teaspoons hot paprika
2 teaspoons turmeric powder, roasted
2 teaspoons cummin seeds, roasted and ground
120 ml olive oil
6 × 400 g squabs
30 g ghee
24 red shallots, peeled
6 cloves garlic, minced
2 teaspoons freshly minced ginger
100 g squab livers
1.5 litres squab or game stock
12 large green olives, pitted and quartered
1 teaspoon saffron threads
1 Preserved Lemon, finely chopped (see page 24)
30 ml lemon juice, strained
½ teaspoon black pepper, freshly ground
40 g unsalted butter
1 tablespoon coriander leaves

1 Mix half the paprika, turmeric and cummin with the olive oil. Clean and prepare the squabs and brush inside and out with the spiced olive oil.

2 Slice 12 of the shallots. In a large saucepan, fry the sliced shallots, garlic, ginger and squab livers in the ghee over moderate heat until softened and aromatic. Add the remaining paprika, turmeric and cummin and cook for 2 minutes.

3 Add the stock to the saucepan and bring to a boil. Reduce the heat and simmer gently until the stock has reduced by half and has developed a rich colour and taste. Skim regularly with a mesh spoon. Pass the sauce through a fine-mesh sieve, pressing firmly to extract all juices.

4 Bring the strained sauce to a boil, add the remaining whole shallots and simmer for 15 minutes until the shallots have softened. Add the olives, saffron and lemon and simmer for a further 5 minutes. (The sauce can be made to this stage ahead of time and finished off as you are ready to serve when the squabs have been roasted.)

5 Preheat the oven to 300°C or as high as your oven will go. To cook the squabs, place the birds, breast-side down, in a cast-iron frying pan or dish and roast for 8 minutes. Remove from the oven and allow to rest in a warm place for 10 minutes to allow the juices to settle.

6 To serve, carve the breasts off the bone and slice each breast in half diagonally. Remove the legs from each carcass and leave whole (reserve the carcasses to make extra stock later). Finish the sauce by whisking in the lemon juice, pepper and butter, to give it a gloss, and stir in the coriander leaves.

7 Place 2 legs in the centre of each serving plate and arrange the 4 pieces of breast meat on top. Pour the sauce around the meat and serve immediately.

Serves 6

Rare Roasted Squab with Saffron, Green Olives and Preserved Lemon

baked quails stuffed with rice, pine nuts and preserved lemons with a spiced tomato sauce

This recipe is another popular adaptation of the flavours of northern Africa suited to our style of cooking. The most difficult part of this preparation is boning out the quails but if you can buy them already boned, the rest is relatively easy. This dish is quite versatile in that it can be served as an entrée (1 bird each) or as a main course (2 birds each) or as part of a centre-table spread where there are many things to taste.

100 ml olive oil
3 tablespoons finely minced brown onion
1 tablespoon minced garlic
seeds of 4 cardamom pods, ground
1 teaspoon ground cinnamon
1½ cups cooked long grain rice
150 g pine nuts, lightly roasted
3 tablespoons flat parsley leaves, shredded
1 Preserved Lemon, finely chopped (see page 24)
1 teaspoon sea salt
2 teaspoons black peppercorns, freshly ground
24 prepared vine leaves
12 large quails, boned out
2 litres chicken stock

Spicy Tomato Sauce
8 large, ripe tomatoes
5 cloves garlic, unpeeled
250 ml olive oil
1 brown onion, minced
1 stick cinnamon
2 teaspoons cummin seeds, roasted and ground
1 teaspoon black peppercorns, cracked
200 ml white wine

1 To make the Spicy Tomato Sauce, preheat the oven to 250°C. Roast the tomatoes and garlic in a baking pan for about 30 minutes or until the tomatoes are coloured and split open.

2 Heat a wide-based braising pan and add 100 ml of the olive oil and fry the onion until softened and aromatic, stirring to prevent it sticking and burning. Add the cinnamon stick, ground cummin and cracked black peppercorns and stir until fragrant. Add the roasted tomatoes, garlic and the white wine and simmer gently for 30 minutes.

3 Remove the pan from the heat and pass the sauce through a fine conical sieve. Pour the sauce into the bowl of a food processor. With the motor running, slowly pour in the remaining olive oil in a thin stream to emulsify the sauce. Check the seasoning and adjust with sea salt and pepper if necessary. Set the sauce aside until required.

4 To prepare the stuffing for the quails, heat the olive oil in a frying pan and gently sauté the onion and garlic without colouring. Add the cardamom and cinnamon to the pan, stirring to mix. Remove from the heat. Stir in the cooked rice, pine nuts, parsley, lemon, salt and pepper and allow to cool.

5 Wash the vine leaves to remove the brine. Stuff the quails with the cooled rice mixture and wrap each quail around its middle with 2 vine leaves, securing them with a skewer.

6 Sit the quails in a single layer in a wide-based braising pan that is just large enough to hold the birds snugly. Bring the chicken stock to a boil in another saucepan and pour over the quails to cover. Cover with a lid and simmer gently for 10 minutes until the quails are pink. The quails are done if the juices run clear with a touch of pink when a skewer is inserted into the breast.

7 Preheat the oven to 250°C.

8 Take the braising pan off the heat and remove the quails gently from the stock with a slotted spoon. Sit the quails on a baking tray and crisp in the hot oven for 4 minutes. Reheat the sauce, if necessary, while the birds are baking.

9 Remove the skewers, place the quails on serving plates and spoon the hot sauce over and around the birds.

Serves 6 or 12

tasmanian salmon fillet baked in chermoula with preserved lemon and buttered spinach

This dish was on our first Paramount menu and continues to make regular appearances, particularly in the warmer summer months when the Tasmanian salmon is at its best. The flavours are not cloying or rich – the emphasis is on the freshness of all the components – and the chermoula marinade provides an aromatic presence that blends perfectly with the luscious spinach. The whole thing has a melt-in-the mouth sensation. The flesh and flavour of the freshwater salmon from Victoria's Yarra Valley that has recently come onto the market is equal in the quality to that of its ocean cousin and works just as well in this recipe. Make sure that the fillets are taken from the thickest part of the fish. The chermoula can be made up to 3 days in advance.

6 × 200 g salmon fillets
3 bunches of spinach leaves, stalks removed
75 g unsalted butter
½ teaspoon sea salt
½ teaspoon black peppercorns, freshly ground
pinch of freshly grated nutmeg
½ Preserved Lemon, finely chopped (see page 24)
60 ml virgin olive oil

Preserved Lemon Chermoula
4 large cloves garlic
2 red bird's-eye chillies
10 red shallots, finely sliced lengthwise
¼ cup flat parsley leaves, finely chopped
½ cup coriander leaves, finely chopped
½ cup spearmint leaves, finely chopped
1 teaspoon cummin seeds, roasted and ground
½ teaspoon black peppercorns, freshly ground
1 Preserved Lemon, finely chopped (see page 24)
200 ml virgin olive oil

1 To make the chermoula, mince the garlic and chillies together. Mix the shallots, herbs, spices and lemon in a bowl and stir in the olive oil to bind the mixture together. Refrigerate until ready to use.

2 To prepare the fish, cut 6 sheets of baking paper and 6 sheets of foil, each 20 cm square. Remove any bones in the salmon fillets with a pair of tweezers. Spread 1 tablespoon of chermoula onto each piece of baking paper, and position a piece of salmon on it. Spread another tablespoon of chermoula on top of the fish. Fold each piece of paper over to make a secure package and then wrap in a foil square. Allow the salmon parcels to marinate in the refrigerator for 3–5 hours before cooking.

3 Wash the spinach leaves thoroughly and blanch in boiling water for 30 seconds. Refresh immediately in iced water to stop the cooking process and retain the colour. Squeeze out all excess water and set aside.

4 Preheat the oven to 200°C and bake the salmon fillets in their foil parcels on a baking tray for 6–8 minutes, depending on their thickness. The fish should retain a rosy blush in the middle and not be cooked right through as it has a tendency to dry out. (Fish, like meat, is best served rare to get full benefit of flavour and texture.)

5 While the fish is baking, heat a frying pan and melt the butter gently. Add the spinach, salt, pepper and nutmeg and stir continuously over a medium heat until the spinach softens and warms through. Don't let it burn or become crisp.

6 Stir the chopped Preserved Lemon into the virgin olive oil.

7 When the fish is ready, remove it from the oven and unwrap the parcels. Spoon the spinach onto serving plates and slide the fish on top. Pour over the excess juices from the parcels. Spoon over the lemon and oil and serve immediately.

Serves 6

Chilli Pastes

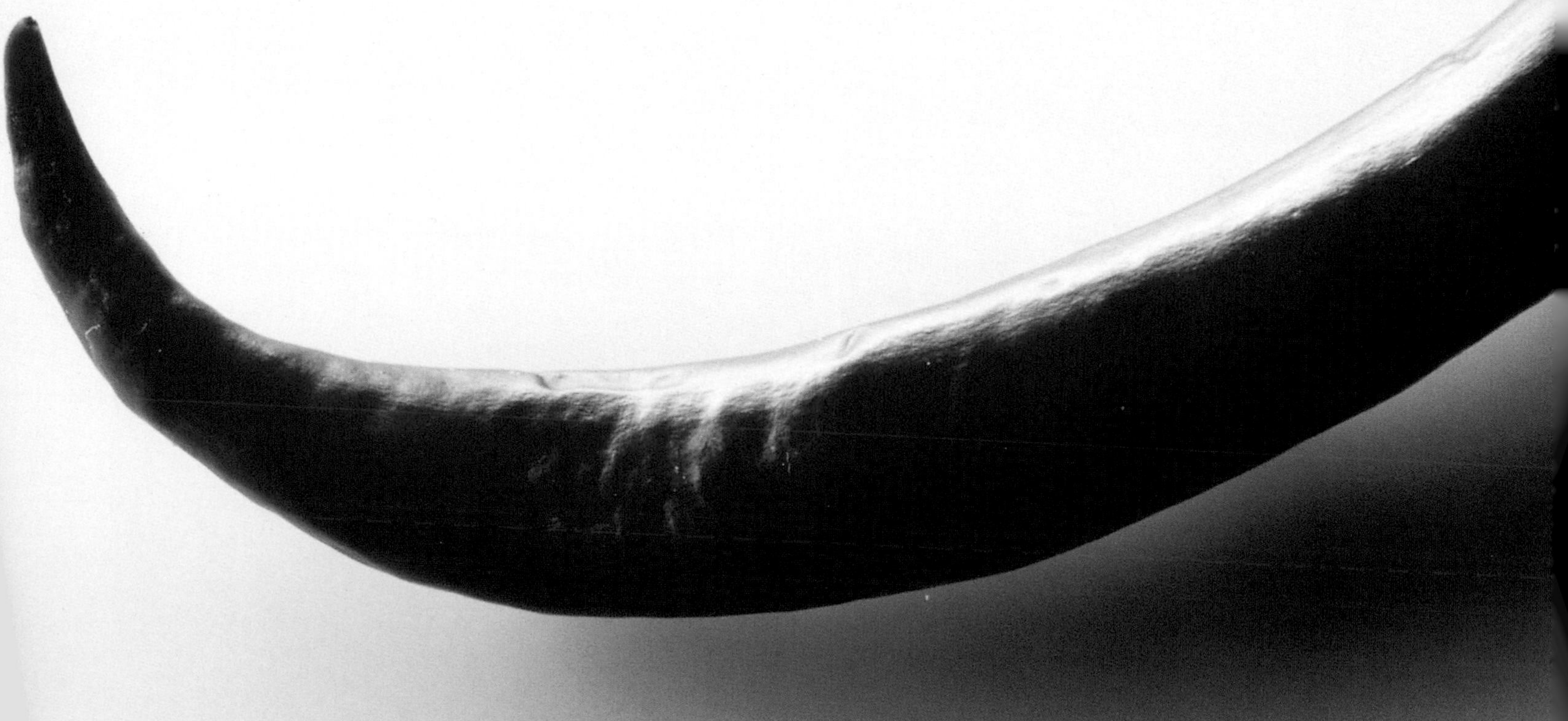

I can't imagine cooking without the beloved chilli, life would be too boring and dull. Chillies are a flamboyant element of the cooking process. They create heat, fire and really get the palate going. As a raw ingredient, they are a symbol of strength and versatility. The origin of the chilli can be traced back to South America well before trade routes were established. Today the use of chillies in cooking can be found in many cuisines of the world. They have become an essential and indispensable ingredient in the historical development of food. There are many varieties of chilli, each giving a specific flavour, pungency, aroma and heat. For the regular chilli consumer, their taste is addictive.

When selecting chillies, the basic guideline is that size determines heat: the smaller they are, the hotter they are, with most of the heat being stored in the seeds and membrane. Green chillies are usually hotter as they sweeten slightly as they ripen to a red colour. Chillies that grow in a hot tropical climate tend to give off the most heat. Tolerance to their heat grows with use, so the best advice to give when reading or cooking a particular recipe is to taste the chilli carefully in its raw state first to determine how much to use. Chillies deserve to be used in a proper context, not thrown in haphazardly without any basic understanding of their effect on the finished product – that is tantamount to abuse and indiscriminate use displays ignorance for the fundamental aspects of cooking. Their diversity lies in their many varieties and possible cooking treatments. They can be used raw, fried, stewed, smoked, dried, roasted, ground, grilled or stuffed. They also form the bases for oils, pastes, sambals, sauces, preserves and spice mixes.

The use of chilli in current cooking methods in Australia has a direct relationship with the development of our food culture. Our white history is one of immigrant status, where each ethnic group has brought with it its particular cooking style and ingredients. These practices have been adopted and adapted to suit our changing needs and desires. The emergence of an identifiable Australian food culture and cuisine develops as we grow confident enough not to rely on borrowed terms to define what we are doing in terms of professional technique and everyday cooking and eating. Chillies have become part of our diet: they grow abundantly, suit our climate, are good for our health, are no longer deemed foreign, are readily obtainable and feature on restaurant, bistro and café menus across the country. As a group of people, Australians have become much more adventurous eaters. Chillies can even spark philosophical, political and social debate – such is their strength!

At the Paramount, chillies show their faces in many preparations, sometimes with subtlety, sometimes with strength. As cooks, we embrace them with passion. We keep on hand four types of fresh chilli at any one time, not allowing for the imported American/Mexican dried varieties that are also used in abundance. Their dried state reduces some of their heat but heightens other facets of their flavours. We use mostly the green or red bird's-eye chillies, the small Asian variety commonly found in the shops, and the longer and larger, not-so-hot, red or green chillies. When available, we also sparingly use a tiny chilli that has enormous heat. According to my learned colleague David Thompson of Sydney's Darley Street Thai Restaurant, its Thai name *prik kii noo suan* means 'garden mouse chilli', but it is commonly referred to as the 'scud' chilli by aficionados. Apparently, in Queensland, where they are grown, they are referred to as 'ornamental chillies'.

When using any type of chilli, it is important to remember it must balance with the other flavours and not override them, so don't let the heat kill the palate. Chilli should be detectable for its fragrance as well as its heat. Experimentation is the key to understanding and gaining confidence with chilli – make it work for you and you will have a friend forever.

We make a variety of chilli pastes for use in dishes offered in the Restaurant and some of these are duplicated for purchase in the Store.

chilli jam

Chilli jam is always on hand at home and in the Restaurant because of its versatility and is a favourite with some as a simple spread on toast (mind you, a healthy chilli appetite and tolerance is needed to cope with this method of consumption). It can be simmered in coconut cream and used as a sauce for fish or chicken; it can be spooned over grilled meat, or used as part of a marinade. Use it as you would any other chilli sambal. Chilli jam keeps for 3 months, refrigerated.

1.5 kg large red chillies
300 g red bird's-eye chillies
8 large brown onions
15 large cloves garlic
1 litre vegetable oil
300 ml tamarind juice
125 g palm sugar, shaved

1 Chop the chillies, onions and garlic and then blend in a food processor to a fine paste with the oil.

2 Cook the chilli mixture in a heavy, wide-based braising pan on a low heat until the paste changes colour to a dark red. This will take up to 12 hours of continuous slow cooking.

3 Add the tamarind juice and the palm sugar to the chilli paste and cook for a further 2 hours on very low heat.

4 To store, spoon the jam into jars, cover with oil, seal and refrigerate.

lemongrass and chilli paste

This most fragrant paste brings a simple stir-fry to life and gives food a fiery zing. The flavours are released immediately with the application of heat and respond better to a quick, high blast than a slower approach, which only results in a stewy mess. This paste wins the popularity stakes at the Store as the biggest-selling item. Customers feel comfortable using it and stir-frying has become one of the most common cooking methods in the domestic arena these days. This paste keeps for 2 months, refrigerated.

10 stalks lemongrass
12 red bird's-eye chillies
15 cloves garlic
8 coriander roots
6 fresh kaffir lime leaves
200 ml vegetable oil
3 teaspoons black peppercorns, freshly ground
50 ml fish sauce

1 Finely chop the lemongrass, chillies, garlic, coriander roots and lime leaves (doing this before blending the ingredients makes a finer paste).

2 Blend the chopped ingredients in a food processor with the oil. Add the pepper and fish sauce and blend until the paste is quite fine. Check for taste and adjust if necessary.

3 To store, spoon into a jar, cover with oil, seal and refrigerate.

harissa

Like chilli jam, harissa can be eaten as is. It is the North African counterpart of the Asian sambals, though very much hotter as it has not been mellowed with cooking or by the addition of sugar. Harissa is a relish served as an enhancer of salads, cooked fish and meats and is an automatic addition to couscous. Test the water, so to speak, and then use accordingly. Harissa seems to keep, refrigerated, forever!

75 g dried large red chillies, chopped
100 ml water
2 large cloves garlic, minced
2 teaspoons cummin seeds, roasted and ground
¼ teaspoon caraway seeds, ground
1 teaspoon sea salt
50 ml tomato purée
60 ml olive oil

1 Soak the chopped chilli in the water for 2 hours.

2 Blend the chilli, water and garlic in a food processor to a purée. Add the spices, salt and tomato purée and blend well. With the motor running, slowly pour in the olive oil and mix thoroughly.

3 To store, spoon into a jar, cover with oil, seal and refrigerate.

laksa paste

This chilli paste has its origins in the Nyonya cooking of Malaysia and Singapore, food that is renowned for it heady spiciness and richness. Laksa paste needs to be cooked to make it palatable and desirable. The heat brings out the subtlety of the flavours as they infuse the added liquid, usually stock and coconut milk. It is a great paste to have on hand to throw together a fabulous soup at the last minute and it keeps for 1 month, refrigerated.

2 teaspoons belacan (shrimp paste)
2 small red onions, chopped
4 cloves garlic, sliced
1 teaspoon lime zest
1 stalk lemongrass, finely sliced
1 teaspoon freshly chopped galangal
1 teaspoon freshly chopped turmeric
4 red bird's-eye chillies
25 g candlenuts
1 teaspoon dried prawns, roasted and ground
2 dried chillies, roasted and ground
1 teaspoon coriander seeds, roasted and ground
2 coriander roots, chopped
1 teaspoon turmeric powder
1 tablespoon coriander leaves
1 tablespoon Vietnamese mint leaves
120 ml vegetable oil

1 Dry-roast the belacan in a frying pan over a medium heat. (This brings out the flavour of the paste.) Blend all the ingredients together in a food processor until a smooth paste forms.

2 To store, spoon into a jar, cover with oil, seal and refrigerate.

aromatic curry paste

Curry has become a common element of everyday cooking in Australia. Long gone are the Anglo-Saxon bastardisations, where everything from canned pineapple, apple, sultanas and cream were added to the bland curry powders that were synonymous with the 'exotic' cooking of the fifties and sixties. Our shelves have been invaded with myriad choices and we are learning about the subtleties of curry flavours as well as developing an understanding of their complexities and origins.

The making of curry powders and pastes is considered an art in Asian countries: the blending of spices is the essence of cooking in India, just as curry pastes are of prime importance in Thai cooking.

Combinations vary according to regions and the types of food they are to be cooked with and all are distinctive. This particular curry paste is inspired by the flavours of southern India and the combination of spices makes for a heady, aromatic and slightly sweet concoction. It can simply be infused in coconut milk, along with your desired choice of protein, or used as a marinade for meat or fish to be barbecued or grilled. This curry paste keeps for 2 months, refrigerated.

1 large brown onion, finely diced
3 cloves garlic, minced
1 tablespoon freshly minced young ginger
40 ml vegetable oil
2 teaspoons turmeric powder
2 teaspoons dried red chillies, roasted and ground
2 teaspoons cummin seeds, roasted and ground
3 teaspoons coriander seeds, roasted and ground
1 teaspoon white peppercorns
pinch of freshly grated nutmeg
seeds of 2 cardamom pods, ground
100 ml tomato purée
4 ripe tomatoes, peeled and roughly diced
200 ml coconut cream
1 stick cinnamon
10 fresh curry leaves
50 ml fish sauce

1 Fry the onion, garlic and ginger in the oil in a wide-based frying pan until softened and aromatic. Add the spices and stir over the heat until they become fragrant. Stir in the tomato purée and diced tomato and cook until soft.

2 Pour in the coconut cream and add the cinnamon and curry leaves. Cook, uncovered, for 20 minutes on a low to medium heat, stirring often to prevent sticking, until the paste thickens. Add the fish sauce, taste and adjust if necessary.

3 To store, spoon into jars and refrigerate.

spiced tomato and chilli pickle

This paste is of Indian origin and rich in spices and the sweetness of the tomatoes is balanced by the gentle heat of the chilli. It is an adaptation of the tomato kasaundi in Charmaine Solomon's Complete Asian Cookbook. *It is a variation of the traditional tomato chutney, pickle or relish served as a condiment with Indian breads and fish dishes. The paste has the appearance of chutney and has the sweet-sour-spicy characteristic of Indian preserves. It is made even more luscious when a lashing of butter is quickly stirred into it once it has been heated. This pickle keeps well for 2 months, refrigerated.*

1 tablespoon brown mustard seeds
125 ml cider vinegar
2 teaspoons turmeric powder
pinch of ground cloves
2 tablespoons cummin seeds, roasted and ground
125 ml vegetable oil
2 tablespoons freshly minced ginger
10 cloves garlic
10 red bird's-eye chillies
2 kg ripe tomatoes, peeled and quartered
75 g palm sugar, shaved
60 ml fish sauce

1 In a small saucepan, cook the mustard seeds in the vinegar for 10 minutes. Remove from the heat and allow to cool for 2 hours.

2 In a large saucepan, fry the turmeric, cloves and cummin gently in the oil until fragrant.

3 Purée the ginger, garlic, chillies, mustard seeds and vinegar in a food processor until smooth and add to the oil and spices with the tomato quarters. Cook for 1 hour on a low heat, stirring often.

4 Add the palm sugar and fish sauce to the saucepan. Cook for 30 minutes on a low heat. Taste and adjust if necessary.

5 To store, spoon into jars, cover with oil, seal and refrigerate.

crispy-skinned, twice-cooked baby chicken with sticky black rice and chilli jam

This has been one of our menu staples since the early days of the Paragon and the demand for it remains constant. The technique for the preparation of the chickens is a classic Chinese one that results in the birds taking on the aromatic flavours of the stock and the skin developing a lacquered and crisp appearance. The flavours used in the stock are reinforced in the black rice and the Chilli Jam balances the spices and the textures, giving a hot sweetness.
The Master Stock can be used and reused, its flavour intensifying with age, so once you have made it, use it or boil it once a week and it will live on almost indefinitely. The sticky rice can be prepared in advance and reheated just before serving, if you like. To do so, spoon the cooled rice into individual oiled moulds and steam for 10 minutes.

6 × 500 g baby chickens
6 litres vegetable oil for deep-frying
1 tablespoon sea salt
2 teaspoons five-spice powder
1 teaspoon sichuan peppercorns, roasted and ground
6 teaspoons Chilli Jam (see page 34)

Master Stock
3 litres chicken stock
300 ml dark soy sauce (preferably Elephant brand)
250 ml light soy sauce
100 ml Chinese brown rice wine (shaosing)
1 small lump yellow rock sugar (about 1 tablespoon)
2 whole star anise
1 piece cassia bark
1 teaspoon fennel seeds
1 teaspoon sichuan peppercorns
1 black cardamom pod, cracked open
2 pieces dried tangerine peel
2 red bird's-eye chillies
4 slices fresh ginger
2 slices fresh galangal
3 pieces licorice root

Sticky Black Rice
1 brown onion, finely diced
2 red bird's-eye chillies, finely diced
2 cloves garlic, finely diced
1 teaspoon freshly diced ginger
50 ml vegetable oil
2 pieces dried tangerine peel, soaked and cleaned
1 teaspoon fennel seeds, roasted and ground
2 black dates, minced
250 g sticky (glutinous) black rice, washed
750 ml chicken stock
25 ml fish sauce
1 teaspoon black pepper, freshly ground

1 To make the Master Stock, bring all the ingredients to a boil in a large stockpot. Cook for 1 hour on a gentle simmer and then strain through a fine-mesh sieve. Discard the refuse and bring the Master Stock to a boil in a 10 litre stockpot.

2 Clean the chickens and remove the wings at the elbow. Dry thoroughly with a clean tea towel, inside and out.

3 Turn the stock down to a mere simmer and submerge the chickens, making sure they are completely covered. Cook the chickens for 18 minutes and remove immediately with a wire sieve, being careful not to damage the skin. At no time during this process should the stock be allowed to boil.

4 Cover a tray with a clean, dry tea towel and drain any residual stock from the chickens. Place chickens breast-side down on the tray and refrigerate overnight.

5 Make the Sticky Black Rice before finishing off the chickens (the whole process takes about 30 minutes). Fry the onion, chilli, garlic and ginger in the oil in a large saucepan until aromatic and softened. Finely mince the tangerine peel and stir into the onion mixture with the ground fennel and dates and cook for a minute or two. Add the rice and fry a little more, stirring to coat the rice in the spices and the oil.

6 Bring the chicken stock to a boil and add to the rice. Cook over a low heat until the liquid has been absorbed. The rice should be sticky but not soggy or sloppy. Stir the fish sauce and pepper into the rice and set aside.

7 Just before serving, heat the vegetable oil to 180°C in a deep-fryer or a deep saucepan. Deep-fry the chickens 2 or 3 at a time for 5 minutes, depending on the size and capacity of your deep-fryer. Drain well.

8 Remove the chickens from the oil and drain upright on paper towel to allow any oil to escape. Cut each bird into quarters and remove the backbone by cutting along either side of it. Then separate the legs from the breasts by slicing through, following the line of the leg.

9 Put the rice into the centre of each serving plate and sit the two breast pieces on either side of the rice. Place the 2 legs on top of the breasts so the bird appears to have been rejoined.

10 Mix together the sea salt, five-spice powder and the ground sichuan peppercorns and sprinkle over the meat.

11 Spoon the Chilli Jam on top of the rice and serve immediately.

Serves 6

rare kangaroo medallions with smoked eggplant, harissa and spicy masala sauce

I take my lead here from the hedonistic flavours and textures of the Middle East but give the dish a particularly Australian twist by using kangaroo meat. It is a bold combination that enlivens the palate, the components working together to make a perfect whole. I tend to use strong and complex flavours with kangaroo; it is a meat that holds its own in assertive company, its flavour not being lost in the process. Kangaroo is a beautiful meat to work with, as long as you treat it with care and don't overcook it. The dish works well, too, when lamb, beef or venison is used instead of kangaroo.
The Smoked Eggplant Purée is a variation of the well-known Lebanese baba ghannouj and has been adapted from Claudia Roden's classic New Book of Middle Eastern Food.

1 teaspoon black peppercorns, freshly ground
1 teaspoon coriander seeds, roasted and ground
6 × 150 g kangaroo striploin (sirloin, backstrap or saddle) fillets, trimmed
olive oil
vegetable oil for deep-frying
6 × 2 cm thick slices eggplant
6 teaspoons Harissa (see page 36)

Spicy Masala Sauce
2 teaspoons belacan (shrimp paste)
75 ml vegetable oil
25 ml sesame oil
1 brown onion, finely chopped
4 large cloves garlic, finely chopped
1 tablespoon freshly minced ginger
2 slices fresh galangal, finely chopped
5 red bird's-eye chillies, finely chopped
2 slices fresh turmeric, finely chopped
4 coriander roots, minced
1 teaspoon sichuan peppercorns, roasted and ground
2 teaspoons dried prawns, roasted and ground
1 teaspoon cumin seeds, roasted and ground
2 teaspoons coriander seeds, roasted and ground
1 teaspoon turmeric powder
pinch of freshly grated nutmeg
8 fresh curry leaves
1 stick cinnamon
100 ml tomato purée
150 ml coconut cream
50 g palm sugar, shaved
1.5 litres beef or veal demi-glace
25 ml fish sauce

Smoked Eggplant Purée
4 large eggplants, smoked and peeled
8 cloves garlic
2 teaspoons sea salt
180 ml tahini
120 ml lemon juice, strained
1 teaspoon cumin seeds, roasted and ground
200 ml virgin olive oil

1 To make the Spicy Masala Sauce, dry-roast the belacan in a frying pan over a medium heat.

2 Heat a large, wide-based saucepan, add the oils and fry the onion, garlic, ginger, galangal, chilli, fresh turmeric and coriander roots until the onion just begins to take on colour.

3 Add the dried prawns and spices, stirring until the mixture becomes fragrant. Stir in the tomato purée, coconut cream and palm sugar and cook on a gentle heat for a few minutes until the mixture starts to bubble.

4 Add the demi-glace to the saucepan, bring to a boil, then reduce the heat and simmer the sauce for 1 hour to reduce until the sauce coats the back of a spoon. Skim to remove any excess oil and scum. Remove from the heat, sieve to extract all juices, and discard the cooked solids. Add the fish sauce, taste and adjust the seasoning if necessary. Set aside.

5 To make the Smoked Eggplant Purée, squeeze out any liquid from the warm eggplants, then chop them. Blend the garlic with the salt in a food processor. Add the chopped eggplant and blend until smooth. Add the tahini and lemon juice alternately, pulsing between additions, and then add the cummin. With the motor still running, slowly pour in the olive oil until a smooth paste forms. Refrigerate until required.

6 To prepare the meat, mix the pepper and coriander and sprinkle over the kangaroo fillets. Brush well with olive oil.

7 Heat a heavy-based frying pan large enough to hold the fillets in a single layer until very hot. Sear the oiled meat on both sides for 2–3 minutes. Do not overcook. Rest in a warm place for 5 minutes.

8 Heat the vegetable oil in a deep-fryer and fry the eggplant rounds until golden on both sides. Drain.

9 To serve, reheat the Smoked Eggplant Purée in a steamer and bring the sauce to a boil. Check the meat; it may need to be reheated in a hot oven for 1 minute. Spoon $1\frac{1}{2}$ tablespoons of the purée in the centre of each serving plate and top with a disc of fried eggplant. Cut each kangaroo fillet into 4 or 5 slices and arrange on top of the eggplant. Spoon some sauce around the purée and add a teaspoon of Harissa to the top of the meat.

Serves 6

clay pot of red emperor fillets with aromatic curry sauce and rice pilaf

This is a popular and convenient way of serving a curry at the table in an elegant manner. The fish curry is gently cooked in two clay or sand pots that are taken straight from the oven to the table. Clay pots in varying sizes can be found in Asian food stores at very reasonable prices. They need to be seasoned when new and should not be placed on a direct flame or heat. Cooking in a clay pot allows the natural juices of the food to be sealed in.

12 bok choy hearts
900 g red emperor fillets (or any other reef or white flesh fish), cleaned and trimmed
6 snake beans, cut into 3 cm lengths
coriander leaves to garnish

Curry Sauce
18 red shallots, peeled
vegetable oil
6 tablespoons Aromatic Curry Paste (see page 38)
600 ml coconut milk
600 ml fish stock
6 large red chillies, split open
12 fresh curry leaves
50 ml fish sauce
coriander leaves for garnish

Rice Pilaf
250 g basmati rice
2 brown onions
50 ml vegetable oil
3 cloves garlic
1 tablespoon ghee
1 teaspoon nigella seeds
½ teaspoon cardamom seeds, ground
1 bay leaf
4 whole cloves
½ stick cinnamon
1 litre water
25 g unsalted butter
1½ teaspoons sea salt
1 teaspoon freshly ground black pepper

1 To make the Rice Pilaf, soak the rice in cold water for 1 hour, then rinse and strain.

2 Preheat the oven to 250°C. Finely slice one of the onions lengthwise. In a wide-based braising pan, cook the sliced onion in the oil until golden and slightly crispy. Drain the oil from the onion and set the onion aside.

3 Finely mince the remaining onion and the garlic and cook in the ghee until softened. Add the spices and seasoning to the onion and stir for a minute to release the flavours. Add the washed rice and the water, cover the pan with a lid and cook in the oven for 15 minutes until the rice is cooked and the liquid has been absorbed. Remove the pan from the oven and discard the bay leaf, cloves and cinnamon stick. Add the reserved crispy onion and keep warm. Turn off the oven and open the oven door to help cool it down quickly. (The clay pots need to go into a cool or cold oven in due course.)

4 To make the Curry Sauce, soften the shallots in a little oil in a frying pan over medium heat until golden. Mix the curry paste with the coconut milk and fish stock in a clean saucepan and add the cooked shallots, split chillies and curry leaves. Stir and bring to a boil. Reduce the heat and simmer, uncovered, for 20 minutes, then add the fish sauce.

5 While the sauce is simmering, bring a large saucepan of water to a boil and blanch the bok choy hearts for 1 minute only. Refresh immediately in iced water to stop the cooking and retain the colour. Drain.

6 Put the clay pots into the oven and turn up the heat as far as it will go.

7 Clean and trim the red emperor fillets and cut into 10 cm lengths (the fillets usually divide naturally into about 3 pieces). You should end up with 24 pieces of fish (4 per person) that are all about the same size, which will ensure even cooking.

8 Divide the fish fillets, snake beans and blanched bok choy hearts between the warmed clay pots and spoon the Curry Sauce over. Mix thoroughly with a spoon or pair of tongs. Cover the pots with their lids and return to the oven for 5 minutes until the fish is just cooked.

9 Just before serving, stir the butter through the rice and check the seasoning. Put the hot clay pots on underplates and carefully remove the hot lids. Sprinkle each dish with some coriander leaves and cover the pots with cool lids (so fingers don't get burnt) and take to the table. Serve the hot rice from another bowl or spoon onto serving plates.

Serves 6

duck and fennel sausage with duck livers, spiced lentils and chilli jam

Sausage-making requires time and patience, so if you have neither, buy some spicy sausages from a reliable butcher and proceed with the rest of the recipe. I have included the sausage recipe because the textures and flavours work so well together and the sausages are well worth persevering with. The ingredients will yield about 24 sausages, which need to be hung for at least three days. They will keep for up to 2 weeks in the refrigerator.

120 g red lentils
50 ml olive oil
1 brown onion, minced
3 garlic cloves, minced
3 tablespoons Spiced Tomato and Chilli Pickle (see page 39)
250 ml chicken stock
50 g unsalted butter
1 teaspoon sea salt
1 teaspoon black peppercorns, freshly ground
12 large duck livers, brushed with olive oil
3 handfuls of small spinach leaves, washed and stems removed
6 teaspoons Chilli Jam (see page 34)

Duck and Fennel Sausages
20 sausage skins (available from butchers)
1 × 1.7 kg duck
10 dried shiitake mushrooms
1 tablespoon freshly minced ginger
4 cloves garlic, minced
1 dried chipotle chilli, roasted and ground
2 teaspoons chopped garlic chives
3 tablespoons diced fennel bulb
12 water chestnuts, diced
2 coriander roots, minced
2 drops of sesame oil
2 teaspoons sea salt
1 teaspoon sichuan peppercorns, ground
1 teaspoon white peppercorns, freshly ground

1 To make the Duck and Fennel Sausages, soak the sausage skins in cold, salted water for 24 hours.

2 Remove the flesh and fat from the duck, discard the bones and skin (or keep them to make a stock), chop the meat and fat roughly and refrigerate until very cold. Pass the chilled meat and fat through a mincer on a coarse grind.

3 Soak the mushrooms in a little warm water for 30 minutes to reconstitute them. Drain and slice the mushrooms.

4 In a large bowl, mix together all the sausage ingredients except the skins until well amalgamated and evenly distributed.

5 Drain and wash the sausage skins and fill them with the prepared mixture, using a piping bag and nozzle. Do not overfill the casings or they will burst when you twist them into lengths, so leave a little slack. Twist the filled casings at 10 cm intervals, tie with a piece of string to secure and hang the sausages in the refrigerator for 3 days before using.

6 Soak the lentils for 30 minutes, then drain and wash them.

7 Heat the oil in a wide-based saucepan, add the onion and garlic and sauté until softened. Add the pickle and sauté for a minute or two, stirring, then stir in the washed lentils.

8 Pour the stock into the saucepan, bring to a boil and reduce the heat. Simmer until the liquid has been absorbed by the lentils, which should be soft by this stage. Stir in the butter, salt and pepper.

9 Grill 6 of the sausages until the skins become crisp and they are cooked through (about 5 minutes). Rest in a warm place.

10 Heat a heavy-based frying pan and, when hot, quickly sear the oiled livers on both sides, allowing them to remain quite rare. Remove from the heat.

11 To serve, slice each sausage in half on the diagonal. Stir the spinach leaves into the lentils until they begin to wilt. Spoon the lentils and spinach onto serving plates and top with a sliced sausage, livers and a teaspoonful of Chilli Jam. Serve immediately.

Serves 6

wok-seared tuna and tatsoi with lemongrass, chilli, basil and roasted peanuts

Every time this dish appears on our menu, it almost walks out the door. Make it when you can use the very best tuna in season, preferably sashimi-quality. Its firm flesh responds brilliantly to the lemongrass and chilli and the fast cooking method and with all the basic preparation being done in advance, you can pull a great trick out of your hat in the blink of an eye. As with most Chinese or Asian cooking, the time is consumed in the preparation, making the final cooking and assembly very quick and effortless.
The end result will be much better if each serve is cooked separately in a small wok as the cooking relies on using a quick, high heat to ensure that the ingredients don't stew. Small Teflon woks are available from Asian food stores. The Tamarind Dressing keeps for 3 months, refrigerated.

1 × 1 kg piece yellowfin belly tuna, uncleaned
6 tablespoons Lemongrass and Chilli Paste (see page 35)
70 ml peanut oil
20 ml sesame oil
2 small carrots, cut into julienne
1 long cucumber, shaved lengthwise
6 teaspoons holy basil leaves
12 spring onions, cut into 2 cm pieces
2 large red chillies, cut into julienne
½ daikon radish, cut into julienne
6 handfuls of tatsoi leaves
6 teaspoons raw peanuts, roasted and crushed

Tamarind Dressing
400 ml tamarind juice
60 g palm sugar, shaved
300 ml fresh lime juice, strained
50 ml ginger juice
100 ml fish sauce
50 ml sesame oil

1 Trim the tuna, removing the bloodline, and cut the fish into 2 cm square cubes (you should have about 750 g left after cleaning the fish).

2 Mix the lemongrass paste with the oils in a large bowl and add the tuna cubes. Coat well and marinate for 1–2 hours in the refrigerator.

3 While the tuna is marinating, make the Tamarind Dressing. Heat the tamarind juice with the palm sugar until the sugar has dissolved. Allow to cool.

4 Mix all the dressing ingredients together in a bowl and taste. The three prominent flavours (sweetness from the sugar, sourness from the tamarind and lime and saltiness from the fish sauce) should be in harmony. Adjust if necessary. To store, pour the dressing into jars and refrigerate.

5 Heat the woks and, when hot, add the tuna and marinating juices and toss for 1 minute over a high heat to seal. Add 360 ml of the Tamarind Dressing with the carrot, cucumber, basil, spring onion, chilli and radish and continue to toss with a pair of tongs.

6 Add the tatsoi leaves and toss once. Do not overcook. Pile the stir-fry onto serving plates, sprinkle with the crushed peanuts and serve immediately.

Serves 6

Wok-seared Tuna and Tatsoi with Lemongrass, Chilli, Basil and Roasted Peanuts

prawn and coconut laksa with prawn wontons

Laksa soups have become a perennial favourite snack or meal in everyday eating in Australia, everyone seeming to know of the best *place that makes a laksa, regardless of which city you may be in. Laksa seems to have become the most celebrated dish of Nyonya cooking and we often have our own version of the classic on the Paramount menu, its richness greatly admired and appreciated. The wontons used in this dish can be made up to 2 hours beforehand and refrigerated.*

3 tablespoons Laksa Paste (see page 37)
450 ml coconut milk
450 ml prawn stock
2 teaspoons fresh lime juice, strained
30 ml fish sauce
3 teaspoons fried shallot slices
3 teaspoons coriander leaves
3 red bird's-eye chillies, finely sliced
3 teaspoons Vietnamese mint leaves

Prawn Wontons
120 g green prawn meat, cleaned and minced
1 teaspoon freshly minced galangal
2 fresh kaffir lime leaves, finely shredded
3 teaspoons coriander leaves, chopped
½ teaspoon black peppercorns, freshly ground
18 fresh wonton skins
egg white
rice flour

1 To prepare the Prawn Wontons, mix the prawn meat, galangal, lime leaves, coriander and pepper thoroughly in a bowl.

2 Arrange the wonton skins on a flat, cool surface in a single layer and brush each one with egg white. Spoon a little of the prawn mixture onto the centre of each wonton skin and fold in half to form a triangle. Press the edges to seal. Sprinkle a tray with rice flour and transfer the wontons to it. Sprinkle the tops of the wontons with rice flour and set aside until the soup is ready.

3 To make the soup, stir the Laksa Paste into the coconut milk in a large saucepan and gently bring to a boil. Reduce the heat and simmer, uncovered, for 10 minutes.

4 Add the stock to the saucepan and bring to a boil. Reduce the heat and simmer, uncovered, for a further 15 minutes. Season with the lime juice and fish sauce. Taste and adjust if necessary.

5 Just before serving, add the wontons to the boiling soup for 2 minutes. Ladle the soup into 6 deep bowls, allowing 3 wontons per bowl and garnish with the fried shallot slices, coriander, chilli and Vietnamese mint leaves.

Serves 6

steamed snapper fillet with saffron noodles and spiced tomato chilli sauce

To eat and enjoy fish cooked in this manner is to understand the meaning of ambrosial indulgence and pleasure. Saffron has the ability to bring about such delight and, used in this context, offers a subliminal experience. Use only the freshest firm-textured fish (preferably cut from a large, deep-sea fish) for the best results. Small, thin fillets will not give a good result.

6 × 150 g thick snapper fillets
150 g saffron butter, softened
9 tablespoons Spiced Tomato and Chilli Pickle (see page 39)
9 ripe tomatoes, peeled, seeded and quartered
½ teaspoon sea salt
½ teaspoon black peppercorns, freshly ground

Saffron Noodles
½ teaspoon saffron threads
25 ml reduced tomato essence
225 g plain flour
50 g gluten flour
½ teaspoon sea salt
1 teaspoon white peppercorns, freshly ground
3 large (61 g) eggs
rice flour

1 To make the Saffron Noodles, infuse the saffron in the tomato essence over a gentle heat and allow to cool. Blend all the noodle ingredients except the rice flour in a food processor until the dough forms a ball. Refrigerate the dough, wrapped in plastic foodwrap, for 1 hour.

2 Divide the chilled dough into 6 pieces. Flatten each piece with a rolling pin and then work the dough through the rollers of a pasta machine, starting on the widest setting and working and stretching the dough each time until you reach the second-finest setting. Each time the dough passes through the rollers, sprinkle it with some rice flour to prevent it sticking. Pass each sheet of dough through the spaghetti cutters on the pasta machine. Hang the noodles over a broom handle until ready to cook.

3 Brush the snapper fillets with 60 g of the softened saffron butter.

4 Bring the pickle to a boil in a saucepan and add the tomato and remaining saffron butter. Stir over the heat until the butter has been incorporated. Season with the salt and pepper and keep warm.

5 Bring a saucepan of water to a rapid boil and cook the noodles for 2 minutes, then strain.

6 Grill the snapper fillets for 5–6 minutes depending on their thickness. Be careful not to overcook them.

7 Spoon the tomato sauce onto 6 serving plates, make a nest of saffron noodles in the centre of the sauce puddle and sit the grilled fish on top of the noodles. The fish should be glistening and a rich yellow from the saffron.

Serves 6

Pickled Ginger

Green or young ginger is an integral ingredient in our cooking at the Paramount, invaluable because it gives a spiciness and freshness to prepared foods. It aids digestion, cutting the richness and fattiness of particular dishes, and has a distinctive flavour and aroma that cannot be substituted by any other ingredient. A rhizome that grows on an underground stem just as turmeric and galangal do, ginger is used prolifically in food preparations of Asian origin and particularly in China where it is used in abundance. It is used medicinally as well as in cooking and acts as a preservative and a warming and clarifying agent.

Pickled ginger is a staple of Japanese cooking. Young ginger roots are preserved in a vinegar solution and used as a seasoning and a condiment, traditionally with grilled meats, sashimi and sushi. When we pickle ginger for use in the Restaurant and the Store, we choose ginger that is green. It has been picked at a young age and has not been left in cold storage or allowed to mature: the skin is smooth, translucent and soft and needs little or no peeling, the flesh is firm but not fibrous and the tips have a pink blush. The ginger is cut into tissue-thin slices and covered with a vinegar solution. It is an ingredient I always have on hand to toss into seafood salads, add to stir-fries, sprinkle over fried spring rolls or fish cakes, or as an addition to a plate of thinly sliced raw fish and seafood. The effect of pickling mellows the flavour of the ginger, which gives a refreshing and gentle lift to the ingredients it accompanies.

pickled ginger

Ready for use a few days after pickling, Pickled Ginger keeps for a lengthy time, refrigerated.

300 g green ginger knobs, peeled and trimmed
350 ml rice vinegar
50 ml fresh lime juice, strained
25 ml fish sauce

1 Cut the ginger into extremely fine slices, using either a sharp knife with a fine blade, a mandolin or a sharp, thin-bladed cleaver.

2 Mix the rice vinegar, lime juice and fish sauce together in a jug. Pack the sliced ginger into sterilised jars, cover with the vinegar and mix well. Seal and refrigerate until ready to use.

tea and spice smoked quail with pickled cucumber and ginger

The smoking mixture used in this recipe imparts wonderful aromas to the meat but the kitchen tends to reek afterwards, so keep the window open and the fan on! The quantity given here is sufficient for two 'smokes' and the mixture seems to keep forever.

6 large quails
1 teaspoon five-spice powder
1 teaspoon sea salt
½ teaspoon sichuan peppercorns, roasted and ground
2 small eggplants, smoked, peeled and sliced
2 continental cucumbers
1 tablespoon finely diced red onion
2 tablespoons Pickled Ginger, cut into julienne (see page 52)
2 teaspoons purple basil leaves, finely sliced
2 red radish, cut into julienne
24 small radicchio leaves

Tea and Spice Smoking Mixture
1 tablespoon oolong tea leaves
1 tablespoon jasmine tea
zest of 1 orange
2 pieces dried tangerine peel, broken up
2 tablespoons jasmine rice
2 tablespoons brown sugar
3 whole star anise
2 teaspoons sichuan peppercorns
3 pieces cassia bark

Sweet and Sour Dressing
100 ml vegetable oil
2 red bird's-eye chillies, chopped
2 small cloves garlic, finely sliced
60 ml light soy sauce
100 ml cider vinegar
150 ml sugar syrup

1 Clean the quails and, using a sharp knife, split each one open down the backbone. Flatten the quails and arrange on a tray, skin-side up.

2 Mix together the five-spice powder, sea salt and ground sichuan pepper. Sprinkle this mixture over the quails, cover and cure for 3 hours in the refrigerator. Allow the quails to come back to room temperature before smoking, otherwise the smoking time will be affected.

3 While the quails are curing, make the Tea and Spice Smoking Mixture by combining all the ingredients. Store at room temperature in an airtight container.

4 To make the Sweet and Sour Dressing, heat the oil in a saucepan with the chilli and garlic over a low heat until the garlic becomes golden but does not burn. Add the soy sauce, vinegar and sugar syrup and bring to a boil. Remove from the heat, allow to cool, then strain and store in the refrigerator until ready to use.

5 To smoke the quails, line a large wok with foil. Put a strip of baking paper down the middle of a metal steamer tray that fits neatly over the wok. Be sure to leave some gaps along the sides of the tray when putting in the paper or the smoking will not be as effective.

6 Put the foil-lined wok, without the steamer tray in position, over a high flame or heat. Arrange the quails skin-side up on the baking paper in the steamer tray, making sure they do not overlap (it may be necessary to do this in 2 batches to ensure even smoking).

7 Sprinkle 4 tablespoons of the smoking mixture over the base of the hot wok and, when it starts to smoke seriously and burn at the edges, place the steamer tray with the quails over it and cover the wok with a tight-fitting lid. Use foil to secure the lid further, if necessary. (This must be done under an effective exhaust vent or you will smoke and smell out your kitchen.)

8 Smoke the quails for 6 minutes. Remove the steamer tray immediately, fold the burnt foil over on itself and discard outside straight away. (Throw these burnt offerings in the bin when they have cooled down.) Take the quails out of the steamer and allow to cool.

9 Remove the breast meat from the quails, then take the leg meat off the bone and discard the carcasses. Slice the breasts and the leg meat in two.

10 Warm the Sweet and Sour Dressing over a gentle heat. Put the quail meat into half the dressing with the smoked eggplant and marinate for 3 minutes.

11 Using a vegetable peeler, peel the cucumbers and shave into long strips, discarding the skin and the core of seeds. Pickle the cucumber shavings in the remaining dressing in a large bowl for 3 minutes only (any longer and the cucumber will start to disintegrate).

12 Add the remaining ingredients to the cucumber with the quail and eggplant and mix thoroughly to ensure even distribution. Pile carefully onto serving plates and serve immediately.

Serves 6

steamed custards of yabbies, shiitake mushrooms and ginger

These custards are an adaptation of the delicate Japanese chawan-mushi savoury custards that make a perfectly light start to a meal. Don't expect the custards to set firm as the liquid dispelled from the ingredients during the cooking will give the custards a generous wobble and, when the surface is broken with eating, the custard will take on a soupy appearance, which is why they are served in the bowls in which they are steamed. Experiment with other ingredients and come up with your own combinations, remembering these custards are a delicate treat and therefore ingredients with subtle flavours work best.

1.5 litres fish stock
12 green yabbies in their shells
30 ml tomato essence
30 ml mirin
6 fresh shiitake mushrooms, each cut into 5 strips
3 teaspoons Pickled Ginger, cut into julienne (see page 52)
6 teaspoons finely sliced spring onions
2 teaspoons coriander leaves
6 large (61 g) eggs
3 drops chilli oil

1 Put the fish stock in a stockpot and bring to a boil over a high heat. Add the yabbies and reduce the heat to medium, so the stock just bubbles. Cook the yabbies for 2 minutes only, just enough to loosen the flesh from their shells.

2 Remove the yabbies from the stock and plunge into icy water to stop the cooking. Remove the meat from the yabbies, devein the tails and set aside until ready to use. Add the yabby shells to the stock and simmer for 30 minutes.

3 Strain the stock through a fine-mesh sieve or piece of muslin and measure out 900 ml (reserve the remaining stock for later use). Return the 900 ml stock to the heat in a clean saucepan, add the tomato essence and the mirin and simmer for 5 minutes. Remove from the heat and allow to cool.

4 Bring a large saucepan of water to a gentle boil.

5 Arrange 6 small Japanese or Chinese round-based bowls on a metal steamer tray that will fit snugly over the saucepan of boiling water. To each bowl add 2 yabby tails, 5 slices of mushroom, 1/2 teaspoon of ginger, 1 teaspoon of sliced spring onions and a few coriander leaves.

6 Gently whisk together the eggs, chilli oil and 960 ml of the reserved stock without aerating the mixture and pour carefully over the ingredients in the bowls.

7 Place the steamer tray over the saucepan of gently boiling water and cover with a tight-fitting lid. Reduce the heat to low so the water is just simmering (any more than this and the custards will separate). Steam for 20 minutes or until the custards have just set and still have a slight wobble in the centre.

8 Remove the steamer from the heat and carefully take out the bowls of custard. Serve immediately with each bowl on a flat underplate with a napkin between the two to prevent sliding.

Serves 6

seared beef fillet with
lemongrass, ginger and pickled green papaya

A refreshing and easy warm salad to make, with great flavours that tingle the palate. Serve as an entrée or as part of a combination of dishes served together. The Pickled Green Papaya will keep, refrigerated, for 1 month.

500 g beef eye fillet, trimmed
30 ml vegetable oil
200 ml Tamarind Dressing (see page 44)
1 stalk lemongrass, finely minced
1 red bird's-eye chilli, minced
2 coriander roots, finely minced
2 fresh kaffir lime leaves, finely shredded
zest of 1 lime
2 teaspoons minced galangal
1 teaspoon minced ginger
1 teaspoon dried shrimp, roasted and ground
1 teaspoon jasmine rice, roasted and ground
1 teaspoon sesame seeds

Pickled Ginger Salad
6 teaspoons pickled ginger, drained
6 cm daikon radish, peeled and finely shredded
1/2 cucumber, peeled, seeded and finely sliced lengthwise
12 red shallots finely sliced
1 tablespoon finely shredded Vietnamese mint leaves
2 cups watercress leaves

Pickled Green Papaya
1 small green papaya
100 ml fresh lime juice, strained
80 ml fish sauce
60 g palm sugar, shaved
1 red bird's-eye chilli, minced

1 To make the Pickled Green Papaya, wash the papaya and quarter it lengthwise. Remove the seeds and slice very finely using a mandolin or slicer. Mix the rest of the ingredients together and add the sliced papaya. Allow to pickle for at least 3 days before using.

2 Brush the beef fillet with the oil and sear on all sides very quickly in a hot pan over high heat, ensuring that the meat remains very rare in the middle. Remove from the pan and rest in a warm place for 10 minutes.

3 In a large bowl, mix together the remaining ingredients. Rest the beef fillet in the dressing for 5 minutes, turning once.

4 In another bowl, mix together the salad ingredients.

5 Slice the beef into 1 cm thick slices and mix with the salad. Add enough dressing to wet the ingredients without drowning them and pile onto 6 serving plates. Top with some slices of the Pickled Green Papaya and add a little extra dressing if necessary. Serve immediately.

Serves 6

blue swimmer crab, shaved coconut and mint salad with fried shallots

This dish, with its clean and refreshing flavours, is the perfect summer salad or light entrée for a lunch or dinner and a must for when the crabs are at their best. While I recommend using blue swimmer crabs here, it also works very well with mudcrabs. Its success lies in everything being absolutely fresh and very fine knife work, so that the flavours and textures work harmoniously together. The Coconut Dressing keeps well for a week, refrigerated.

6 uncooked blue swimmer crabs (to yield 500 g crab meat)
3 tablespoons finely shaved fresh coconut flesh
6 spring onions, finely sliced
1 large red chilli, seeded and very finely sliced
1 tablespoon Pickled Ginger, cut into julienne (see page 52)
½ cucumber, seeded and cut into julienne
1 tablespoon mint leaves, finely shredded
2 tablespoons Vietnamese mint leaves, finely shredded
1 tablespoon coriander leaves
3 teaspoons finely sliced red shallots
8 fresh kaffir lime leaves, very finely shredded
2 handfuls of mitsuba leaves, washed
betel or banana leaves for serving (optional)
6 teaspoons fried shallot slices

Coconut Lime Dressing
100 ml fresh lime juice, strained
100 ml coconut vinegar
25 ml fish sauce
25 ml sugar syrup
2 pinches of freshly ground black pepper
3 drops sesame oil
25 ml olive oil

1 To make the Coconut Lime Dressing, whisk the ingredients together in a bowl. Taste for seasoning and adjust if necessary. Refrigerate in a sealed container until ready to use.

2 Fill a stockpot large enough to fit the crabs with water and bring to a boil. When the water reaches a rolling boil, add the crabs and cook for 6 minutes (10 minutes if using mudcrabs). Remove the crabs from the water and immediately plunge them into icy-cold water to prevent further cooking. Remove the flesh from the crabs and discard the shells (or reserve them to make a crab stock for later use). Ensure that the crab meat is free of any hard membrane and shell.

3 In a large bowl, mix together the crab meat, coconut, spring onion, chilli, ginger, cucumber, mints, coriander, red shallots and lime leaves. Pour in the dressing and allow to stand for 3 minutes only, just long enough for the flavours to mingle.

4 Dry the mitsuba leaves thoroughly. Toss the leaves in the dressed crab and mix carefully.

5 If desired, arrange betel leaves or a round of banana leaf on each serving plate. Pile the salad onto the plates and sprinkle over the fried shallot slices. Serve immediately.

Serves 6

Blue Swimmer Crab, Shaved Coconut and Mint Salad with Fried Shallots

Mustard and Horseradish Pastes

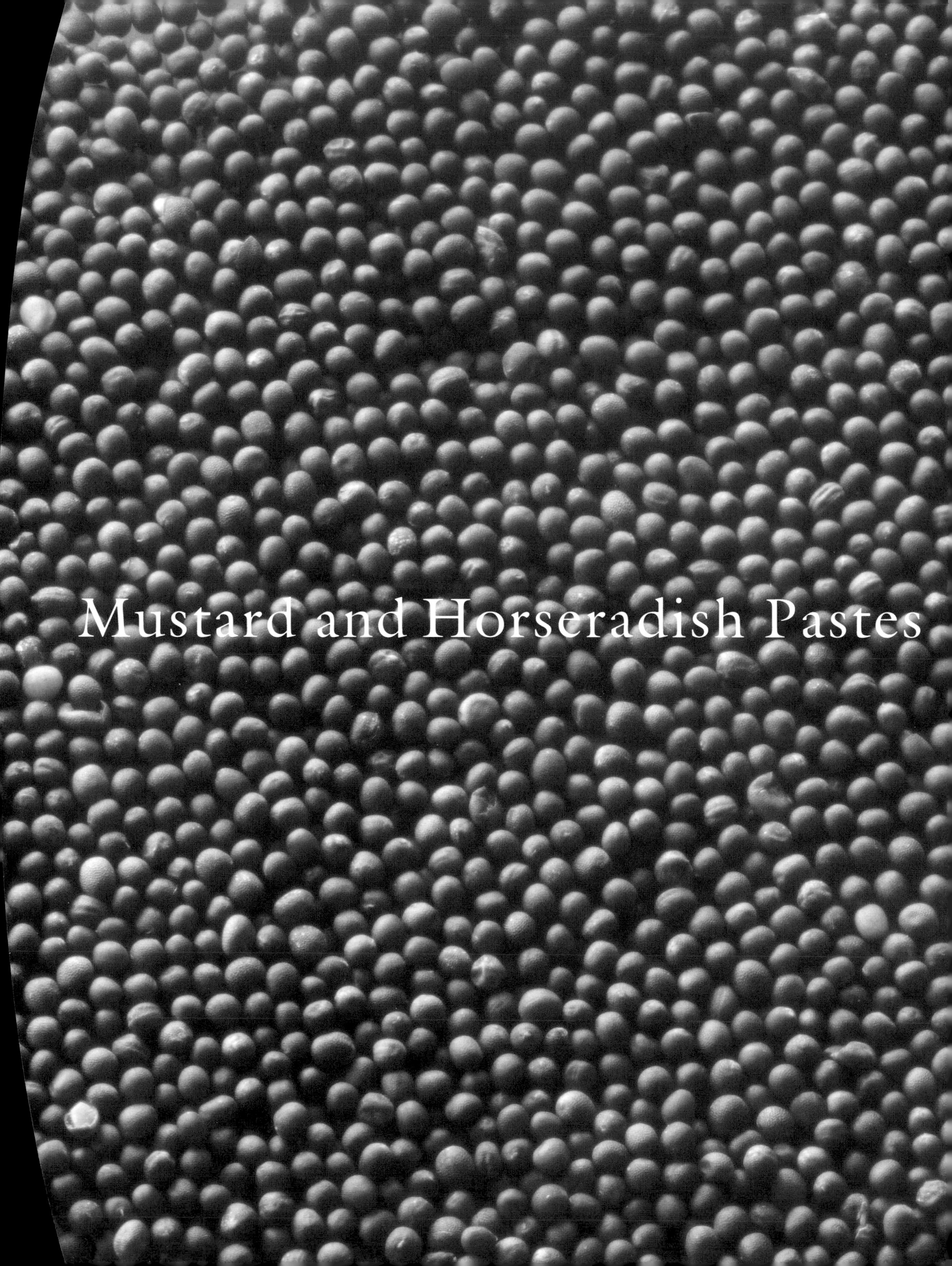

Horseradish and mustard are two of the world's strongest and most evocative tastes, ones that are acquired and usually associated with the adult palate rather than infant or adolescent desires. Both are members of the cabbage family but infinitely more challenging than the common garden-variety cabbage.

Horseradish grows as a long, cylindrical root and has an appearance similar to parsnip, with a brownish skin and creamy-white, firm flesh. Its flavour is hot and pungent. Historically, it appears that horseradish was used for medicinal purposes long before it was held in any culinary regard. It has been referred to as having warming and cleansing properties as well as being an appetite enhancer. Today, it can be found in many cuisines of the world as it grows easily everywhere, particularly near the sea.

Prepared horseradish does not have the invigorating quality of fresh horseradish, which becomes quite apparent when peeling and grating the root. It is worth the effort of seeking out a supply of fresh horseradish if you find yourself addicted to the taste, or if you are a purist at heart. Select roots that are straight, dry and hard and keep them in plastic in a cool, dry place for up to a month. Horseradish loses its sharpness and pungency as soon as heat is applied, so for maximum flavour and benefit it is added to hot food at the last minute or mixed with either vinegar or sour cream to disguise its potency. Grated finely and mixed with a little wine vinegar, horseradish also preserves well.

Once a year, mustard plants yield brown, black or white seeds, depending on the variety. The black seeds are the hottest and not commonly available as they need to be harvested by hand. The brown seeds are larger and milder than the black and the white seeds, which in fact are pale-yellow, are the seeds most readily available on the market and commonly used in mustard preparations. Dijon in France is noted for its unparalleled production and preparation of mustard. It is a condiment in its own right, aids digestion and is similar to horseradish in that it has a distinctive, sharp and pungent flavour that dissipates when applied to high heat. Mustard is a natural thickening or binding agent but does not respond well to boiling as it tends to separate, so when adding it to a sauce, watch it carefully. There are many varieties available – French, English, German, American, smooth, seeded and flavoured – so use a mustard that is appropriate for what you are serving. Mustard, whatever variety, is very versatile as a flavour enhancer and is a necessity for any kitchen.

At the Store we always stock a few items based on mustard or horseradish, pastes that can enliven a basic food item and make the cooking process a quick and painless operation when time is of the essence and flavour is essential. The base recipes in this chapter are also in constant use in the Restaurant in many of our preparations, due to the strength of flavour and complexity they offer.

garlic and mustard marinade paste

This paste enriches the flavour of any meat marinated in it. It can also be used to coat poultry or oily fish that is to be barbecued; mixed with a stuffing to give a more complex flavour; added to a dressing for a warm potato salad, or cooked into a basic cream sauce to serve with chicken or white-fleshed fish. It will keep for up to 3 weeks in the refrigerator.

10 large cloves garlic, minced
3 tablespoons smooth Dijon mustard
5 tablespoons thyme leaves
2½ teaspoons freshly ground black pepper
125 ml lemon juice, strained
150 ml olive oil

Put all the ingredients except the oil in a food processor and pulse to a paste. With the motor still running, drizzle the oil in gradually and process until smooth. Put the paste into a container, seal and refrigerate until required.

horseradish cream

This luscious cream is a great one to keep on hand for giving snacks a lift. It makes grilled meat or sausages more appealing and is wonderful spooned onto scrambled eggs with smoked salmon or used to spike a savoury tart. It keeps for a week refrigerated and is best made several hours ahead.

3 tablespoons crème fraîche or sour cream
1 tablespoon finely grated fresh horseradish
½ teaspoon freshly ground white pepper
2 teaspoons finely chopped chives

Gently mix all the ingredients together in a bowl with a spoon. Keep refrigerated in an airtight container until ready to use.

mustard and horseradish relish

The headiness and pungency of mustard and horseradish sit well together and make this relish a great accompaniment to cold meats, smoked fish, root vegetables, cooked offal (such as liver, brains or sweetbreads) and a charcuterie plate. It will keep, refrigerated, for 2 weeks.

2 tablespoons seeded Dijon mustard
1 tablespoon hot smooth mustard
1 tablespoon freshly grated horseradish
2 teaspoons castor sugar
1 teaspoon white peppercorns, freshly ground
2 tablespoons tiny capers, washed
3 teaspoons tarragon leaves
5 tablespoons Aïoli (see page 76)

Mix together all the ingredients except the Aïoli. Stir this mixture into the Aïoli. The relish should be quite firm with enough body to hold its own weight. To store, spoon into a container, seal and refrigerate.

smoked salmon with potato pikelet, nori omelette and horseradish cream

This dish has been with us since our days at the Paragon and the combination of flavours is a perennial favourite. The effect of stacking one layer upon another gives it a spectacular appearance, demanding that it be noticed and tasted immediately. The Pikelet Mix lasts for about 5 hours before it starts to oxidise, so don't make it too far in advance.

12 slices smoked salmon
6 teaspoons Horseradish Cream (see page 63)
2 teaspoons chopped chives
3 teaspoons fresh salmon roe

Pikelet Mix
350 g waxy potatoes, peeled and chopped
2 teaspoons chopped chives
1 large (61 g) egg
1 tablespoon plain flour
1 teaspoon freshly grated horseradish
1 teaspoon wasabi powder
1 teaspoon sea salt
½ teaspoon freshly ground black pepper
50 ml thick (45%) cream

Nori Omelettes
12 large (61 g) eggs
pinch of sea salt
½ teaspoon black pepper, freshly ground
1 teaspoon sesame oil
1 teaspoon fish sauce
2 nori seaweed sheets, toasted
vegetable oil

1 Make the Pikelet Mix by briefly blending all the ingredients except the cream in a food processor. Add the cream and pulse until just incorporated. Pour the mixture into a plastic jug, cover and refrigerate until ready to use.

2 To make the Nori Omelettes, whisk the eggs until light but not aerated and season with the salt, pepper, sesame oil and fish sauce. Cut the nori into short strips and stir into the egg mixture.

3 Heat a 20 cm Teflon frying pan and brush lightly with oil. Ladle in 40 ml of the egg mixture and spread thinly over the pan as you would a crêpe. Cook until just set and turn out onto a clean tea towel. Continue the process with the remaining mixture, stacking the omelettes on top of each other.

4 Roll up each omelette into a roulade, then wrap firmly in plastic foodwrap, securing the ends to keep the shape firm and intact. Allow to cool for 30 minutes before slicing.

5 To cook the pikelets, heat a Teflon frying pan and oil it lightly. Pour the Pikelet Mix into 6 oiled egg rings (you may need to do 3 at a time, depending on the size of your pan). Cook over a medium heat until bubbles start to appear in the batter. Flip the pikelets over to cook on the other side.

6 To assemble, cut the rolled omelettes into 1.5 cm thick slices (you will need 6 slices). Place a hot pikelet in the centre of each serving plate and top with an omelette slice. Add 2 slices of the smoked salmon, rolled into a rosette, if you desire, per plate, then a teaspoon of the Horseradish Cream and sprinkle with chives and salmon roe. Serve immediately.

Serves 6

rare venison pepper steak with glazed beetroots and horseradish cream

This dish is so vibrant, it almost speaks to you. Venison is one of those meats best cooked and eaten rare if you are to appreciate its flavour and texture. Because it has no fat, like kangaroo, it quickly becomes tough and chewy if it is overcooked or not rested properly, losing its tenderness and moisture. As it is an expensive cut of meat, treat it with the respect it deserves. The flavour of the meat is highlighted by the strength of the beetroot and horseradish, a harmonious combination. You may want to turn your oven up high just before serving in case the venison needs to be reheated for a minute or two. This recipe makes twice as much Pepper Glaze as required; the remainder can be frozen.

3 teaspoons cracked black pepper
6 × 175 g venison medallions, cut from the trimmed striploin (sirloin, backstrap or saddle) fillet
18 small beetroots, trimmed and peeled
50 g unsalted butter
50 ml olive oil
pinch of sea salt
pinch of black pepper, freshly ground
a little extra olive oil
2 teaspoons freshly grated horseradish
6 teaspoons Horseradish Cream (see page 63)

Pepper Glaze
1 brown onion, chopped
3 large cloves garlic, sliced
3 sprigs of fresh thyme
1 tablespoon black peppercorns
½ tablespoon sichuan peppercorns
100 ml brandy
200 ml red wine (preferably shiraz)
2 litres veal or beef demi-glace

Beetroot Purée
50 g unsalted butter
6 beetroots, peeled and sliced
2 small waxy potatoes, peeled and sliced
75 ml thick (45%) cream
½ teaspoon sea salt
½ teaspoon black peppercorns, freshly ground

1 To make the Pepper Glaze, heat a large stockpot, brush it with a film of oil and fry the onion, garlic, thyme and peppercorns until the onion has softened and the mixture is fragrant. Add the brandy and flame it, then add the red wine. Cook until reduced by a third and then add the demi-glace.

2 Bring the glaze to a boil and then reduce the heat. Simmer for 1 hour until reduced by half. Skim the surface occasionally to remove any scum and keep the glaze clear.

3 Pass the glaze through a conical sieve and then a fine-mesh sieve to remove all sediment and coarse particles. Taste and add some ground black pepper if necessary. Set aside until ready to use.

4 To make the Beetroot Purée, preheat the oven to 200°C and grease a gratin dish generously with most of the butter. Add the sliced beetroot and potato in layers and dot with the remaining butter. Pour over the cream and season with salt and pepper. Cover with foil and bake for 30 minutes or until the beetroot is soft when tested with a skewer. Purée the beetroot and potato in a food processor and then transfer to a blender and purée again until very fine. Taste for seasoning and adjust if necessary. Set aside.

5 Cut the beetroots into quarters lengthwise. Heat the butter and oil in a frying pan and, when foaming, add the beetroot slices and toss to coat. Cook on a low heat, stirring regularly, until the beetroots have softened and become glazed. Season with salt and pepper and set aside until ready to serve.

6 Sprinkle the cracked black pepper evenly over both sides of the venison medallions. Heat a heavy-based frying pan until very hot. Add a splash of olive oil and immediately toss in the peppered venison and seal for 2 minutes per side. Rest the meat in a warm place for 10 minutes.

7 While the meat is resting, gently reheat the Beetroot Purée in a steamer and bring the Pepper Glaze to a boil in a saucepan. Add the glazed beetroot slices to the sauce and simmer for 5 minutes. Stir the grated horseradish into the sauce just before serving.

8 To serve, put the meat into a hot oven for 1–2 minutes, if necessary. Spoon the purée onto the centre of 6 serving plates, cut each piece of venison into 4 thick slices and lay on top of the purée and arrange the beetroots and sauce around the meat. Add a teaspoonful of Horseradish Cream to the meat and serve immediately.

Serves 6

Rare Venison Pepper Steak with Glazed Beetroots and Horseradish Cream

mudcrab omelette with horseradish cream and caviar

This is food for the gods, an ethereal taste sensation created by a combination of flavours: the sweetness of the crab meat, the iodine saltiness of the caviar and the creaminess of the omelette and the horseradish cream. Make it with tender, loving care and your pains will be rewarded with heavenly applause and lip-smacking responses. The omelettes work best if made individually, so have on hand a couple of small 15 cm Teflon omelette or frying pans to cook two at a time.

2 × 1 kg uncooked mudcrabs
12 large (61 g) eggs
a few drops of sesame oil
25 ml mirin
25 ml fish sauce
3 teaspoons freshly chopped chives
2 pinches of freshly ground white pepper
60 g unsalted butter
6 teaspoons Horseradish Cream (see page 63)
6 teaspoons osietra or sevruga caviar
virgin olive oil
extra chives for garnish

1 Bring a large saucepan of water to a rolling boil, add the crabs and cook for 6 minutes. The shells will go red during the cooking process and the meat will be easier to remove from the shell. Remove the crabs from the saucepan and immerse in icy-cold water to stop the cooking process. When the crabs have cooled enough to handle, take out of the water and remove the meat. (Keep the shells to make a stock for a soup base, if desired.)

2 Lightly whisk the eggs in a bowl and stir in the sesame oil, mirin, fish sauce, chives and pepper.

3 To make the omelette, heat two 15 cm Teflon frying pans until warm and preheat the griller of your stove. Add a teaspoon of butter to each pan and, as it melts, pour in enough omelette mixture to coat the base generously. As the omelette begins to set on the bottom, sprinkle on some crab meat so it cooks into the soft egg. Flash the pans under the heated griller for a few seconds to seal the top of the omelettes and immediately turn out onto serving plates. Fold the omelettes over in the middle, being careful not to crack them. Rest the cooked omelettes in a warm place (but not the oven) while cooking the remaining serves. (The cooking process is so quick the omelettes should stay hot until being taken to the table.)

4 Top each omelette with a teaspoon each of Horseradish Cream and caviar, drizzle very lightly with virgin olive oil, sprinkle over a few snipped chives and serve.

Serves 6

milk-fed veal tenderloin with pancetta, creamed parsnips and mustard sauce

Make this dish with the best veal you can lay your hands on; the result will be far superior than if made with yearling beef, which is commonly passed off as veal. The tender age of milk-fed or suckling veal gives it a sublime, buttery and melt-in-the-mouth texture, a quality that cannot be matched. The silkiness of the parsnip cream matches the veal beautifully, as well as blending in with and highlighting the pungency of the mustard.

6 × 150 g veal tenderloin fillets, trimmed
30 thin slices pancetta
50 g unsalted butter
1 kg parsnips, peeled and sliced
175 ml thick (45%) cream
½ teaspoon sea salt
½ teaspoon white peppercorns, freshly ground
2 extra parsnips for chips (optional)
vegetable oil for deep-frying (optional)
2 tablespoons smooth Dijon mustard
200 ml Pepper Glaze (see page 66)

1 Preheat the oven to 180°C. Wrap each piece of veal fillet with five slices of pancetta and set aside.

2 Grease a deep-sided baking dish with most of the butter, add the sliced parsnips and stir in 75 ml of the thick cream and the remaining butter. Sprinkle with salt and pepper, cover with foil and bake for 30 minutes or until the parsnips are cooked when tested with a skewer.

3 Blend the baked parsnip in a food processor to make a thick, smooth cream. Set aside until ready to use. To reheat, spoon the parsnip cream into a baking dish, cover with foil and gently warm in a low oven so the cream does not burn. Remove from the oven and turn the temperature up high (you do this in case the meat needs reheating just before serving).

4 To make parsnip chips, use a vegetable peeler to shave the parsnips lengthwise. Heat the oil in a deep-fryer or deep saucepan and fry the shaved parsnip until crisp but not coloured. Drain on paper towels.

5 Heat a cast-iron or heavy-based frying pan, add a drizzle of oil to prevent the meat from sticking and seal the prepared fillets on all sides. This should take 5–6 minutes, by which time the pancetta will have started to crisp. Allow the meat to rest in a warm place for 8 minutes.

6 Whisk the mustard into the remaining 100 ml of thick cream. Bring the Pepper Glaze to a boil in a saucepan and stir in the mustard cream. Allow the sauce to come back to a boil to incorporate the cream and then remove from the heat.

7 Reheat the veal in the hot oven for 1 minute, if necessary, and then slice each fillet into 3 medallions. Spoon the parsnip cream onto the centre of 6 serving plates and top with the meat. Spoon the sauce around the meat and add some deep-fried parsnip chips, if using.

Serves 6

roasted corn-fed chicken with garlic mustard crust and steamed mustard greens

This dish is a tribute to the quality of the chickens bred by Glenloth Farm at Wycheproof, Victoria, giving us poultry as it should taste, not the battery-hen variety made tasteless and boring by conditions not designed for a quality product. Ask for corn-fed chickens from your supplier and take your tastebuds to new heights. The marinade paste makes this an interesting alternative to the usual roast chicken as it forms a tasty crust, sealing the juices in the meat.

180 g breadcrumbs (made from day-old, crusty white bread)
3 large (61 g) eggs, beaten
6 tablespoons Garlic and Mustard Marinade Paste (see page 62)
6 teaspoons brown mustard seeds
3 × 900 g corn-fed chickens
12 cloves garlic
6 sprigs of thyme
1 teaspoon sea salt
1 teaspoon black peppercorns, freshly ground
100 ml olive oil
150 g mustard greens, washed

1 Preheat the oven to 250°C. In a large bowl, mix together the breadcrumbs, eggs, marinade paste and mustard seeds until well incorporated.

2 Wipe the chickens inside and out with a clean, dry tea towel. Place 4 garlic cloves and 2 sprigs of thyme into the cavity of each bird, and season with salt and pepper.

3 Pack the mustard crust liberally onto the outside of the birds, covering their entire surface, and truss with either a skewer or string. Put the birds in an oiled baking dish and bake for 25 minutes or until cooked. Test with a skewer, piercing the flesh near the leg joint; if the juices are clear with a touch of pink, the chicken is ready. Take the chickens out of the oven and rest in a warm place for 5 minutes.

4 Heat the olive oil in a frying pan until warm. Add the mustard greens, cover immediately with a lid and toss over a medium heat until the greens are wilted but not coloured. Season with salt and pepper and arrange on 6 serving plates.

5 Divide each chicken in two by slicing down the breastbone and backbone, then carve each half in two, separating the leg from the breast. Sit a chicken leg and breast on top of the mustard greens on each plate and pour over any excess pan juices.

Serves 6

seared beef fillet with celeriac and mustard and horseradish relish

This is a celebration of the wonderful celeriac, a root vegetable available during the colder months of the year. It is commonly used in European cooking, particularly French, and has a creamy-coloured flesh that tastes like a celery-flavoured potato. The celeriac harmonises perfectly with the Mustard and Horseradish Relish, so make the most of it when it is in season.

1 × 1.5 kg beef fillet, trimmed
25 ml olive oil
2 teaspoons cracked black pepper
2 heads of celeriac
6 tablespoons Mustard and Horseradish Relish (see page 64)

1 Preheat the oven as high as it will go.

2 Brush the fillet with the oil and sprinkle with the cracked pepper. Bake the beef in a baking dish for 8 minutes. Turn the fillet over and cook a further 5 minutes. The meat should be quite rare. Take the meat out of the oven and rest in a warm place for 10 minutes to allow the juices to settle.

3 Peel the celeriac, then grate it into a bowl of acidulated water to prevent it from discolouring.

4 Bring a saucepan of water to a boil. Take the grated celeriac out of the acidulated water and blanch for 30 seconds in the boiling water. Remove the celeriac with a sieve and run cold water over it to stop the cooking. Drain the celeriac, put it into a bowl and allow to cool. Stir the relish into the cooled celeriac.

5 Cut the hot beef fillet into 1 cm thick slices. Spoon the celeriac on to 6 serving plates. Place the sliced beef on top of the celeriac and serve.

Serves 6

Aïoli

Aïoli, a luscious amalgamation of garlic, egg yolks and olive oil, has its origins in Provençe in the south of France. Essentially a mayonnaise heavily spiked with crushed garlic, it can be served simply with grilled or barbecued fish or meat, stirred at the last minute into a vegetable soup to give it a creamy lift, added to a fish stew as in the French classic *bourride*, spread on sandwiches with cured or smoked meats or spooned onto fried sardines, taken to a picnic and added to a salad at the last minute or served with prepared salt cod, crudités or vegetables. The diversity of its use is a celebration of garlic, an ingredient around which festivals are based.

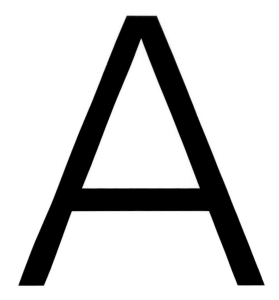

At the Restaurant, we make aïoli in two different ways. One uses freshly crushed garlic which gives a powerful blast to the palate since the garlic is digested raw. The second involves roasting a head of garlic wrapped in foil in the oven until it softens; the roasted garlic is squeezed into the emulsion, giving it a gentle and well-rounded taste. Which is chosen simply depends on the context of the dish and the preferred style. With the addition of some diced roasted red capsicum and a couple of red chillies, you have a more fiery mayonnaise known as rouille. Hailing from Marseilles, in the south of France also, it is traditionally added to bouillabaisse, a fish soup or stew; some of the stock is often used to flavour the mayonnaise.

With all mayonnaise preparations, be careful to add the oil in a thin, steady stream to ensure the emulsion thickens properly and does not separate.

aïoli

It is the emulsion of egg yolks enriched with juicy young garlic that gives Aïoli its distinctive character and taste. Like any other mayonnaise preparation, it keeps for approximately 1 week, refrigerated, in a sealed container.

6 fresh cloves garlic
2 pinches of sea salt
25 ml lemon juice, strained
25 ml white wine vinegar
3 pinches of freshly ground white pepper
2 egg yolks
250 ml virgin olive oil
250 ml vegetable oil

1 Crush the garlic with the salt in a mortar and pestle to release the aroma and flavour the salt.

2 Blend the garlic and salt in a food processor with the lemon juice, vinegar, pepper and egg yolks until well incorporated.

3 With the motor running, slowly drizzle in the combined oils in a thin, steady stream until incorporated and the mayonnaise has become thick.

4 To store, spoon the mayonnaise into a container, seal and refrigerate.

roasted garlic aïoli

This recipe requires roasted garlic but is otherwise made the same way as Aïoli. It keeps for up to 1 week, refrigerated.

1 head of garlic
2 pinches of sea salt
25 ml lemon juice, strained
25 ml white wine vinegar
3 pinches of freshly ground white pepper
2 egg yolks
250 ml virgin olive oil
250 ml vegetable oil

1 Preheat the oven to 180°C and wrap the head of garlic in foil. Bake the garlic for 30 minutes or until soft.

2 Squeeze out the soft garlic cloves and mix with the salt in a mortar and pestle.

3 Blend the garlic and salt in a food processor with the lemon juice, vinegar, pepper and egg yolks until well incorporated.

4 With the motor running, slowly drizzle in the combined oils in a thin, steady stream until incorporated and the mayonnaise has become thick.

5 To store, spoon the mayonnaise into a container, seal and refrigerate.

rouille

Add chilli and capsicum as you make Aïoli (see page 76) for a more fiery alternative.

1 quantity of Aïoli (see page 76)
1 red capsicum, roasted, peeled and chopped
2 bird's-eye chillies, seeded and minced

Make the Aïoli as directed, adding the minced chilli and chopped capsicum to the food processor with the eggs.

snapper and tomato soup with duck-egg pasta and roasted garlic aïoli

The success of this soup relies on using a good, clear, jellied snapper stock as a base. You need to procure a couple of fresh snapper heads to achieve the best results. Aïoli, by its very nature, lends itself to those flavours we associate with the Mediterranean. The Duck-egg Pasta gives the soup an added richness.

30 ml olive oil
1 brown onion, finely chopped
3 cloves garlic, finely chopped
½ small bulb fennel, finely chopped
10 tomatoes, roasted
150 ml tomato purée
100 ml white wine
1 litre fish stock (made with snapper bones)
1 teaspoon sea salt
1 teaspoon black peppercorns, freshly ground
300 g snapper fillet, skin on
2 tablespoons diced tomato
12 flat parsley leaves, finely shredded
6 teaspoons Roasted Garlic Aïoli (see page 77)

Duck-egg Pasta
200 g plain flour
50 g gluten flour
½ teaspoon sea salt
2 large duck eggs
20 ml olive oil
rice flour

1 To make the Duck-egg Pasta, sieve the flours and add to the bowl of a food processor with the salt.

2 Lightly beat the eggs and the oil, and pour into the food processor with the motor running until the dough forms a ball. Wrap the dough in plastic foodwrap and refrigerate for 2 hours.

3 Cut the dough into 5 pieces. Flatten each piece with a rolling pin on a surface lightly dusted with rice flour so that the dough will pass easily through the rollers of the pasta machine. Pass each piece of dough through the rollers of the pasta machine, starting at the widest setting and working the dough through to the thinnest setting, dusting each time with some rice flour.

4 Pass each piece of worked dough through the tagliatelle cutters of the pasta machine or, alternatively, cut the dough into strips with a sharp knife. Hang the pasta over a broom handle to dry for 30 minutes.

5 To prepare the soup, heat a large saucepan or stockpot, add the oil and gently sauté the onion, garlic and fennel until aromatic and softened. Add the roasted tomatoes and their juices, the tomato purée and the white wine and simmer, stirring often, for 30 minutes to reduce the wine slightly.

6 Add the snapper stock to the saucepan and cook over a gentle heat for 30 minutes. The soup should be bubbling lightly during this time.

7 Pass the soup through a conical sieve, pressing to extract all juices. Season the strained soup to taste with the salt and pepper and reheat to boiling point when ready to serve.

8 To cook the pasta, bring a large saucepan of water to a rolling boil, add the pasta and cook for 2 minutes. Strain and refresh the cooked pasta under cold water to stop the cooking process, then drain and toss in a little olive oil to prevent it sticking.

9 To serve, cut the snapper into 6 × 50 g pieces. Lightly oil the fillets with olive oil and grill until translucent.

10 Ladle the boiling soup into 6 deep bowls and add the tomato dice, hot pasta and grilled fish. Sprinkle with the shredded parsley and top with a generous dollop of aïoli. Serve immediately.

Serves 6

parmesan-crumbed

sardine fillets with crisp black noodle pancake, roasted tomato sauce and aïoli

The textures and flavours that make up this dish capture the spirit of balmy nights by the sea. Black noodles are a personal favourite and they complement the oily iodine taste of sardines, octopus and scallops in particular. Squid ink, available from fishmongers and some specialty food shops, gives the noodles their colour.

150 g fine breadcrumbs (made from day-old, crusty bread), sieved
100 g freshly grated parmesan cheese
½ teaspoon sea salt
½ teaspoon black peppercorns, freshly ground
½ teaspoon chilli powder
24 sardine fillets
rice flour
3 eggs, beaten
120 g brioche crumbs
3 tablespoons flat parsley leaves, finely sliced
30 ml olive oil
vegetable oil for deep-frying
6 teaspoons Aïoli (see page 76)

Black Ink Noodles
3 large (61 g) eggs
2 teaspoons olive oil
2 teaspoons squid or cuttlefish ink
320 g plain flour
pinch of sea salt
rice flour

Roasted Tomato Sauce
1 head of garlic
12 ripe tomatoes
75 ml olive oil
½ teaspoon sea salt
½ teaspoon black peppercorns, freshly ground

1 To make the Black Ink Noodles, blend the eggs, oil and squid ink in a food processor until well incorporated. Add the flour and salt and blend again until the dough forms a ball. Refrigerate the dough, wrapped in plastic food wrap, for 1 hour.

2 Divide the chilled dough into 6 pieces. Flatten each piece with a rolling pin and then work the dough through the rollers of a pasta machine, starting on the widest setting and working and stretching the dough each time until you reach the second-finest setting. Each time the dough passes through the rollers, sprinkle it with some rice flour to prevent it sticking. Pass each sheet of dough through the spaghetti cutters on the pasta machine. Hang the noodles over a broom handle until ready to cook.

3 Bring a large saucepan of water to a rapid boil and cook the noodles for 2 minutes. Refresh the noodles immediately under cold, running water to stop the cooking. Drain, toss in a little oil and set aside.

4 To make the Roasted Tomato Sauce, preheat the oven to 300°C or as high as it will go. Brush a baking tray with a little olive oil and wrap the head of garlic in foil. Bake the garlic and tomatoes for 30 minutes until the tomatoes have coloured and the skins have split and the garlic has softened (the cloves should fall out of their skins when squeezed).

5 Pass the roasted tomatoes and garlic through a conical sieve, pressing firmly to extract all juices. While the mixture is still hot, blend in a food processor, adding the oil in a slow drizzle to bind the sauce. Season with salt and pepper.

6 To prepare the sardines, mix the breadcrumbs, half the parmesan cheese, salt, pepper and chilli powder in a bowl.

7 Dust the sardine fillets with rice flour, then coat with egg and then with the breadcrumb mixture. Arrange the sardines on a tray in a single layer and refrigerate until ready to cook.

8 To make the noodle pancakes, mix together the cooked noodles, brioche crumbs, remaining parmesan, parsley and olive oil. Heat a 12 cm cast-iron frying pan and brush it with oil. Distribute some crumbed noodles evenly over the base of the pan and cook over a medium heat until the noodles start to crisp. Flip over the noodle pancake and cook the other side. Turn out onto a warm plate and repeat the process until you have the necessary number of serves.

9 Heat the prepared tomato sauce until it comes to a boil.

10 Heat vegetable oil in a deep-fryer or saucepan until it reaches 180°C and fry the sardine fillets 6 at a time until they puff up in the oil (this usually takes only 2 minutes). Cook the sardines in small batches so the oil temperature doesn't drop, making the fish oil-sodden.

11 Spoon the hot sauce onto the plates, top with a crisp noodle pancake and layer the sardine fillets on top. Finish with a dollop of Aïoli.

Serves 6

Parmesan-crumbed Sardine Fillets with Crisp Black Noodle Pancake, Roasted Tomato Sauce and Aïoli

squid stuffed with bacon, capsicum and herbs with salsa verde and rouille

When preparing this dish, you need to obtain squid tubes of even size for a common cooking time. The squid can be stuffed and prepared up to a day in advance, so you don't need to get yourself into a mad panic at the last minute. Follow the principle of organising yourself beforehand and you can produce a miraculous feast with ease. These flavours and textures make the palate feel alive – there is depth, complexity and strength. The Salsa Verde used here, a heavenly paste from Italy's Emilian region, is a must to have on hand. Its uses are diverse and it provides an instant addition to an antipasto plate, livens up a piece of grilled or barbecued meat or fish and can even be spread on crusty bread to appease a hunger attack. It's quick and simple to make and is best eaten within a week of being made.

6 squid (each 12 cm long)
1 tablespoon diced onion
3 cloves garlic, minced
1 red bird's-eye chilli, minced
100 ml olive oil
160 g rindless bacon slices, cut into matchstick lengths
40 g fresh breadcrumbs (made from crusty white bread)
20 g roasted red capsicum, diced
20 g roasted yellow capsicum, diced
2 teaspoons shredded parsley leaves
2 teaspoons shredded basil leaves
1 teaspoon thyme leaves
25 g salted, tiny capers, rinsed thoroughly
3 anchovy fillets, chopped
50 ml lemon juice, strained
½ teaspoon sea salt
½ teaspoon black peppercorns, freshly ground
2 litres fish stock
6 teaspoons Rouille (see page 78)

Salsa Verde
25 g stale white bread
100 ml olive oil
75 g flat parsley leaves
40 g small capers, rinsed
2 large cloves garlic, minced
3 anchovy fillets, chopped
1 tablespoon finely minced red onion
30 ml lemon juice, strained
½ teaspoon black peppercorns, freshly ground

1 Clean each squid by removing the tentacles and internal sac. Discard the sac and lightly oil the tentacles and set aside. Remove the transparent pen from the body section and discard. Cut the wings away from the body, mince finely and set aside. Ensure the squid tubes are clean and free of membrane and rinse well under cold, running water.

2 Sauté the onion, garlic and chilli in the olive oil in a frying pan until the onion is golden and soft. Transfer the mixture to a bowl.

3 Fry the bacon in another pan to render it of its fat until it is slightly crisp. Drain and add to the onion mixture with the breadcrumbs, capsicums, herbs, capers, anchovy and minced squid wings. (If the mixture feels a little dry at this stage, add some more oil, but only enough to wet the mixture.) Season with lemon juice, salt and pepper.

4 Spoon the stuffing into the squid tubes until nearly full. Pack it tightly to ensure there are no air pockets and sew across the tops with a needle and thread to secure.

5 To make the Salsa Verde, soak the bread in a tablespoon of the oil. In a food processor, blend the parsley, capers, garlic, anchovy, onion, lemon juice and soaked bread until smooth. With the motor still running, slowly drizzle in the remaining olive oil until the mixture has emulsified. Season with pepper, taste and adjust if necessary. To store, spoon into a jar, seal and refrigerate.

6 Heat the fish stock in a wide-based braising pan until it comes to a boil. Turn to low and add the squid tubes. Cook them very gently in the stock for 20 minutes or until they feel firm to the touch. Roll regularly with a slotted spoon to ensure even cooking. They should float in a single layer in the pan, not on top of each other. Remove the cooked squid tubes carefully from the stock and allow to rest for a few minutes before slicing (letting the stuffing settle prevents them from splattering).

7 Just before serving, heat a frying pan and quickly toss the reserved squid tentacles over high heat for a minute or two only until they just start to curl. Season lightly.

8 To serve, spread the Salsa Verde on 6 plates, slice the squid into thin diagonal rounds and arrange on the sauce. Top with the fried squid tentacles and a dollop of Rouille. Serve immediately.

Serves 6

grilled rare tuna steak with fennel, green garlic and roasted garlic aïoli

This is a wonderful, easy-to-prepare number for a summer lunch or outdoor dinner that blends the subtle flavour of green garlic (immature garlic picked before the cloves have developed) with the aniseed taste of fresh fennel in a gently stewed lemon emulsion that complements the oiliness of the tuna and aïoli. The best results are achieved by minimal cooking. Well-cooked tuna belongs in a can, so if you go to the bother of buying a beautiful piece of fresh tuna, do it justice and cook it rare.

6 × 150 g trimmed tuna steaks (2 cm thick)
100 ml olive oil
2 small bulbs fennel, finely sliced
3 green garlic stems, finely sliced
5 cocktail onions, caramelised and cut into quarters
25 ml lemon juice, strained
50 ml virgin olive oil
pinch of sea salt
pinch of freshly ground white pepper
3 teaspoons chopped green fennel tops
6 tablespoons Roasted Garlic Aïoli (see page 77)

1 Preheat a chargrill pan or barbecue. Brush the tuna steaks with half the olive oil and set aside.

2 Heat a frying pan, add the remaining olive oil and gently sauté the fennel and green garlic until just softened. Add the caramelised onion and warm through. Transfer the vegetables to a bowl.

3 Make a vinaigrette by mixing the lemon juice and virgin olive oil with the salt and pepper. Stir the vinaigrette into the fennel mixture with the fennel tops, then spoon the vegetables onto 6 serving plates.

4 Quickly sear the tuna steaks on the hot grill for 1 minute on each side – just enough to seal and colour the surface, leaving the inside very rare and pink but warmed through.

5 Put the fish on the sautéd fennel and garlic and spoon over some aïoli. Serve immediately.

Serves 6

Pies and Pastries

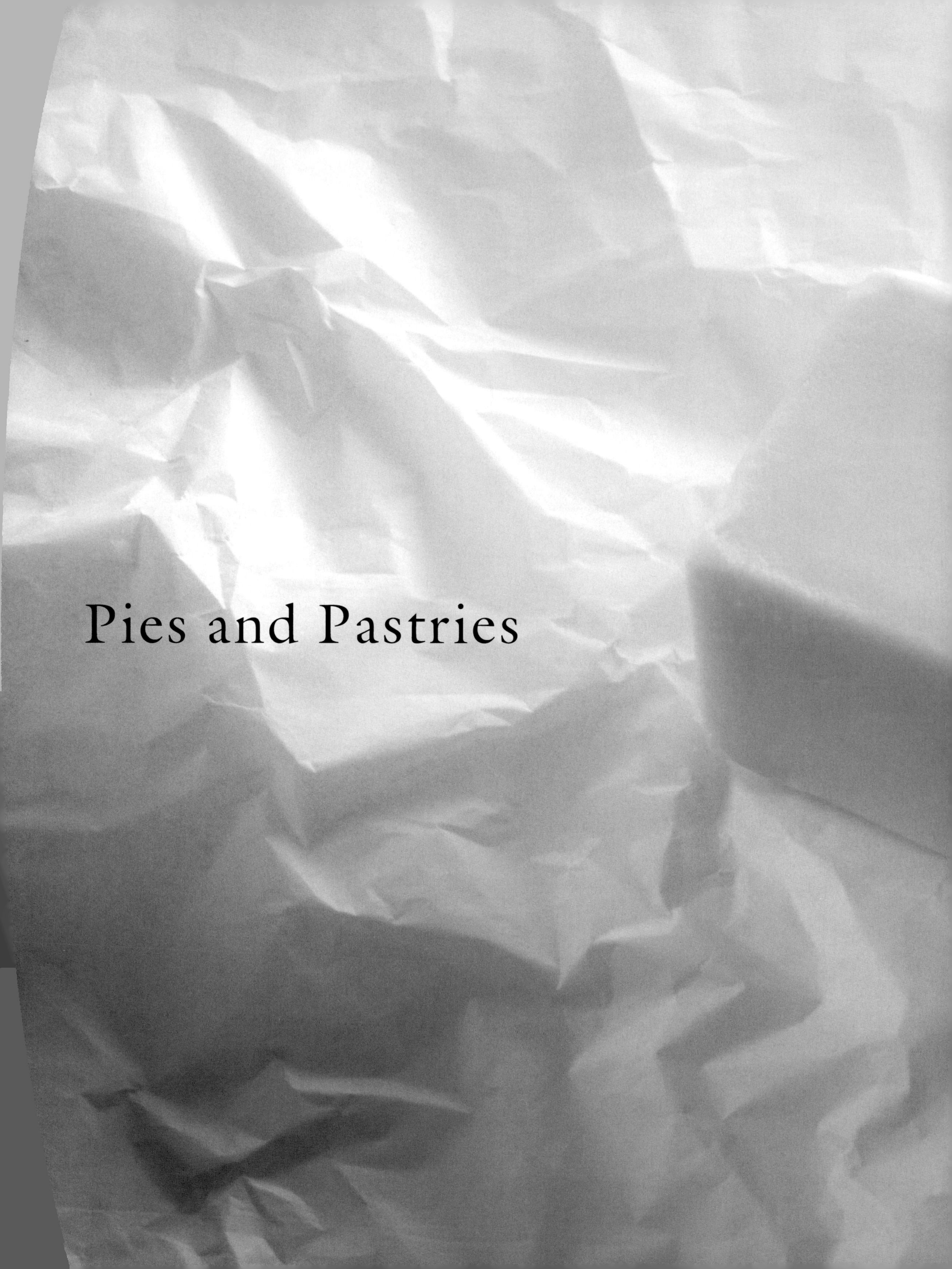

In professional haute-cuisine cooking, pastry is traditionally studied and practised separately from the rest of the cooking process, such is its depth and intensity. I find it an interesting, challenging and productive part of my cooking repertoire. The uses for pastry are many and varied; it is the perfect receptacle for carrying other foods.

Making pastry requires patience, care, feeling and skill. It can be fickle and bothersome, difficult and contrary until you develop a deft hand, feel and understanding for it. It requires only a few basic concepts to understand and achieve the most rewarding results. As with any other aspect of cooking, there are certain rules to follow and procedures to adopt to guarantee a successful result. Temperature (of the ingredients, room, equipment and workbench) is one of the primary deciding factors. Pastry must be made and dealt with in a cool environment (under 18°C) with the fat content (butter, shortening, cream and so on) best at refrigerator temperature. Proceed with pastry preparation for short intervals to ensure that the correct temperature is maintained and not varied. It is also important not to overwork the dough; the gluten should remain undeveloped, unlike bread where the opposite rule of thumb applies.

The way the fat, flour, liquid and sugar react together depends on the way the pastry is constructed: elasticity is created through beating, as in a brioche; incorporating butter through repeated rolling and folding produces puff pastry, and working the pastry dough quickly to inhibit gluten development results in short, sweet and shortbread pastry doughs. As with most things in cooking, the quality of the ingredients and careful handling bear a direct relationship to the final outcome. Resting pastry in the refrigerator between the making, the rolling and the baking is of paramount importance, as it prevents shrinkage and allows the glutens to relax.

When making most of the pastry doughs in this chapter, any excess quantity can be wrapped and frozen for later use. Prepared pastry kept frozen can often come in handy at the last minute.

shortcrust pastry

This is the most simple and straight-forward of all the pastry doughs and is very versatile. It is a more resistant pastry to use for tarts as it has the capacity to hold juicy and wet fillings without leaking or becoming soggy. This pastry will yield 12 individual tart cases or 2 × 20 cm tart cases and can be made in advance and frozen.

240 g plain flour
1/2 teaspoon sea salt
180 g unsalted butter, chilled and diced
80 ml sparkling mineral water, chilled

1 Chill the bowl and blade of a food processor in the refrigerator.

2 Blend the flour, salt and butter in the cold food processor bowl until the mixture resembles breadcrumbs.

3 Pour in the mineral water with the motor running and blend until the dough forms a ball. Wrap the dough in plastic foodwrap and rest for 1 hour in the refrigerator.

4 Roll out and cut the pastry according to the directions of the recipe and refrigerate for 30 minutes before baking.

sweet pastry

When sugar is added to pastry, it produces a crisper pastry that is similar to short-crust. This is quite a resistant and versatile pastry to use when making desserts or sweet things. As with the other pastries, work quickly to stop the glutens from developing, ensure all ingredients are of the same temperature to prevent shrinkage and rest the pastry in the refrigerator between making, rolling and baking. I usually bake it blind before filling it. This pastry will yield 6 individual tart cases or 1 × 20 cm tart case and can be made in advance and frozen.

50 g icing sugar
125 g plain flour
75 g unsalted butter, chilled and diced
2 egg yolks
seeds from ½ vanilla pod

1 Chill the bowl and blade of a food processor in the refrigerator.

2 Sift the icing sugar and the flour and incorporate with the butter in the food processor until the mixture resembles fine breadcrumbs.

3 Add the yolks and vanilla seeds and blend until the dough just comes together. Wrap the dough in plastic foodwrap and rest in the refrigerator for 2 hours.

4 Roll out and cut the pastry according to the directions of the recipe and refrigerate for 30 minutes before baking.

shortbread pastry

A higher ratio of fat to flour produces a shorter pastry that is harder to handle and softer in texture than others with more flour. This pastry is fragile and is at its best when served fresh as it is highly perishable. It can be used as a base for a tart or rolled and cut out to make biscuits. This quantity will yield 20 × 6 cm biscuits or a 20 cm tart shell. If used to line a tart tin, prick the base with a fork before resting so the pastry holds its shape during cooking. This pastry can be made in advance and frozen.

100 g unsalted butter
50 g icing sugar
1 egg yolk
1/2 tsp vanilla essence
125 g plain flour

1 Chill the bowl and blade of a food processor in the refrigerator.

2 Cream the butter in the food processor until soft. Sift in the icing sugar and work until thoroughly blended. Add the egg yolk and vanilla and mix lightly. Sift in the flour and pulse until the dough just comes together. Wrap the dough in plastic foodwrap and rest in the refrigerator for at least 2 hours.

3 Roll out and cut the pastry according to the directions of the recipe and refrigerate for 1 hour before baking.

chocolate pastry

This is a fabulous pastry from one of Australia's most celebrated chefs and culinary writers, Stephanie Alexander. It is like a chocolate shortbread, very moist with a fine crumb and used as a base for Chocolate Mocha Tart (see page 131). It can also be used to hold other chocolate fillings, such as chocolate mousse or chocolate butter cream.
Unlike other pastries, I find it easier to work this pastry into the tart shell as soon as it has been made, while it is still soft and pliable, using my fingers to press it into the shape of the tin. I have never had much success at rolling it out after it has become firm in the refrigerator. This quantity will yield 1 × 24 cm tart shell.

85 g unsalted butter, softened
85 g castor sugar
½ teaspoon vanilla essence
100 g plain flour
35 g Dutch cocoa

1 Cream the softened butter and the sugar together in an electric mixer (or by hand) until pale. Mix in the vanilla.

2 Sift the flour and cocoa together and mix into the butter until a dough is formed. The dough will feel quite wet.

3 Grease a 24 cm fluted flan tin, preferably one with a removable base, and press the pastry into the sides and over the base with your fingertips, ensuring it is evenly distributed. Allow the pastry shell to rest in the refrigerator for 1 hour.

4 Bake the pastry shell for 10 minutes in a 180°C oven. The pastry will bubble up slightly and slip down the sides a little, so when you take it out of the oven, and while it is still hot and malleable, press the pastry back into its original shape using a clean tea towel. Work quickly because once the pastry cools it holds its shape.

puff pastry

The nature of puff pastry lies in its preparation, where the layers of butter and flour are multiplied through the process of repeated folding and rolling. With the application of heat, the air that has been trapped between the layers expands and the water evaporates, causing the layers to separate and push up. It is the most complicated pastry to make, temperature being as important as the resting time between turns; the surface of the dough must not be broken during the rolling process or the butter will escape. I find this quantity of pastry most satisfying to work with. Follow the instructions and cut out the pastry into desired weights and freeze them for further use. Once cooked, this pastry should be served the same day as it deflates when stored.

500 g plain flour
250 ml sparkling mineral water, chilled
1 teaspoon sea salt
½ teaspoon strained lemon juice
250 g unsalted butter, chilled

1 Chill the bowl and blade of a food processor in the refrigerator.

2 Process the flour, salt, lemon juice and mineral water in the food processor bowl until incorporated. Refrigerate for 1 hour.

3 Rework the cold dough in the food processor a second time to work the glutens; this gives elasticity and prevents shrinkage. Wrap the dough in plastic foodwrap, making sure it is airtight. Rest for 1 hour in the refrigerator.

4 Roll the dough out on a cold surface to make a 40 cm × 30 cm rectangle about 1 cm thick.

5 Cut the cold butter into 1 cm thick slices and arrange in a single layer down the middle of the rectangle. Fold the edges in; the butter should be encased by the dough. It is important that the dough and the butter are of the same temperature and equal thickness to give uniformity to the layers when rolling. Flatten the dough with a rolling pin, dust with flour and refrigerate for 30 minutes, wrapped in plastic foodwrap.

6 Each time you work the pastry, dust it with flour and work on a cool surface. Using even pressure, roll the dough into a rectangle until it is 90 cm × 40 cm. Fold it over 3 times to end up with a piece of dough that is 30 cm × 40 cm. Turn the dough to your right and repeat the rolling and folding process, continuing until you have turned the dough twice.

7 Rest the dough in the refrigerator for 1 hour. (It is important to rest the dough at these intervals to prevent the dough from heating and to inhibit the glutens from building up through overworking.)

8 Continue the rolling and turning process until you have made 6 turns, refrigerating the dough for 1 hour after every second turn.

9 Roll and cut the pastry according to the directions of the recipe, brush with egg wash and refrigerate for 30 minutes before baking.

crème fraîche flaky pastry

This is a very short pastry because of the high ratio of fat to flour, which gives it its flakiness and richness. This pastry is best used for pies that have relatively dry fillings, as it does not need any extra moisture. It is not recommended for tart cases as it is too short and will crumble and fall apart. The pastry responds best when fresh and I don't recommend freezing it. This quantity will yield 6 individual pies or 1 large one.

190 g unsalted butter, chilled
300 g plain flour
½ teaspoon sea salt
190 g crème fraîche, chilled

1 Chill the bowl and blade of a food processor in the refrigerator.

2 Chop the butter into chunks and, while still cold, mix with the flour and salt in the cold food processor until the mixture resembles breadcrumbs.

3 Add the crème fraîche and pulse until the cream has just been incorporated. Don't overwork at this stage or the pastry will be quite difficult to handle when rolling.

4 Work the pastry into a ball by hand, wrap in plastic foodwrap and refrigerate for 2 hours.

5 Roll out and cut the pastry according to the directions of the recipe, brush with egg wash and refrigerate for 1 hour before baking.

sweet potato pastry

Chinese pastries are celebrated with the daily consumption of yum cha – a ritual of eating small amounts of many things, many encased in pastry. Chinese pastry differs from French pastry in its ingredients, construction and cooking. Dim-sum pastries are many and varied. There are pastry wrappers that are paper-thin and made from rice flour and water or with egg; spring-roll wrappers made with wheat flour; and dumpling pastries that use some form of vegetable starch as a base and are bound with duck fat, lard or oil. For this particular pastry I use sweet potato but it works with any other starchy root vegetable, such as potato, taro or yam. The dough is quite moist and needs to be worked on a bench floured with tapioca starch to stop it from getting sticky. When the pastries are filled and deep-fried, they become very puffy, flaky and aerated, with the filling steamed inside. This quantity will yield 24 dumplings.

750 g sweet potato, peeled and cubed
25 g castor sugar
40 g tapioca flour
25 g sweet potato flour
pinch of five-spice powder
60 ml vegetable oil
extra vegetable oil for deep-frying

1 Steam the sweet potato until soft and mash it while hot.

2 Mix all the ingredients together in a food processor. Remove the dough, wrap it in plastic foodwrap and allow it to rest in the refrigerator for 1 hour until firm.

3 Knead the dough and shape into the size of golf balls. Dust your hands with tapioca flour and flatten each ball into a flat disc about 4 cm in diameter. Put a teaspoon of your chosen filling onto the centre of each disc.

4 Fold each pastry over into a half-moon shape and press the edges together (you may need to use a little water to seal the edges). Rest the pastries on a floured tray until ready to cook.

5 Deep-fry 6 pastries at a time until golden and flaky and they float on the surface of the oil. This will take about 4 minutes. Drain on paper towels and serve hot.

Serves 8

brioche dough

Brioche is a type of bread dough, leavened with yeast and made rich with the addition of eggs and butter. The dough is beaten with a dough hook until it becomes very elastic and shiny and can be used to encase savoury or sweet fillings. Because of its elasticity, this pastry can withstand fillings that are quite wet but not too sloppy. The quantity given here will yield one brioche loaf baked in a regular-sized bread tin (ideal for breakfast) or will be enough to make any of the brioche recipes that follow.

250 g plain flour
pinch of sea salt
10 g compressed fresh yeast
50 ml warm milk
1 tablespoon castor sugar
2 large (61 g) eggs
125 g unsalted butter, softened

1 Put the flour and salt in the bowl of an electric mixer. In another bowl, mix the yeast into the warm milk with the sugar.

2 Whisk the eggs. Incorporate the yeast mixture into the flour with a dough hook on low speed. Add the eggs and turn the speed up to high. Mix for 5 minutes or until the dough appears elastic. Add the butter in small chunks until combined and the dough is smooth and shiny.

3 Put the dough into a greased bowl, cover with plastic foodwrap and allow to rise in a warm place for about 45 minutes or until it has doubled in size.

4 Punch the dough down and roll or knead it. Proceed according to the directions of the recipe. If making a loaf, put the dough into a bread tin, brush the surface with egg wash and allow the brioche to rise in a draught-free, warm place for 30 minutes. Bake the loaf over a water bath at 200°C for 40 minutes or until a skewer comes out clean. Turn onto a wire rack to cool.

baked goat's cheese tart with rocket and pickled walnut salad

Another perennial favourite on the Restaurant menu, this tart is made and baked to order and the balance between the cheese, custard, rocket and walnuts is perfect. You can make these tarts as individual ones, as a larger one or even as tiny tartlets that can be served as a canapé or appetiser (remember that the cooking time will vary accordingly). This tart was devised as a tribute to the wonderful fresh goat's cheeses being made in Australia, particularly by Gabrielle Kervella at Gidgegannup, Western Australia, and David Brown at Milawa, Victoria.

1 quantity of Shortcrust Pastry (see page 88)
6 large (61 g) eggs
3 teaspoons crème fraîche
1/4 teaspoon sea salt
1/4 teaspoon white peppercorns, freshly ground
6 teaspoons caramelised onions
6 tablespoons crumbled fresh goat's cheese
2 handfuls of perfect rocket leaves, trimmed
6 teaspoons finely diced red onion
3 pickled walnuts, sliced
30 ml balsamic vinegar
30 ml walnut oil
75 ml virgin olive oil
pinch of sea salt
pinch of freshly ground black pepper

1 Roll the pastry out on a cool, floured surface and line 6 × 12 cm Teflon flan tins. Refrigerate the pastry shells for 30 minutes.

2 Preheat the oven to 180°C. Blind bake the pastry shells for 20 minutes. Remove the paper and rice weights and let the tart shells cool. Leave the oven on.

3 Make a custard by whisking together the eggs, crème fraîche, salt and pepper.

4 Spoon the caramelised onion over the bases of the tart shells, add the crumbled goat's cheese and pour the custard over gently until the tart shells are full. Bake for 9 minutes until the custard has just set. The tart filling should have the same consistency as a soufflé mix, not too firm or the eggs will be overcooked and dry.

5 Carefully lift the baked tarts out of their tins onto plates and serve with a salad made at the last minute with the rocket leaves, red onion dice and pickled walnuts, dressed with a vinaigrette made with the vinegar, oils and the salt and pepper.

Serves 6

deep-fried sweet potato dumplings filled with prawn, chicken and water chestnuts

We serve these pastries at the Restaurant as an entrée with a chilli sauce or float one in a sweet potato soup. Either way, they are delectable. They will keep, refrigerated, up to 24 hours before they need to be cooked.

500 ml chicken stock
2 chicken breasts
25 ml fish sauce
15 ml fresh lime juice, strained
40 ml tamarind juice
2 tablespoons mint leaves
1 teaspoon jasmine rice, roasted and ground
200 g green prawn meat
1 tablespoon water chestnuts, blanched and finely chopped
1 tablespoon straw mushrooms, blanched and finely chopped
1 quantity of Sweet Potato Pastry (see page 94)

Coriander Paste

2 teaspoons minced garlic
½ teaspoon black peppercorns, freshly ground
a few sichuan peppercorns, ground
3 coriander roots
25 ml vegetable oil
2 teaspoons fish sauce
2 teaspoons strained lime juice
½ cup coriander leaves, chopped

1 To make the Coriander Paste, fry the garlic, peppers and coriander roots in the oil until softened and fragrant. Remove from the heat and stir in the fish sauce, lime juice and coriander leaves. Refrigerate until ready to use.

2 Bring the chicken stock to a boil in a saucepan and reduce the heat. Simmer the chicken breasts for 8 minutes. Turn off the heat and allow the meat to sit in the stock for another 5 minutes.

3 Remove the breasts from the stock, chop up roughly and blend in a food processor with the fish sauce, lime juice, tamarind juice, mint and ground rice until the mixture resembles mince. Do not overwork – the meat should not become a paste. Allow the mince to cool.

4 In a large bowl, mix together the chicken mince, prawn meat, water chestnuts, straw mushrooms and 1 tablespoon of the Coriander Paste.

5 Assemble and cook the dumplings according to the directions in the recipe for the Sweet Potato Pastry (see page 94).

Makes 18

five-spice duck and shiitake mushroom pies with ginger glaze

This pie made its début on our menu at the Phoenix and has been a permanent fixture since. The outward appearance of the pie pays homage to the French pithivier, *a hand-moulded dome, while its filling looks towards China. This dish is proof that the humble pie can achieve elegant status and refined technique. Start the preparations at least a day in advance. The duck can be cooked and the sauce and pastry made ahead of time, leaving only the assembly.*

1 × 1.7 kg duck, cleaned and trimmed
1 large brown onion, diced
3 cloves garlic, chopped
1 teaspoon chopped ginger
1 red chilli, split open
2 spring onions, chopped
100 ml vegetable oil
1 whole star anise
1 teaspoon fennel seeds
1 teaspoon sichuan peppercorns
2 litres duck stock
1 quantity of Crème Fraîche Flaky Pastry (see page 93)
egg wash

Ginger Glaze
60 ml vegetable oil
20 ml sesame oil
1 brown onion, chopped
3 cloves garlic, chopped
1 tablespoon finely shredded ginger
1 red bird's-eye chilli, split open
2 spring onions, chopped
1 whole star anise
1 teaspoon fennel seeds
1 teaspoon sichuan peppercorns
1 piece cassia bark
100 ml Stone's Green Ginger Wine
30 ml Chinese brown rice wine (shaosing)
20 ml fresh ginger juice
extra 1 tablespoon finely shredded ginger

Shiitake Mushroom Mix
50 g dried Chinese black mushrooms
1 brown onion, finely diced
2 cloves garlic, minced
2 teaspoons minced ginger
50 ml vegetable oil
200 g shiitake mushrooms, finely sliced
3 spring onions, finely sliced
2 teaspoons five-spice powder
1 teaspoon sea salt
1 teaspoon freshly ground black pepper
2 teaspoons flat parsley leaves, finely sliced

1 Begin preparing the duck at least a day before. Prick the duck all over with a skewer to release the fat and fry in vegetable oil until the skin is golden. Set aside.

2 In a deep-sided saucepan just big enough to hold the duck, fry the onion, garlic, ginger, chilli and spring onion until fragrant. Add the star anise, fennel seeds and sichuan peppercorns and stir until fragrant. Add the stock and bring to a boil. Reduce the heat, add the whole duck and simmer until the meat feels tender and is almost falling off the bone (this will take about 1½ hours). Turn the duck over a couple of times to ensure even cooking.

3 Remove the duck from the stock and allow to cool enough to handle. Strain the stock and skim off any fat. Refrigerate overnight for later use in the Ginger Glaze.

4 While the duck is still warm, take off all the meat, discarding the rest. Shred into uniformly small pieces and set aside.

5 The next day, make the Ginger Glaze (this will take about 2 hours). Heat a large saucepan and add the oils. Fry the onion, garlic, ginger, chilli and spring onion until softened. Stir in the star anise, fennel seeds, sichuan peppercorns and cassia bark and cook until fragrant. Deglaze the saucepan with the wines and cook, stirring, until reduced slightly.

6 Discard any fat from the reserved duck stock. Add the ginger juice and the duck stock and bring to a boil. Reduce the heat so the stock continues at a gentle boil and cook, skimming occasionally, until the sauce is reduced by half and has developed a shiny and sticky glaze. Remove from the heat and pass through a sieve to remove any sediment. Allow the sauce to become cold and settled and skim off any fat.

7 To make the Shiitake Mushroom Mix, soak the dried mushrooms in hot water until softened, then slice finely. Cook the onion, garlic and ginger in the oil in a frying pan until fragrant and softened. Stir in the sliced shiitake and black mushrooms and cook for 15 minutes until soft and any liquid has evaporated. Add the spring onion and cook until just softened, then add the five-spice powder, salt, pepper and parsley. Set aside to cool.

8 Mix the duck meat with an equal amount of the mushroom mixture until well incorporated. Form the mixture into balls slightly larger than a tennis ball.

9 Roll out the pastry on a floured surface to 5 mm thickness. Cut 6 bases 14 cm in diameter and 6 lids 16 cm in diameter. Brush the bases with egg wash, sit the balls of filling on top and cover with the pastry. Press the edges together with your fingers and smooth with a paring knife. Brush the lids with egg wash and score 6 or 7 arcs around the dome, working from the top centre down. Refrigerate the pies for at least 1 hour before baking.

10 Preheat the oven to 220°C. Bake the pies for 16 minutes on a baking tray until golden.

11 To reheat the Ginger Glaze, bring to a boil and add the extra ginger at the last minute. Use a spatula to slide the cooked pies from the tray to each plate. Serve with the glaze.

Serves 6

puff pastry baked with meredith farm sheep milk blue cheese and apple jelly

This pastry provides an interesting alternative to the usual cheese plate. I sometimes include it on a set menu as a small taste between main course and dessert. It is also ideal as a follow-up to a light lunch. Other boutique cheeses being made in Australia that would be equally suitable include Milawa Chevre or Milawa Blue, or even Kervella's Affiné, a matured goat's milk cheese. Of course, French roquefort or Italian gorgonzola will work just as well, depending on your preference.

½ quantity of Puff Pastry (see page 92)
250 g Meredith Farm Sheep Milk Blue Cheese
egg wash
6 tablespoons Apple Jelly (see page 142)

1 Roll out the pastry on a cool, floured surface and cut 6 rectangles each measuring 8 cm square and 1 cm thickness.

2 Cut 6 slices of the cheese the same size as the pastry.

3 Put the pastry sheets on a baking tray, brush with egg wash and score the tops diagonally with a sharp knife. Refrigerate the pastry until very cold again before baking.

4 Preheat the oven to 200°C. Bake the pastry sheets for 8 minutes or until golden. Remove from the oven and allow to cool on a wire rack. Reduce the oven temperature to 150°C.

5 Split the pastries open through the centre, spread each side carefully with Apple Jelly, put a slice of the cheese on each pastry base and top with the pastry lid.

6 Bake for 4 minutes until the cheese starts to soften. Serve immediately.

Serves 6

ocean trout fillet, leeks and mushrooms baked in pastry with tomato chive sauce and salmon roe

This is an adaptation of coulibiac, *which is a hot fish pie of Russian origin made popular by the French. It is a wonderful pie to cook for a group of friends. The preparation is done beforehand, so you will not be slaving over the stove and missing all the fun; when the pie is ready, you simply slice and serve it. At the Restaurant, we make this as a smaller individual piece as, once it is cooked, it needs to be served and eaten immediately. It is equally delicious made with freshwater salmon.*
The Tomato Chive Sauce can be made ahead of time up to the stage where the butter is added. Once the butter has been added, the sauce must be served immediately. I suggest you use the time the fish is baking to finish off the sauce.

1 × 1 kg ocean trout fillet
50 g butter
6 leeks, washed and finely sliced
1 tablespoon chopped garlic chives
sea salt
freshly ground white pepper
6 shallots, finely sliced
24 swiss brown or button mushrooms, sliced
1 quantity of Crème Fraîche Flaky Pastry (see page 93)
egg wash
6 teaspoons fresh salmon roe

Tomato Chive Sauce
1 brown onion, sliced
175 g unsalted butter
100 ml riesling or other white wine
6 ripe tomatoes
75 ml thick (45%) cream
1 teaspoon sea salt
1 teaspoon white peppercorns, freshly ground
3 tablespoons finely chopped chives

1 To make the Tomato Chive Sauce, sweat the onion in 25 g of the butter in a saucepan until softened. Add the white wine, bring to a boil and reduce by a third.

2 Purée the tomatoes in a food processor, add to the saucepan and cook until the liquid has been reduced by half again.

3 Pass the sauce through a conical sieve, pressing firmly to extract as much juice and pulp as possible. Discard the remaining solids.

4 In a clean saucepan bring the tomato sauce base and the cream to a boil. Set aside.

5 Trim the fish, removing its skin and bones and cutting away the tail end and belly piece to leave a fillet of even thickness weighing about 750 g. The fillet must be a constant thickness to ensure even cooking in the pastry.

6 Melt half the butter in a frying pan and gently sauté the leek until softened. Stir in the chives, season with a little salt and pepper and cool.

7 Melt the remaining butter in another frying pan and cook the shallots and mushrooms together until softened. Season with salt and pepper and cool.

8 Roll the pastry out on a cool, floured surface to make a 40 cm × 25 cm rectangle of 5 mm thickness. Brush the edges of the dough with egg wash. Spoon the mushroom mixture down the middle of the pastry, then put the fish on top and sprinkle with a little salt and pepper. Distribute the leeks evenly over the fish. Fold in the ends, then roll up the pastry to make a secure parcel. Rest seam-side down on a buttered baking tray. Brush the surface with the egg wash and refrigerate for 30 minutes before baking.

9 Preheat the oven to 220°C and bake the pie for 20 minutes until the pastry is cooked and golden – the fish should be just cooked. Don't be tempted to leave the pie in the oven any longer than 20 minutes.

10 Finish off the Tomato Chive Sauce while the pie is baking. Reheat over a medium heat and add the remaining butter, a piece at a time, stirring to incorporate each piece before adding the next (this is known as mounting the sauce). Stir constantly to prevent the sauce from separating. When all the butter has been added, take the saucepan off the heat and stir in the salt, pepper and chives. Taste and adjust if necessary.

11 To serve, cut the pie into 6 and put on serving plates. Spoon the sauce around and dot with some salmon roe.

Serves 6

Ocean Trout Fillet, Leeks and Mushrooms Baked in Pastry with Tomato Chive Sauce and Salmon Roe

baked apple and muscatel brioche with mascarpone

This is a popular patisserie item at the Store, where it is made each day and sold by the slice. You can experiment with other fruits and sweet fillings that take your fancy, the method remains the same. You can also serve the brioche with clotted cream if you wish.

1 quantity of Toffee Apples (see page 133)
50 g dried muscatels
60 g brown sugar
1 teaspoon ground cinnamon
250 g crème fraîche
2 teaspoons cornflour
1 quantity of Brioche Dough (see page 95)
egg wash
6 tablespoons Vanilla Mascarpone (see page 121)

1 Prepare the apples as directed and allow to cool.

2 Add the muscatels, brown sugar, cinnamon, crème fraîche and cornflour to the apples and mix well.

3 Roll out the brioche dough on a cool, floured surface to make a 30 cm × 18 cm rectangle of 1 cm thickness. Transfer the dough to a baking tray and brush the edges of the dough with egg wash. Place the filling along one long side of the dough. Fold in the ends, then fold the pastry over the filling and tuck it under so the parcel rests on its seam. Brush the surface with egg wash and allow the brioche to prove in a warm, draught-free place for 30 minutes.

4 Preheat the oven to 180°C and bake the brioche for 20 minutes or until golden.

5 Remove the brioche from the oven (sprinkle with some cinnamon sugar, if you like) and allow to cool slightly before slicing. Serve with a generous spoonful of Vanilla Mascarpone.

Serves 6

lemon tart with lemon verbena ice-cream

The classic lemon tart is a part of every self-respecting cook's repertoire. This particular recipe is an adaptation of Marco Pierre White's wonderful lemon tart from his book White Heat. *It is one of those things that demands to be eaten immediately as it does not keep well at all. Although some people serve this type of tart with cream, I prefer to accentuate the flavour with Lemon Verbena Ice-cream (see page 124), which, to my palate, is a much better complement to the tart. (We should move beyond the idea that cream is served on the side of every dessert, regardless of its content, structure and taste.) Of course, the tart is also perfect served unadorned, its beauty being its simplicity.*

1 quantity of Sweet Pastry, made with 1 teaspoon minced lemon zest (see page 89)
1 egg white, beaten
6 large (61 g) eggs
110 g castor sugar
450 ml thick (45%) cream
225 ml lemon juice, strained
1 quantity of Lemon Verbena Ice-cream (see page 124)

1 Roll out the pastry on a cool, floured surface and line a 20 cm flan tin that has been buttered. Refrigerate for 1 hour.

2 Brush the pastry with the beaten egg white and refrigerate for another 15 minutes.

3 Preheat the oven to 180°C and blind bake the pastry shell until lightly coloured, about 18 minutes. Remove from the oven.

4 Beat the eggs and sugar until pale and foamy. Mix in the cream, then add the lemon juice at the last minute. Pour the lemon custard into the hot pastry shell and bake until just set, 25–30 minutes. Remove from the oven and allow to cool for 30 minutes before removing from the flan tin. Dust with icing sugar, slice and serve immediately with Lemon Verbena Ice-cream.

Breads

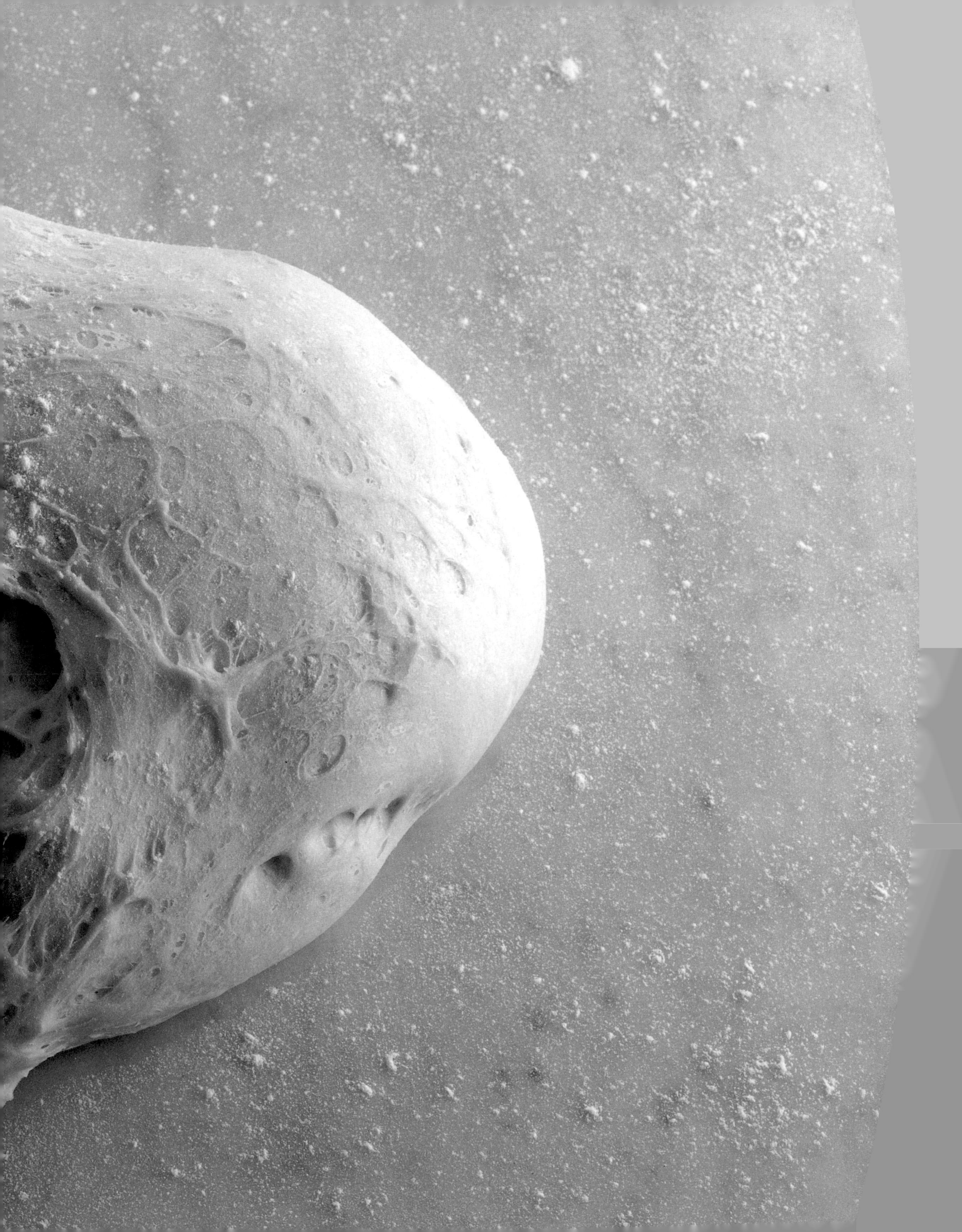

Bread is the staff of life, part of our historical development and a mainstay of our modern diet, offering roughage, energy, flavour and sustenance and acting as a carrier for other foods. The breaking of bread at the table symbolises a bond of friendship, giving and generosity. The making of bread is a comforting and empowering one, a response to some primal urge and a skill too often overlooked and ignored in our acceptance of the instant and the immediate. To understand and practise the art of breadmaking is to have a close relationship with a necessary food source and its preparation is an act of providing for our wellbeing!

I believe it is a moral sin to charge for bread when diners are paying for their food – it is mean-spirited. While there appears to be a resurgence of interest in good, well-made and tasty bread at the consumer level, this has not been translated into broad-based restaurant practice, with most establishments relying on a mass-produced, commercial and often inferior product. As a restaurateur, I adopt the philosophy that it is my responsibility to make and offer bread to customers as a sign of welcome. For me, a good cook means being generous, extravagant and knowledgeable and this should be apparent in all aspects of restaurant life. Anything else amounts to failure and a lack of soul.

The skill of breadmaking is easily acquired, especially through enthusiasm, practice and repetition. It requires a 'feel', particularly for texture and temperature, a good machine, strong arms and, most importantly, time. Strong flour is required to give the best results, that is, flour that has a higher gluten content than regular plain flour. Yeast has a life of its own and can be temperamental. When introduced to flour and water, it acts as a leavening agent, allowing the dough to rise and double in volume and become elastic. It can be obtained in fresh or dried form, depending on preference. The general rule is that a recipe calling for fresh yeast uses twice as much as dried yeast. Kneading is an important part of the process as it develops the glutens in the dough to give a lighter texture and finer crumb. Hand-kneaded bread usually has a denser texture and heavier feel than bread that has been worked by a machine.

For an even result and consistent crumb, allow the dough to double its volume in the first rising, then punch down the dough, knead and roll into the desired shape, glaze if necessary and allow the prepared dough to rise and double in volume a second time before baking. This second rising determines the look and feel of the bread. If fractures or cracks appear in the baking, it is usually because insufficient time was allowed for the second rising; the bread will feel heavier than it should and will have lost its shape. Remember that rising times are not absolute as how quickly the dough rises depends on the weather and the atmosphere in which you are working. Try to develop a feel for the dough so you can tell when it is ready, when it needs attention and so forth – instincts are much better than a clock! Failing the procedure a few times teaches you a lot more about the dynamics and what to look out for than an instant success.

The various ways we roll our bread are offered with each recipe but are not blueprints for reproduction; feel free to use your imagination. After all, texture and taste take precedence over shape, so this is where energies should be directed. Bread bakes best in a hot and humid oven, so it is advisable to spray the oven with water at regular intervals during baking to give a good crust. Baking bread on an unglazed clay tile in the bottom of the oven gives the bread a better crust again. Bread made with milk instead of water gives a softer dough with little or no crust.

At the Restaurant, we make bread for each service and three different kinds of bread are baked at the Store throughout the day. This chapter is an ode to the clever Barbara Alexander, the great cook who manages our Store and works closely with me in the Restaurant. She understands the importance of bread and how to make it and the good effect it can have. Her skill is matched by her imagination, and some of her creations are ingenious.

Sweet Curds and Creams

lemon curd

This is one of those delectable basics to always have on hand, even if you just want to spread it on toast. Use it to fill a 20 cm tart shell, spread it between layers of sponge or serve it in a pot alongside brioche toast and candied lemon. It is also referred to as lemon butter.

5 large egg yolks
100 g castor sugar
110 ml lemon juice, strained
125 g unsalted butter

1 Whisk the egg yolks and sugar until they are light and fluffy. Add the lemon juice and cook over a bain-marie until thick, stirring constantly.

2 Add the butter, piece by piece, allowing each piece to incorporate before adding the next. The mixture should have become thicker by the time the last piece of butter has been added. Remove from the heat and set the bowl over ice to cool.

3 To store, spoon into a jar and refrigerate.

vanilla mascarpone

Mascarpone is a cooked cream curd of northern Italian origin and has a texture similar to clotted cream but is not as high in fat. The method I use for making mascarpone has been adapted from that mentioned by Glynn Christian in his World Guide to Cheeses *but I add vanilla to give the mascarpone more depth of flavour. If you want to make a plain mascarpone, omit the vanilla. The mascarpone will keep, refrigerated, for 1 week.*

2 limes
1 litre single (35%) cream
1 vanilla pod, split open and scraped
1 scant teaspoon citric acid

1 Zest and juice the limes.

2 Bring the lime zest, cream and vanilla pod to a vigorous boil in a deep, stainless steel pot. Boil for 5 minutes until the cream separates.

3 Add the lime juice and citric acid to the cream and bring back to a boil. Simmer for 1 minute and remove from the heat. Pour the cream through a fine-mesh sieve into a bowl. Sit the bowl in the refrigerator until it starts to set.

4 Line a conical sieve with a double layer of wet muslin and sit it over a 2 litre bucket. Pour in the cream, cover the sieve with plastic and let the sieve stand for 24 hours to separate the whey from the curd.

5 Scoop the mascarpone into a plastic container, seal and refrigerate until ready to use.

passionfruit bavarois

A light, mousse-like cream tasting of passionfruit set just enough to still wobble, ethereal to the palate and one of my particular favourites. I am predictable in my constant use of passionfruit.

125 ml milk
4 large egg yolks
150 g castor sugar
100 ml passionfruit juice
2 gelatine leaves
250 ml thick (45%) cream, whipped until stiff

1 Heat the milk in a saucepan to simmering point.

2 Whisk the egg yolks and sugar together in a bowl until pale and creamy. Add the passionfruit juice, then whisk in the warm milk. Cook to the consistency of custard over a bain-marie, stirring constantly.

3 Soak the gelatine leaves in cold water until softened, then squeeze out the water and stir into the custard until the gelatine has dissolved.

4 Strain the custard through a fine-mesh sieve and cool over ice in the refrigerator. When almost set, whisk in the whipped cream.

5 Spoon the mixture into 6 plastic bavarois or dariole moulds and allow to set in the refrigerator for 4 hours or overnight, covered with plastic foodwrap.

6 To turn out each bavarois, hold the mould in hot water for a few seconds. Slide the custard out of its mould onto the serving plate.

Serves 6

honey bavarois

A bavarois is a flavoured custard base set lightly with gelatine and whipped cream and moulded before being turned out for serving. It gives the illusion of eating air, due to its ever-so-light texture, and takes on the intensity of the chosen flavouring. When making Honey Bavarois, choose a honey that has a flavour you like, but make sure it's not too strong or sweet otherwise it will mask the flavours of its accompaniment.

4 large egg yolks
100 g castor sugar
320 ml milk
60 ml honey
2½ gelatine leaves
250 ml thick (45%) cream

1 Whisk together the egg yolks and sugar in a bowl.

2 In a saucepan, heat the milk and honey to a simmer. Pour the milk onto the eggs, whisk and then stir over a bain-marie until the mixture is the consistency of custard.

3 Soak the gelatine leaves in cold water until soft, then squeeze out the water and stir into the custard until the gelatine has dissolved.

4 Strain the custard into a clean bowl and cool over ice.

5 Fold the cream into the cooled custard. Spoon the mixture into 6 plastic bavarois or dariole moulds and allow to set in the refrigerator for 4 hours or overnight, covered with plastic foodwrap.

6 To turn out each bavarois, hold the mould in hot water for a few seconds. Slide the custard out of its mould onto the serving plate.

Serves 6

pineapple sorbet with candied fruit

The best way to obtain fresh pineapple juice is to purée very ripe, sweet pineapples and pass the purée through a fine-mesh sieve. Alternatively, an electric juicer that produces fibre-free juices can be used.

75 g castor sugar
500 ml fresh pineapple juice, strained
1 tablespoon finely chopped glacé pineapple
1 tablespoon finely chopped candied citron (*cedru*)
100 g liquid glucose

1 Whisk the sugar into the pineapple juice with the glacé pineapple and the citron.

2 Melt the glucose in a bowl over a bain-marie until it becomes liquid and stir into the juice, mixing well.

3 Churn the mixture in an ice-cream machine according to the manufacturer's instructions. Store in the freezer.

raspberry sorbet

Sorbet has a more intense fruit flavour than ice-cream and when served with ice-cream it helps to cut some of the richness and creaminess – a great balance. Fresh raspberries need to be puréed and then passed through a fine-mesh sieve to give the required amount of juice. Raspberry seeds have no place in sorbet, the initial effort gives the most rewarding results.

125 g castor sugar
25 ml fresh lime juice, strained
750 ml sieved raspberry purée
150 g liquid glucose

1 Stir the sugar and lime juice into the raspberry purée until the sugar has dissolved.

2 Soften the glucose in a bowl over a bain-marie until it becomes liquid. Whisk the glucose into the purée until well incorporated.

3 Churn the mixture in an ice-cream machine according to the manufacturer's instructions. Store in the freezer.

Serves 6

lime mousse

This mousse is cooked slowly over a bain-marie like a custard, but is enriched with butter. The whipped cream is folded in when it has cooled to give it a mousse-like texture. The lime juice helps to counteract the fatty taste it would otherwise have.

5 large egg yolks
100 g castor sugar
1/4 teaspoon cornflour
110 ml fresh lime juice, strained
1 gelatine leaf
125 g unsalted butter
200 ml thick (45%) cream

1 Whisk the egg yolks and sugar in a bowl until light, then add the cornflour, followed by the lime juice. Place the bowl over a bain-marie and continue to whisk over heat until the mixture starts to thicken.

2 Soak the gelatine leaf in cold water until softened, then squeeze out the water and stir into the custard until the gelatine has dissolved.

3 Gradually add the butter to the custard a piece at a time, adding more as each piece melts into the custard, which should start to thicken and expand during the process. When all the butter has been worked into the custard, remove the bowl from the heat and cool over ice, whisking occasionally.

4 Whip the cream until thick and fold into the cooled custard to transform it into a mousse. Cover the mousse with plastic foodwrap and refrigerate until ready to use.

lemon verbena ice-cream

This is a fabulously refreshing ice-cream, the milk having been infused with the heady aroma of the leaves and flowers of lemon verbena. It is a must to make in summer when the plant becomes prolific. I also use the leaves as a base for tisane, a herbal tea that aids digestion. At the Restaurant we serve a slice of this ice-cream sandwiched between praline wafers – a play on the commercially produced Eskimo Pie. It is also wonderful served alongside the Lemon Tart (see page 103).

1 cup lemon verbena leaves, washed
500 ml milk
6 large egg yolks
200 g castor sugar
500 ml single (35%) cream

1 Infuse the lemon verbena leaves in the milk in a saucepan over very low heat for 2 hours, being careful not to reduce the volume of liquid.

2 Whisk the egg yolks and sugar together in a large bowl until pale and creamy.

3 Pour the hot milk through a fine-mesh sieve, discarding the leaves, and stir the scented milk into the eggs. Cook the milk mixture over a bain-marie on the stove until it reaches the consistency of custard, stirring constantly to keep smooth.

4 Pass the mixture through a fine-mesh sieve into another bowl and add the cream. Allow the mixture to cool completely.

5 Churn the cooled mixture in an ice-cream machine according to the manufacturer's instructions. Store in the freezer.

Serves 6

strawberry ice-cream

There is no substitute for good ice-cream. Fruit-based ice-cream should taste of fruit-enriched cream and not have ice splinters in it. This particular ice-cream does not have an egg custard base, giving it a more intense flavour. Use very ripe strawberries for the best results. The best way to purée strawberries is to blend them in a food processor.

250 ml strawberry purée
180 g castor sugar
25 ml lemon juice, strained
250 ml single (35%) cream

1 Pass the strawberry purée through a fine-mesh sieve to remove the seeds and give a finer texture. Mix the sugar and lemon juice into the purée thoroughly with a whisk.

2 Stir the cream into the mixture and churn in an ice-cream machine according to the manufacturer's instructions. Store in the freezer.

Serves 6

passionfruit ice-cream

Another perfect use for passionfruit, once again using the sieved juice to its best advantage. I incorporate the juice into the beaten egg yolk and sugar cold as I find the taste of the juice loses its intensity once it has been heated directly.

200 g castor sugar
6 egg yolks
500 ml single (35%) cream
250 ml passionfruit juice

1 Whisk the sugar and eggs together in a bowl until pale.

2 Heat half the cream in a saucepan to simmering point.

3 Stir the passionfruit juice into the egg mixture then pour in the hot cream, stirring well to incorporate, and cook over a bain-marie until the mixture is the consistency of custard. Remove from the heat and strain the custard through a fine-mesh sieve. Add the remaining cream to the custard and allow to cool.

4 Churn the mixture in an ice-cream machine according to the manufacturer's instructions. Store in the freezer.

Serves 6

Tropical Cassata Ice-cream

tropical cassata ice-cream

The ice-creams we serve at the Paramount tend to be spectacular, moulded affairs. Moulded ice-creams allow the eater to taste all the flavours with the scoop of a spoon, as well as providing a visual challenge, giving food a witty character and taking it beyond the ordinary. Making ice-cream at home does not need to involve this degree of detail as the moulds that are used in restaurants are often specially made. Get the flavours right and you can serve them as you wish. A simple layered effect, where you churn each flavour separately and lay one on top of the other in a plastic, rectangular storage container, works very well, and, when you turn it out, you can just slice and serve. Choose flavours that work together, that compliment each other. Make ice-cream in good quantities, perhaps layering some and leaving others plain. This way you always have a wonderful dessert to hand.

1 quantity of Strawberry Ice-cream (see page 125)
1 quantity of Passionfruit Ice-cream (see page 125)
1 quantity of Raspberry Sorbet (see page 123)
1 quantity of Pineapple Sorbet with Candied Fruit (see page 123)

1 Prepare one flavour of ice-cream at a time as directed. Divide between the desired number of containers and freeze.

2 When the first layer is frozen, prepare the next flavour as directed. Add a layer of ice-cream to the containers and freeze. Repeat this process with the remaining ice-cream.

3 Store the layered ice-cream in the freezer until required. To serve, unmould and cut into slices with a hot, sharp knife.

sauternes sabayon

A sabayon is a light custard that is whisked over heat – not stirred – making it very light and frothy. It needs to be served as soon as it is made. Use good quality sauternes in the cooking, one that you can drink with the dessert when it is made. As with all good cooking, quality ingredients give the best result. This is not a recipe for using up cheap wine.

500 ml single (35%) cream
250 ml sauternes
8 large egg yolks
150 g castor sugar

1 Heat the cream and sauternes in separate saucepans until simmering, making sure neither boils.

2 Whisk the egg yolks and sugar together in a bowl until light and fluffy. Pour the warm cream into the egg mixture in a slow, thin stream and whisk gently. Repeat the process with the warm sauternes.

3 Put the bowl over a simmering saucepan of water and whisk constantly until the mixture reaches the consistency of custard. Pass the sabayon through a fine-mesh sieve and use immediately.

chocolate cream meringues

A simple and satisfying petit four to make and serve with coffee. The meringues will keep in an airtight container for a week, just spread with the Chocolate Cream as you are ready to serve them.

3 egg whites
100 g castor sugar
100 g icing sugar, sifted
15 g cornflour
15 g cocoa powder
1 quantity of Chocolate Cream (see page 120)
extra cocoa

1 In an electric food mixer, beat the egg whites until stiff.

2 Gradually add the castor sugar in a thin, steady stream with the beaters at high speed. Fold in the sifted icing sugar, cornflour and cocoa.

3 Line a tray with baking paper and pipe on the meringue mixture in little peaked drops.

4 Leave in an oven set at 50°C until set, this takes about an hour.

5 To serve, sandwich 2 meringue drops together with Chocolate Cream. Dust with a little cocoa powder.

espresso ice-cream

The great flavour of this ice-cream relies on a base of strong, well-made espresso coffee. Do not be tempted to use an inferior instant substitute. I began making Espresso Ice-cream to accompany the Chocolate Mocha Tart (see page 131) as the textures and flavours work in perfect harmony. It remains a constant and popular feature on our menu.

500 ml single (35%) cream
250 ml milk
100 ml strong espresso coffee
25 ml coffee essence (preferably Trablit)
6 large egg yolks
200 g castor sugar
1 quantity of Chocolate Cream (see page 120)

1 In a saucepan, heat half the cream and the milk, coffee and coffee essence to simmering point.

2 Whisk the egg yolks and sugar in a large bowl until pale and creamy. Pour the hot cream over the eggs, whisking continuously, and cook over a bain-marie until the mixture is the consistency of custard. Pass the custard through a fine-mesh sieve and allow to cool.

3 Stir the remaining 250 ml of the cream into the cooled custard and churn in an ice-cream machine according to the manufacturer's instructions. Store in the freezer.

Serves 6

chocolate mocha tart with espresso ice-cream

Rich is an understatement when describing this double-layered tart. I believe when you use chocolate you should treat it as if you were an addict. Chocolate and moderation do not usually sit well together, so my chocolate desserts are designed for chocolate addicts – it's the full hit. When using chocolate in cooking, use the best couverture chocolate at your disposal, don't settle for low-grade cooking or compound chocolate as it just doesn't taste the same. The best brands are Callebaut (Belgian), Valrhona (French) and Lindt (Swiss). Start this recipe the day before you intend serving it as it needs time to set.

In the Restaurant we serve this tart with Espresso Ice-cream moulded into a spectacular cone shape. The ice-cream sits pointy end up alongside the sharp triangle of tart, making a strong geometric statement. See colour plate on page iii.

1 quantity of Chocolate Pastry (see page 91)
525 ml single (35%) cream
375 g dark couverture chocolate, in small pieces
30 ml coffee essence (preferably Trablit)
340 g milk chocolate, finely chopped
1 quantity of Espresso Ice-cream (see page 130)

1 Prepare the pastry according to the recipe. Bake in a 24 cm flan tin at 180°C for 12 minutes.

2 Bring 275 ml of the cream to simmering point in a saucepan.

3 Put the dark chocolate into a bowl and stir in the hot cream. Keep stirring until it has combined to form a ganache. Pour immediately into the freshly baked pastry shell. Refrigerate straight away and allow to set on an even surface for at least 4 hours.

4 Heat the remaining 250 ml of the cream and the coffee essence to simmering point and pour into a bowl over the milk chocolate and stir until smooth.

5 Remove the tart from the refrigerator and pour the mocha mixture over the dark chocolate layer, filling the tart right to the top of the pastry. Return it to the refrigerator to set firmly, about 3 hours. After the tart has set, cover with plastic foodwrap until ready to use.

6 To serve, unmould the tart and slice with a hot, sharp knife. Accompany it with a scoop of Espresso Ice-cream.

Serves 6

glazed nectarines with sauternes sabayon and toffee wafers

Make this dessert when nectarines are at their prime during summer. Select large, juicy, unblemished fruit to use for the cooking. The Toffee Wafers are much like brandy snaps, only they are smoothed out after cooking to remove their bubbly texture. The result is a smooth, thin wafer that resembles a shard. The wafers deteriorate quite quickly, especially in humid conditions, so be very organised when planning to make them and have a few practices beforehand so you become comfortable with the technique. The wafer mixture can be prepared and refrigerated up to 2 weeks in advance, leaving the cooking only for the day you require them.

9 ripe nectarines
50 g unsalted butter, diced
50 g castor sugar
1 quantity of Sauternes Sabayon (see page 128)

Toffee Wafers
50 g unsalted butter, softened
50 g castor sugar
2 egg whites
50 g plain flour

Toffee
100 g castor sugar
25 ml water

1 To make the Toffee Wafers, cream the butter and sugar in a bowl with an electric mixer until pale and creamy. This will take up to 10 minutes.

2 Fold the egg whites into the mixture a little at a time. Add the flour and work until the dough becomes smooth.

3 With a palette knife, spread a thin layer of the wafer mixture measuring 20 cm × 15 cm onto a buttered baking tray. Put the tray in the refrigerator until the mixture becomes firm, approximately 1 hour.

4 Preheat the oven to 180°C. Bake for 6 minutes until the mixture has set and is pale golden in colour. Remove from the oven. While the wafers are still warm, cut into 6 triangles that are 6 cm wide and 15 cm long. Work quickly to prevent fracturing, using a long-bladed sharp knife.

5 To make the Toffee, cook the sugar and water in a saucepan over a high heat until the mixture caramelises. Remove from the heat. Using a spoon, drizzle threads of toffee over the wafers.

6 Remove from the tray carefully with a flat slide and cool on a wire rack. Store in an airtight container between sheets of baking paper. The wafers are best used the same day as baked.

7 Cut the nectarines in half and remove the stones carefully, letting the fruit hold its shape. Place the nectarine halves on a baking tray, cut-side up, cover with butter cubes and sprinkle liberally with sugar. Grill until the sugar has caramelised and nectarines are glazed.

8 Put 3 nectarine halves into each bowl (flat soup bowls are best), pour over the warm sabayon and accompany with Toffee Wafers. Serve immediately.

Serves 6

toffee apple and vanilla cream tarts

With the preparation done beforehand, these tarts need only a few moments of your time when they are to be served. The tarts are more successful made individually as opposed to one big one as the Vanilla Cream is not made to be cut and hold its shape. The only trick is to have a blow torch on hand, easily acquired with refillable gas containers from any hardware shop for minimal cost. It works more effectively than a brulée iron in this instance and a griller will only heat the custard too much and cause it to separate and become runny.

½ quantity of Sweet Pastry (see page 89)
1 quantity of Thick Vanilla Cream (see page 120)
castor sugar

Toffee Apples
6 golden delicious apples, peeled and cored
100 ml water
500 g castor sugar

1 Prepare and bake 6 × 10 cm tart shells as directed.

2 To make the Toffee Apples, preheat the oven to 200°C. Cut the apples into eighths lengthwise.

3 Butter a baking dish and place the apple slices in a single layer over the base.

4 In a saucepan, bring the water and sugar to a boil and cook over a high heat until it forms a caramel. Pour over the apple.

5 Bake the apple for 7 minutes, then turn the slices over and cook for a further 5 minutes. Remove the apple from the tray while still warm and store on a sheet of baking paper until ready to use.

6 Cover the bases of the tart shells with the warm apple. Spoon over the Thick Vanilla Cream until each tart shell is full. Sprinkle the surface evenly with castor sugar and caramelise with a blow torch. Carefully remove the tarts from their tins and serve immediately.

Serves 6

poached peaches with raspberries and vanilla cream

Using the same flavours of the renowned Peach Melba in a different way, this is an easy dessert to assemble at the last minute provided the necessary preparation has been done. It captures the essence of summer when peaches and raspberries are plentiful and economical. I sometimes take these three flavours and turn them into ice-cream, mould them into layers and create a frozen Peach Melba slice. In this instance, the peach has been poached, the stone has been removed and the peach is then stuffed with raspberries and returned to its original shape.

250 ml sauternes
100 ml riesling
250 ml sugar syrup
25 ml vanilla essence
100 ml orange juice, strained
80 ml lemon juice, strained
zest of 1 orange
zest of 1 lemon
6 ripe yellow slipstone peaches
500 g raspberries
50 g castor sugar
1 quantity of Thick Vanilla Cream (see page 120)

1 In a stainless-steel braising pan, bring the sauternes, riesling, sugar syrup, vanilla, orange juice, 50 ml of the lemon juice and zests to a boil. Reduce to a simmer and add the peaches. Gently poach until the peaches are softened and the skins are just starting to split. Remove the peaches from the syrup and allow to cool. Reserve the syrup for another time (it keeps well refrigerated and with repeated use, the peach flavour intensifies).

2 Purée half the raspberries in a food processor or blender and pass the purée through a fine-mesh sieve to remove the seeds. Stir the sugar and remaining lemon juice into the raspberry purée until well mixed.

3 Peel the peaches and cut each one in half, removing the stones. Be careful not to rip the flesh – the peach halves should be perfectly intact and in shape.

4 Spread some raspberry purée on 6 serving plates and spoon a dollop of the Thick Vanilla Cream in the centre of the sauce.

5 Reassemble the peaches, stuffing some raspberries into the hollow where the stone was. Sit a 'whole' peach on top of the cream and dot a few extra raspberries around the peach on the cream and serve immediately.

Serves 6

honey bavarois with grilled figs and pistachio wafers

I always have this on the menu when figs are in season towards the end of summer and into autumn. The wafers will keep for a day in a sealed container away from heat and moisture.

12 ripe purple figs
icing sugar
1 quantity of Honey Bavarois (see page 122)
pistachio nuts, shelled and crushed

Pistachio Wafers
50 g castor sugar
50 g unsalted butter, softened
2 egg whites
50 g plain flour
25 g pistachio nuts, shelled and crushed

1 To make the Pistachio Wafers, put the sugar and butter into the bowl of an electric mixer and work on medium speed until the mixture is white and creamy, about 10 minutes.

2 Gradually add the egg whites to the creamed mixture and incorporate, then add the flour and work until the dough just comes together. Stir in the crushed nuts and refrigerate the mixture for 2 hours.

3 Preheat the oven to 140°C. For each biscuit, spread a tablespoon of the wafer mixture in a disc on a greased baking tray and bake for 5 minutes until cooked but not coloured.

4 Remove the tray from the oven and, working quickly, remove the biscuit from the tray with a spatula and roll up into a thin cigar shape while the biscuit is still hot, so that it sets into its shape. Allow to cool, then store in an airtight container.

5 Just before serving, cut the figs in half lengthwise and dust liberally with icing sugar. Grill for 2–3 minutes until glazed.

6 Turn out each bavarois onto a serving plate. Place 4 fig halves around the base of each bavarois and serve with a Pistachio Wafer. Sprinkle some extra crushed pistachio nuts on top of the bavarois.

Serves 6

shortbread biscuits with lime mousse and mango

The buttery nature of these biscuits is offset by the tartness and acidity of the Lime Mousse, which in turn is balanced with the sweetness of the ripe mango – the whole bringing to mind edible tropical pleasures. A dessert to have when mangoes are at their best. The biscuits can be stored in a sealed container between layers of baking paper until needed. They are best used the same day they are baked.

1 quantity of Shortbread Pastry (see page 90)
3 mangoes
1 quantity of Lime Mousse (see page 124)
icing sugar

Lime Syrup
50 ml water
250 g castor sugar
3 limes

1 To make the biscuits, roll the pastry out on a cool, floured surface until it is 5 mm thick. Using a 7 cm pastry cutter with a fluted edge, cut out 12 pastries, arrange on a baking tray and refrigerate for 15 minutes.

2 Preheat the oven to 150°C. Bake the biscuits for 6 minutes until firm but not coloured. When the biscuits are cooked, slide them off the baking tray with a spatula onto a wire rack and leave to set for at least 5 minutes.

3 To make the Lime Syrup, boil the water and sugar in a saucepan over a high heat until the mixture forms a pale caramel.

4 Juice and zest the limes and add to the caramel. Cook over a medium heat for a further 15 minutes until it becomes a syrup. Pour the syrup into a stainless steel bowl to stop the cooking process and allow to cool completely before using.

5 Just before serving, slice the cheeks off the mangoes, remove the skin and cut each piece into thin slices.

6 To assemble, spoon some mousse onto each plate over an area a little smaller than one of the biscuits, top with mango, drizzle a little syrup around it and finish off with a shortbread biscuit. Carefully build a second layer on top of the biscuit – first the lime mousse and then some more mango slices and finally another biscuit dusted with icing sugar. Serve immediately.

Serves 6

soft meringue, passionfruit and strawberry roulade

This recipe reworks the very Australian image of the pavlova into a more refined presentation that still captures the flavours and textures of the original form. It is a great standby because it can literally be thrown together in no time, looks spectacular and provides a big impact without impinging on your time when it comes to serving. It's what I call an easy 'slice and serve' dessert. You can adjust the filling according to the season, vary the fruit you use and substitute whipped cream or mascarpone for the Passionfruit Cream. Apply the same principle and make it in summer or for Christmas using mascarpone, cherries, blackberries and lychees.

hazelnut oil
8 egg whites
375 g castor sugar
2 teaspoons vanilla essence
2 teaspoons white vinegar
2 teaspoons cornflour
sifted icing sugar
1 quantity of Passionfruit Cream (see page 120)
500 g strawberries, sliced
2 tablespoons passionfruit pulp

1 Preheat the oven to 160°C. Line a 4 cm deep, 24 cm × 32 cm baking tin with baking paper and lightly grease the paper with hazelnut oil.

2 Beat the egg whites until stiff peaks form. Gradually add the sugar while still beating until the mixture is thick and glossy. Fold in the vanilla, vinegar and cornflour. Spread the meringue into the prepared tin with a spatula, level it off and bake for 20 minutes.

3 Allow the meringue to cool in the tin for a few minutes after removing it from the oven. Turn the meringue out onto a sheet of baking paper that has been dusted with the icing sugar. Allow to cool for 10 minutes.

4 Spread the meringue with the Passionfruit Cream, add half the strawberries and roll up carefully into a roulade using the paper to keep a firm shape. Refrigerate on a baking tray for 3 hours.

5 To serve, slice the roulade into portions and top with the remaining strawberries, drizzle with passionfruit pulp and dust with icing sugar.

Serves 6

Fruit Jellies and Preserves

This chapter is a dedication to the seasonal abundance of fruits that demand we make the most of their perfect ripeness, perfume and flavour and allow them to endure for as long as possible in a suspended preserved state. The art of preservation arrests the process of decay and gives us greater flexibility in our cooking and eating choices and goes beyond the boundaries of limited availability. Although economy plays an important role in the preserving process, it is often the way the ripe 'at-its-peak' fruit is transformed into an even more sensuous and appealing product that gives us the desire to adopt this practice. Summer, in particular, is a time of abundance and we have to work hard to capture the essence and seductive flavours of the heat so we can relive them in the colder, leaner months of winter.

Fruit can be preserved in its original shape steeped in an alcoholic sugar syrup or it can be candied, while over-ripe fruit can be juiced to flavour drinks, syrups and sauces that may accompany other fruit or dessert items. Sugar acts in the same way as salt in the preservation process: it inhibits the growth of bacteria when used in a concentrated form. It also acts as a setting agent, along with the natural acid and pectin found in varying degrees in fruit. The amount of sugar needed is determined by the type of preserve you are making. Fruit 'cheeses' and pastes use more sugar than fruit butters, which in turn use more sugar than jams and jellies.

Preserving all types of food items in the Restaurant has enabled a greater flexibility in our menu-planning decisions, giving us a wider scope and understanding of the science of food. I always question opening a can if I can make it, an important legacy from my days of working at Oasis Seros. I am helping to pass that skill and practice on to the people who work with me in my kitchen now. Preserving is a time-honoured tradition that appears to be disappearing with the advent of fast and frozen food and the modern desire for immediate gratification. It is important, then, that we maintain the skills of food preservation, to be reminded of the source, to respect the produce and the process, even if we don't necessarily do it ourselves. You don't have to go overboard and preserve everything in sight, just use a little of your time occasionally to indulge in the very gratifying experience of prolonging the life of our natural resources.

With all preserving and dessert work, it is imperative that you use only stainless steel or copper equipment to prevent tarnishing and the fruit discolouring. While you are about it, buy a jelly bag, or muslin, some preserving jars and a confectionery thermometer. Don't forget to label your produce – or eat it!

We stock all the preserves mentioned in this chapter at the Store when that particular fruit is in season. I use the preserves throughout the year when planning menus – they are indispensable!

apple jelly

Apples are high in natural pectin, a setting agent necessary for making jelly. Firm red or pink apples give the best flavour and colour to the jelly. Often, apples are added to other fruits when making jellies to give enough pectin for the jelly to reach setting point.

5 kg red apples (preferably Tasmanian pink lady or New Zealand gala)
5 kg castor sugar
2 litres apple juice
1 stick cinnamon

1 Wash the apples thoroughly. Roughly chop the apples and put them into a large stockpot with their peel, cores and seeds.

2 Add the remaining ingredients to the stockpot and bring to a boil gently. Cook over a moderate heat until the apple is very soft.

3 Pour the contents of the stockpot into a prepared jelly bag, or several layers of muslin, that has been suspended over a large bowl or bucket and allow the juices to drain overnight.

4 Tie the muslin or jelly bag to a wooden spoon and twist the spoon around gently to extract as much juice as possible.

5 Pour the strained juices into a large, clean pot and bring to a boil. Cook over moderate heat until it reaches setting point (110°C). To check whether the jelly stage has been reached, test the syrup on the back of a cold spoon.

6 Ladle the jelly into hot, sterilised preserving jars and seal.

apple butter

This recipe works best with tart, green cooking apples to balance the added sweetness. It is delicious spread on toast or brioche or served warm with apple tea cake and lashings of cream.

2 kg granny smith apples
350 ml apple juice
250 g brown sugar
seeds of 4 cardamom pods, ground
1 teaspoon ground cinnamon
½ teaspoon freshly grated nutmeg
1 teaspoon lemon zest, minced

1 Roughly chop the apples, including the peel and cores.

2 In a large stockpot, bring the chopped apple and apple juice to a boil over gentle heat. Stir regularly to prevent sticking.

3 Pour the contents of the stockpot into a conical sieve over another pot and press the solids through the sieve. Discard the contents of the sieve and gently reheat the apple purée with the sugar, spices and zest.

4 Simmer the apple mixture for 50 minutes or until thickened. Ladle the Apple Butter into hot, sterilised preserving jars and seal.

5 Store in the refrigerator.

grape jellies

Make this delicate jelly in individual moulds when grapes are at their best. Don't try using a large mould as the jelly won't set.

1 kg muscat grapes
150 g castor sugar
50 ml liqueur muscat
50 ml lemon juice, strained
4 gelatine leaves
48 seedless green grapes, peeled

1 In a pan, bring the muscat grapes, sugar and liqueur to a boil, then reduce the heat and simmer until the grapes just lose their shape, about 15 minutes.

2 Pass the grapes through a fine-mesh sieve, pressing firmly to extract as much liquid as possible. You should have 750 ml of grape juice. Add the lemon juice.

3 Dissolve the gelatine leaves in cold water until softened. Squeeze out the water and stir into the hot grape juice until the gelatine has dissolved. Strain the grape juice again and allow the mixture to cool slightly.

4 Divide the peeled grapes between 6 individual jelly moulds and pour over the grape liquid. Allow to set in the refrigerator until firm.

5 Turn out the jellies and serve immediately.

Serves 6

quince jelly

The quince is a native of Persia (modern-day Iran), a hot barren land, and is common in Middle Eastern and North African cooking. Readily available at fruit markets just as the summer fruits are fading, quinces come into their own in savoury and sweet cooking (they require treatment before they can be eaten). For further information, refer either to Maggie Beer's Maggie's Farm *or Jane Grigson's* Fruit Book, *both of which include evocative chapters about the virtues of the quince. Like the apple, it is high in natural pectin, so making jelly is quite easy.*

2 kg ripe quinces
4 litres water
castor sugar
250 ml lemon juice

1 Chop the quinces, including the peel and cores, and put them in a large stockpot with the water and cook over a moderate heat until the fruit is very soft.

2 Pour the contents of the stockpot into a prepared jelly bag, or layers of muslin, that is suspended over a bucket or bowl and allow the juices to drain overnight. Do not press or force the juices through the bag, as doing so will make the jelly cloudy.

3 Measure the strained juice with a cup measure, then transfer it to a clean, large saucepan and add an equal amount of sugar. Cook over a low heat – but do not let it boil – until the sugar has dissolved.

4 Stir in the lemon juice and increase the heat until the mixture boils. Skim and continue to boil for 15 minutes or until it reaches setting point (110°C). To check whether the jelly stage has been reached, test the syrup on the back of a cold spoon.

5 Ladle the jelly into hot, sterilised preserving jars and seal.

quince marmalade

A wickedly good and unusual preserve to make and have on hand when quinces are in abundance.

2 kg ripe quinces
500 ml water
500 g castor sugar
75 ml lemon juice, strained

1 Chop half the quinces, including the peel and cores, and put them into a large stainless steel stockpot with the water and bring to a boil over a low heat. Simmer for 30 minutes or until the fruit is very soft.

2 Tip the contents of the stockpot into a prepared jelly bag, or layers of muslin, that is suspended over a bucket or large bowl and let it drain for 12 hours or overnight. Do not press or force the juices through as doing so will make the jelly cloudy.

3 Combine the juices from the bucket with the sugar in a clean, large pot and cook over a low heat, stirring frequently until the sugar has dissolved.

4 While the mixture is cooking slowly, peel and core the remaining quinces and slice the fruit into thin shreds. You may need to keep the quince in acidulated water until ready to use to stop it discolouring.

5 Bring the syrup in the pot to a boil, add the shredded quince and lemon juice. Return to a simmer and continue to cook gently until the fruit is cooked, skimming any froth from the surface regularly. Bring the syrup back to a boil and continue to cook until setting point (110°C) is reached. To check whether the jelly stage has been reached, test the syrup on the back of a cold spoon.

6 Ladle the marmalade into hot, sterilised preserving jars and seal.

seville orange marmalade

This jam is an adaptation of the St Benoît Three-day Marmalade in Jane Grigson's Fruit Book. *Navel or valencia oranges can also be used, but the particular tartness and flavour of the seville oranges give the jam a distinctive character. They are only available for a short time in early summer so look out for them or find someone who has a tree. When they are available, blood oranges also make a wonderful jam with this recipe. If using any other orange than the seville, you would need to add a lemon to the recipe, treated in the same way as the oranges.*

10 seville oranges
castor sugar

1 Slice the oranges into thin rounds, discarding the ends. Remove the seeds and tie in a muslin bag.

2 Place the fruit and seeds in a large bowl or bucket and soak in enough water to cover, with a weight on top, for 24 hours.

3 Put the fruit, seeds and the water into a large stockpot and gently bring to a boil. Simmer for 1 hour and skim the surface with a mesh spoon to remove any scum that forms. Turn the heat off, allow to cool, then cover the stockpot and leave to sit for another 24 hours.

4 Measure the contents of the stockpot and for every kilogram of fruit and juice, add 1.25 kg castor sugar.

5 Bring the fruit and sugar to a boil in a clean, large pot and continue to boil gently, stirring occasionally, until the marmalade reaches setting point (110°C). This will take about 1 hour. To check whether the jelly stage has been reached, test the syrup on the back of a cold spoon.

6 Remove the muslin bag and ladle the marmalade into hot, sterilised jars and seal.

cumquat marmalade

This small oval fruit, with its sweet-and-sour characteristic, is a member of the citrus family and perfect to preserve as it is edible in its entirety.

2 kg cumquats
castor sugar

1 Cut the cumquats in half and remove the seeds. Put the seeds in a muslin bag and tie up.

2 Weigh the cumquats, put them in a bucket, cover with water and refrigerate overnight.

3 Transfer the cumquats, water and seeds to a large, heavy-based stockpot and add sugar to half the weight of the cumquats. Bring the stockpot to a boil and simmer for 1 hour. Turn off the heat and allow to stand overnight.

4 Bring the stockpot to a boil again and cook the marmalade until it reaches setting point (110°C). To check whether jelly stage has been reached, test the syrup on the back of a cold spoon.

5 Ladle the marmalade into hot, sterilised jars and seal.

brandied peaches

Keep the taste of summer alive by preserving peaches when they are in peak season towards the end of summer. You can use them in winter in a trifle, baked in cakes, made into puddings or topped with a crumble. These peaches keep well for a few months.

750 ml sauternes
250 ml riesling
1 litre sugar syrup
1 vanilla pod, split open
16 ripe yellow slipstone peaches, washed
750 ml brandy

1 In a wide-based braising pan, bring the sauternes, riesling, sugar syrup and vanilla pod to a boil and cook for 30 minutes on a gentle boil.

2 Reduce the heat to low, add the peaches and poach very gently for 10 minutes, turning them regularly in the syrup. Remove the peaches from the syrup, allow to cool enough to handle, then peel.

3 Add the brandy to the syrup and remove the vanilla pod.

4 Sterilise 2 × 2 litre preserving jars. Put 8 peaches in each one and pour the hot syrup over until the peaches are covered, then seal.

muscat-poached fruit

Dried fruit is available all year round and by preparing it this way you have a ready-made fruit dessert during the winter months when many varieties of fruit are not in season. Choose fruit that has been recently dried; it will be soft and malleable and taste fresh. Fruit from Australia's riverland is usually of the best quality. Serve this wonderful concoction warm, with clotted cream and toasted fruit bread.

750 ml liqueur muscat
250 ml water
500 g castor sugar
1 vanilla pod, split open
6 dried figs
12 dried apricots
8 dried peaches
6 prunes, pitted
4 dried pineapple rings, quartered
½ cup dried cherries

1 Boil the liqueur, water, sugar and vanilla pod in a large saucepan over a high heat for 20 minutes until the liquid begins to thicken and become syrupy.

2 Reduce the heat and add all the fruit. Simmer for 20 minutes until the fruit is tender and the syrup has reduced slightly. Stir regularly to distribute the fruit evenly in the syrup.

3 Store in a sealed container in the refrigerator.

preserved cherries

Cherries have a very short season around Christmas in Australia, but their shelf life can be extended by preserving them for later use whenever you have the desire to indulge in their taste.

1 litre sugar syrup
400 ml cherry liqueur or cherry brandy
1 stick cinnamon
3 pieces whole dried mace
2 kg black ron cherries, pitted

1 In a large, wide-based stockpot, bring the sugar syrup, liqueur, cinnamon and mace to a boil and simmer for 20 minutes.

2 Add the cherries and simmer gently for 15 minutes, stirring occasionally. Spoon the cherries and their syrup into hot, sterilised jars and seal.

3 Store refrigerated until ready to use.

spiced plums

These plums are very versatile. Used as they are, they make a warming winter dessert; cooked until the fruit has broken down, then sieved, these spicy plums make a sauce that can be preserved in hot, sterilised jars.

2 litres water
2 kg castor sugar
200 ml brandy
300 ml cassis
1 vanilla pod, split open
2 sticks cinnamon
6 cloves
3 pieces whole dried mace
3 kg satsuma or blood plums, washed

1 Put all the ingredients except the plums in a large stockpot and bring to a boil. Simmer for 20 minutes.

2 Add the plums to the syrup and simmer gently for 10 minutes until the plums are softened but not broken down. Pour the plums and their syrup into hot, sterilised preserving jars and seal.

3 When cool, refrigerate and store for 1 month before using. Peel the plums when ready to use.

steamed cumquat sponge puddings with orange sabayon

The construction and gentle steaming of these puddings makes them feathery light. A good balance of fruit acid and sugar, they show off the prepared cumquats to their best advantage.

3 large (61 g) eggs, separated
150 g castor sugar
2 teaspoons Cointreau
30 ml orange-flower water
190 ml milk
1 tablespoon melted butter
280 g self-raising flour, sifted
6 tablespoons Cumquat Marmalade (see page 148)

Orange Sabayon
250 ml single (35%) cream
50 ml milk
zest of 2 oranges
4 egg yolks
75 g castor sugar
75 ml orange juice, strained
15 ml Cointreau
15 ml orange-flower water

1 Preheat the oven to 180°C.

2 Cream the egg yolks and sugar in an electric food mixer until pale and foamy. With the beaters on medium speed, add the Cointreau, orange-flower water and milk, then the butter. Stir in the sifted flour gently.

3 Whisk the egg whites until stiff, then fold into the batter.

4 Butter and sugar 6 × 8 cm wide pudding moulds that are 5 cm deep. Spoon the marmalade into the bases of the moulds and pour in the pudding mixture. Stand the moulds in a baking dish and pour in water to come half-way up the sides of the moulds. Cover with foil and cook for 30 minutes, rotating the moulds at 15 minutes to ensure even cooking.

5 While the puddings are cooking, make the Orange Sabayon. Heat the cream, milk and zest together over a low heat until simmering. Whisk the egg yolks and sugar together in a bowl until pale and foamy. Whisk in the orange juice, Cointreau and orange flower water.

6 Strain the hot cream, discarding the zest, and whisk into the eggs and continue to cook and whisk over a bain-marie until the mixture reaches the consistency of a light and fluffy custard.

7 Remove the moulds from the water bath and allow to cool slightly. Run a small knife around the edges to loosen the moulds and turn out onto serving plates. Serve immediately with the hot Orange Sabayon.

Serves 6

apple butter galette

This is a melt-in-the-mouth, light-as-a-feather dessert. It has to be eaten as soon as it is baked, as reheating makes it soggy. Have the pastry rounds, apple slices and Apple Butter ready and you will be able to whip this up in no time.

1 quantity of Puff Pastry (see page 92)
3 golden delicious apples
6 tablespoons Apple Butter (see page 143)
castor sugar
icing sugar

1 Preheat the oven to 200°C. Roll out the pastry and cut 6 rounds 15 cm in diameter. Refrigerate until required.

2 Peel, core and cut the apples into thin segments.

3 Arrange the pastry rounds on a buttered baking tray and spread with the Apple Butter. Fan the apple slices over the butter, working from the centre out. Sprinkle with castor sugar and bake for 12 minutes until golden.

4 Dust the hot pastries with icing sugar and serve with a rich vanilla or caramel ice-cream.

Serves 6

baked plum and hazelnut crumble

This is one of those heart-warming desserts to indulge in on a cold night by the fire. It takes little time to put together and is served in the gratin dish it is baked in, so really requires no last-minute fuss or bother. One large crumble can be made instead of individual ones, if desired.

24 Spiced Plums (see page 151)
100 g brioche crumbs
125 g plain flour
100 g unsalted butter, softened
75 g hazelnuts, roasted and ground
1 teaspoon ground cinnamon
100 g castor sugar

1 Preheat the oven to 200°C.

2 Peel the plums, cut them in half and remove the stones. Arrange the plums in individual buttered gratin dishes and spoon a small amount of their syrup over them.

3 In a bowl, work together the other ingredients by hand until the mixture resembles wet breadcrumbs. Spoon the crumble mix evenly over the plums.

4 Place the gratin dishes on a baking tray and bake for 12 minutes until the crumble is golden. Serve hot with clotted or thick cream.

Serves 6

brandied peach and raspberry trifle with vanilla cream

This is a favourite dessert served in late summer when the fruit is abundant and at its best.

6 slices Génoise Sponge (see page 158)
6 Brandied Peaches (see page 149)
500 g raspberries
12 tablespoons Thick Vanilla Cream (see page 120)
6 tablespoons thick (45%) cream, whipped

1 Line the bases of 6 trifle dishes with the cake and soak with some of the brandy syrup from the peaches.

2 Slice the peaches and arrange them on top of the cake. Add a few raspberries, fill the dishes with the vanilla cream and cover with the whipped cream. Top with more raspberries and serve.

Serves 6

baked quinces with quince marmalade brioche and cream

Our cool room is stocked with ripe quinces for a good three months of the year, giving off their heavenly, musky sweet aroma, waiting to be transformed into syrup, pickle, jam, jelly, marmalade or paste to serve with cheese or just poached in sugar syrup until they become deep-red and luscious. Because of their less-than-appealing raw state, quinces, often referred to as the fruit of love, have been largely overlooked, but when treated with the respect they deserve, they rise to the challenge and win over your tastebuds.

1 quantity of Brioche Dough (see page 95)
6 tablespoons Quince Marmalade (see page 146)
3 large, ripe quinces
6 tablespoons clotted cream, crème fraîche or fromage blanc

Quince Syrup
4 ripe quinces
castor sugar
1 stick cinnamon
1 vanilla pod, split open

1 To make the Quince Syrup, chop the quinces coarsely, including the peel, core and seeds, and weigh. Put the chopped quince into a large stockpot with an equal weight of sugar and enough water to cover. Add the cinnamon stick and the vanilla pod.

2 Bring the stockpot to a boil and cook on a medium heat for 2 hours or until the fruit becomes a dark, rich red colour and the liquid has become syrupy. Strain the syrup through a fine-mesh sieve or piece of muslin, pressing to extract as much liquid as possible. Discard the pulp.

3 Prepare the brioche as directed. Roll the dough out into a 40 cm × 25 cm rectangle and spread the marmalade over the surface. Roll up into a long sausage, like a roulade, and rest the dough on a baking tray on its seam to rise in a warm, draught-free place for 20 minutes until it has doubled in volume.

4 Preheat the oven to 220°C. Bake the brioche for 40 minutes. Turn out to cool on a wire rack and reduce the oven temperature to 150°C.

5 Peel and core the quinces, then cut into quarters.

6 Bring the Quince Syrup to a boil in a wide-based, ovenproof pan, add the quinces and cover with a lid. Be careful not to boil the syrup or the fruit will break up and lose its shape. Bake the quinces in the syrup slowly for 4 hours or until they are cooked and a deep-red colour. The longer and slower the cooking, the better. (The quinces can be stored in the syrup once they have cooked until they are ready to be used. If that is the case, reheat them gently in their syrup on low heat.)

7 Cut the brioche into 4 cm thick slices and, when ready to serve, toast lightly on each side.

8 Sit the brioche slices on serving plates and top with the cooked quinces, strained from their liquid (reserve the syrup for future quince cooking). Spoon a little Quince Syrup around and serve with clotted cream, crème fraîche or fromage blanc.

Serves 6

chocolate sponge and orange marmalade puddings with chocolate jaffa sauce

This is a great winter dessert, classic in its combination of chocolate and orange and foolproof (almost) in its method. An interesting alternative to the predictable use of marmalade. One large pudding can be made instead of individual ones, if desired.

12 tablespoons Seville Orange Marmalade (see page 147)
100 g dark couverture chocolate
6 large (61 g) eggs, separated
100 g castor sugar
1 teaspoon Cointreau or Grand Marnier liqueur
100 g blanched almonds, ground
50 g fine, fresh brioche crumbs or breadcrumbs

Chocolate Jaffa Sauce
400 ml single (35%) cream
75 g castor sugar
75 ml orange syrup
25 ml Cointreau or Grand Marnier liqueur
250 g dark couverture chocolate

1 Preheat the oven to 180°C.

2 To prepare the puddings, butter and sugar 6 individual pudding moulds. Spoon 1 tablespoon of the marmalade into the base of each prepared mould.

3 Melt the chocolate in a bowl over a bain-marie and allow to cool slightly.

4 Whisk the egg yolks with half the sugar in a bowl until they foam. Stir the liqueur and then the chocolate into the egg mixture.

5 Beat the egg whites until firm, then gradually add the remaining sugar and beat until stiff. Fold the egg whites into the chocolate base with a whisk, keeping the mixture as aerated as possible, and then add the almonds and the brioche crumbs or breadcrumbs.

6 Pour the mixture into the prepared moulds and stand these in a baking dish. Pour in water to come halfway up the sides of the moulds, cover loosely with buttered foil and bake for 30 minutes. Test with a skewer in the centre – if it comes out clean the puddings are ready. (One larger pudding will take longer to cook than the individual ones.)

7 While the puddings are cooking, make the Chocolate Jaffa Sauce. In a saucepan, bring the cream, sugar, syrup and liqueur to simmering point.

8 Shave the chocolate with a knife, place in a bowl and pour over the hot cream. Stir to combine. Use immediately or reheat gently later over a bain-marie.

9 When the puddings are cooked, uncover and lift out of the water bath carefully.

10 To serve, turn the cooked puddings out of their moulds carefully, running a small knife around the edges to loosen them. Heat the extra marmalade and spoon over the tops of the puddings and pour the warm chocolate sauce around their bases.

Serves 6

muscat-poached fruit with meringue, praline and clotted cream

This dessert is an interpretation of the Gaudi architecture in Barcelona. The meringue structure hides the fruit and cream filling from the initial glance but once the wall is broken, the soft and sweet centre is revealed. I enjoy the challenge of creating a visual impact with desserts without being fussy, tricked-up or using unnecessary garnish. The essential flavours should be the strength behind the appearance – you can't have one without the other.

6 tablespoons clotted cream
6 tablespoons Muscat-poached Fruit
(see page 150)

Meringue Cones
3 egg whites
100 g castor sugar
100 g icing sugar
15 g cornflour

Praline
300 g castor sugar
50 ml water
hazelnut oil
250 g hazelnuts, roasted and skinned

1 To make the Meringue Cones, whisk the egg whites until stiff and gradually whisk in the sugar. The whites must hold their stiffness and body at this stage so they don't collapse on the moulds.

2 Sift the icing sugar and cornflour together and gently stir into the egg whites. Spoon the meringue mixture into a piping bag.

3 Line 6 × 10 cm high conical moulds with baking paper, folding the excess paper into the hollow centre to secure. Pipe the meringue onto the moulds in upward, even strokes, working from the bottom up, finishing each time with a flick of the wrist so the meringue forms a spiked peak. Make sure each line joins the next, so there are no gaps.

4 Put the Meringue Cones on a tray lined with baking paper and sit in a 50°C oven for 8 hours or until cooked and firm but not coloured. Remove the meringues carefully from their moulds and store upright in an airtight container until ready to use.

5 To make the Praline, boil the sugar and water in a saucepan over a high heat until the mixture becomes a pale caramel colour.

6 Oil a bench or marble slab with hazelnut oil and sit the nuts on it. Pour the hot caramel over the nuts and allow it to cool. Scrape the toffeed nuts off the bench with a spatula and keep stored in an airtight container in the refrigerator. When you need some praline, process small amounts of the toffeed nuts in a food processor or mortar and pestle until it forms a fine crumb.

7 To assemble, hold the meringues upside-down and spoon in a little clotted cream, then fill with the muscat fruit. Add a spoonful of cream to seal the bottom of each cone and turn up onto a serving plate. Sit a few pieces of the fruit on the tops of the meringues and drizzle over some of the fruit syrup. Sprinkle with praline and serve immediately.

Serves 6

passionfruit miroir

Passionfruit has an appropriate name. I am passionate about them. The fruit is always on the menu in some form or another. Just as any self-respecting dessert list has a chocolate item, mine also has passionfruit. When they are plentiful and cheap, we make litres and litres of juice that we freeze for making ice-cream, sorbet and curd at a later date.
If the Chocolate Mocha Tart is for the chocolate addict, this is the dessert for the passionfruit addict, as it involves layers of different passionfruit-flavoured textures; its name derived from the clarity of the jelly layer that has the appearance of a mirror. The Génoise sponge used here is wonderfully versatile and freezes well. When preparing the Passionfruit Bavarois (see page 122), keep the mixture in a large bowl until it is required rather than making individual bowls.

1 quantity of Passionfruit Bavarois (see page 122)
pulp of 3 passionfruit

Génoise Sponge
5 large (61 g) eggs, separated
150 g castor sugar
150 g plain flour, sifted
1 teaspoon vanilla essence
50 g unsalted butter, melted

Passionfruit Syrup
300 g castor sugar
100 ml water
250 ml passionfruit juice

Passionfruit Jelly
90 ml passionfruit juice
90 ml sugar syrup
1½ gelatine leaves

1 To make the Génoise Sponge, preheat the oven to 160°C. Whisk the egg yolks and sugar in a bowl until pale and creamy. Add the flour, vanilla and melted butter and stir to incorporate.

2 Whisk the egg whites until stiff and gently fold into the cake batter. Pour the batter into a greased 24 cm square cake tin and bake for 20 minutes or until cooked. Test by inserting a skewer into the centre; if it comes out clean, the cake is cooked. Turn the cake out onto a wire rack to cool.

3 To make the Passionfruit Syrup, bring the sugar and water to a boil in a stainless steel saucepan and continue to cook rapidly until the syrup becomes a pale caramel. Add the passionfruit juice, reduce the heat and simmer for 10 minutes. Cool the syrup completely before serving.

4 To make the Passionfruit Jelly, bring the passionfruit juice and sugar syrup to a boil in a saucepan.

5 Soak the gelatine leaves in cold water until softened, then squeeze out the water and stir into the hot juice until the gelatine has dissolved. Pass the syrup through a fine-mesh sieve and allow to cool.

6 To assemble the miroirs, spoon the Passionfruit Jelly just as it begins to set into the bases of 6 plastic dariole moulds 8 cm in diameter so that it is 3 mm thick. Refrigerate until set.

7 Spoon the bavarois on top of the jelly, filling the moulds until 5 mm from the top. Refrigerate until set.

8 Cut the cake into 6 × 8 cm rounds that are 5 mm thick. Position the cake bases on top of the bavarois and cover with plastic foodwrap and refrigerate until ready to serve.

9 When ready to serve, hold the plastic moulds in hot water for a few seconds to loosen them and turn out onto serving plates. Spoon some fresh passionfruit pulp that has been mixed with some Passionfruit Syrup around each miroir.

Serves 6

Passionfruit Miroir

cherry almond cake

This cake features regularly on the Store menu when cherries abound and stays there until the cherry preserves have been used and we have to wait for the next season. It is a very moist cake and keeps well for 3 days in a sealed container.

250 g unsalted butter
500 g castor sugar
6 large (61 g) eggs
1 teaspoon vanilla essence
400 g plain flour
1 teaspoon baking powder
200 g ground blanched almonds
185 g crème fraîche or sour cream
400 g strained Preserved Cherries (see page 151)

1 Preheat the oven to 180°C.

2 Cream the butter and sugar in an electric mixer until pale and creamy. With the beaters at high speed, add the eggs, one at a time, then the vanilla.

3 Sift the flour and baking powder and add to the egg mixture with the ground almonds. Beat for a couple of minutes on medium speed. Add the crème fraîche and beat gently until incorporated. Stir in the cherries by hand.

4 Spoon the mixture into a 24 cm round cake tin that has been greased with butter and then coated with sugar. Bake for 55–60 minutes until golden. Test with a skewer; if it comes out clean the cake is cooked.

5 Serve with some of the cherry syrup and extra crème fraîche.

cherry brioche with cherry syrup

One of my favourite ways of serving brioche is to laden the dough with fruit for sweetness and built-in flavour. There's nothing better than the seductive aroma and taste of fruit brioche served hot from the oven with cream or mascarpone.

1 quantity of Brioche Dough (see page 95)
12 tablespoons strained Preserved Cherries (see page 151)
500 ml syrup from the Preserved Cherries
icing sugar

1 Prepare the brioche as directed. When it is ready to be kneaded, work 6 tablespoons of the cherries into the dough.

2 Butter and sugar a large brioche mould and place the dough in it, adding a little ball of dough on top as in the classic presentation. Allow the dough to rise in the mould for 20 minutes, then bake in a 200°C oven for 40 minutes with a water bath on the shelf beneath.

3 Turn out the freshly baked brioche and dust with icing sugar. Bring the syrup to a boil in a saucepan and allow to reduce to 300 ml. Stir in the remaining cherries, heat through and pour around the brioche.

Glossary

The following ingredients and processes are used throughout this book and may not be familiar to all readers. You will find among them preparations requiring attention before it is possible to proceed with some of the recipes. Many of these are store-cupboard items – always have them on hand and you'll cut your preparation time significantly. I suggest that you familiarise yourself with the contents of the Glossary before you start cooking and stock up on the more frequently used items.

For ease of reading, recipes for the stocks I recommend using can be found at the end of the Glossary.

References to other Glossary entries are indicated by the use of SMALL CAPITALS.

acidulated water Water to which lemon juice has been added. Cut fruit or vegetables are immersed in acidulated water to prevent browning.

bain-marie A saucepan half-filled with water kept at simmering point over which a stainless steel bowl fits comfortably. The water must not touch the bowl. A bain-marie is used for gentle cooking.

bake blind To prevent shrinkage during cooking, baking paper is placed over prepared pastry and weighed down with dried beans, rice or pastry weights. When the pastry has been cooked, the paper and weights are removed and kept for future use.

bavarois moulds *see* dessert moulds

beef stock *see* page 164

belacan A compressed shrimp paste of Malaysian origin, belacan is called *trasi* in Indonesia, *kapi* in Thailand and *mam ruoc* in Vietnam. Shrimp are salted and fermented in the sun, then mashed into a paste. Don't be put off by the smell; when DRY-ROASTED and crumbled belacan gives a complexity to the flavour of the food to which it is added. I prefer the Malaysian variety. It is sold in blocks and is dark-brown, almost black. It keeps indefinitely but, once opened, should be kept very well wrapped in a container in the refrigerator.

candlenut A soft nut with a similar appearance to the macadamia. Very rich in oil, it is used as a thickening agent in laksa pastes and curries. The packet is best kept in the refrigerator once opened. Available from Asian food stores.

capsicums, roasting To prepare, cut blemish-free capsicums into quarters lengthwise. Remove the seeds and membrane, arrange skin-side up on a baking tray and place under a hot grill or salamander. Allow the skin to blacken and blister, then put the charred capsicum in a plastic bag to sweat for a few minutes. When cool enough to handle, peel off the blackened skin, wash off any other black bits, if necessary, and slice lengthwise into strips. Store in a jar, covered with virgin olive oil, until ready to use. Keeps for about 8 days, refrigerated.

cardamom, black A larger pod than the more common green cardamom, with a hard brown shell that is filled with seeds used in cooking to tenderise meat and add flavour. Available from Indian spice shops.

cassia bark Often mistakenly packaged and sold as cinnamon, dried cassia bark is thicker and harder than the related cinnamon bark. As it is a native of India, the best place to buy it is in an Indian spice shop.

chicken stock *see* page 164

chilli, chipotle Of Mexican origin, this is a jalapeno chilli that has been smoked during the drying process. It has a warming heat and a toasted, smoky flavour. Available dried or preserved in vinegar from specialty food shops.

coconut cream The thick cream scooped from the surface of first-pressed COCONUT MILK. This is the richest form of any coconut product. Available tinned or in block form from Asian food stores.

coconut milk Made by pressing the grated flesh of ripe coconuts that has been steeped in hot water. It is rich in oil and high in saturated fat. The first pressing gives the thickest milk; repeated pressings give a more diluted milk each time. Available tinned from Asian food stores. Choose a reliable brand, preferably Thai. The white milk should be unsweetened and have a smooth consistency.

coconut vinegar A mild vinegar with a low acidity level made from coconut water, the milky liquid that spills out when the coconut is cracked open. Two brands are available from Asian food stores. The Thai brand is a clear vinegar; the one from the Philippines has a milky appearance. Either type can be used.

dariole moulds *see* dessert moulds

date, black Of Chinese origin, this dried date has a dense, smoky taste. The seed must be removed before cooking. Available from Asian food stores.

demi-glace A reduced stock used in the preparation of sauces. Reduce BEEF or VEAL STOCK by half until it is thick and shiny and coats the back of a cold spoon. Do not over-reduce or you will end up with something that looks like Vegemite and is very salty. The stock sets to a jelly when cooled.

dessert moulds Some of the dessert recipes in this book call for particular moulds. The dariole moulds I refer to are 5 cm wide × 8 cm high, hold 200 ml each and are made of stainless steel or aluminium. Bavarois moulds are made of either stainless steel or plastic and are 6 cm wide × 5 cm high and hold 100 ml. Slight variations in size and volume are acceptable, but watch out for cooking times and the given yield.

dry-roast *see* instructions under spices, roasting and grinding

duck stock *see* page 164

egg wash Used for glazing pastry and breads and made by beating egg yolks with a fork in a bowl. Use a pastry brush for application.

eggplant, smoked To prepare, prick whole eggplants a few times with a skewer and sit over a barbecue grill or a direct flame until the skin blisters and blackens on all sides. When cool enough to handle, peel off the skin and squeeze out any bitter juices. The flesh will have a smoky flavour. Use while still warm for maximum flavour.

fish sauce Made from small fish that have been fermented in the sun with salt; a form of 'liquid salt' with more complexity and intensity of flavour than table or sea salt. I prefer to use the Thai 'Squid' brand as I find it is not too salty. The salt content of brands varies, so test each recipe if using a different brand; you may need to use less or more. Available from Asian food stores.

fish stock *see* page 165

ginger juice To prepare, cut 2 washed knobs of fresh ginger into a fine dice. Put into a food processor bowl with just enough cold water to wet the ginger. Process for 1–2 minutes, then press through a fine-mesh sieve or muslin to extract as much juice as possible. Store in the refrigerator. The ginger pulp can be used for flavouring a stock or sauce.

gluten flour Used to boost the gluten content of plain or 'soft' flour. It is not necessary to use gluten flour if using the harder bread flour. Higher gluten levels in bread and pasta doughs give greater elasticity and a better end result. Available from health-food stores.

jelly bag A necessary item to have on hand when preserving. Available from specialty shops and some supermarkets or you can improvise by using several layers of muslin cloth or oil-filter bags.

lime leaves, kaffir A staple ingredient in Thai cooking and available fresh, frozen or dried from Asian food stores. There is no substitute for the fresh leaves that are shredded in salads. Use frozen or dried leaves only if cooking; even then they won't impart the same citrus taste as the fresh leaves.

mirin A sweet Japanese cooking wine made from rice. Available from Asian food stores.

mitzuba A salad green or vegetable of Japanese origin known as trefoil, now grown in semi-tropical parts of Australia. The fragrant leaf can be eaten raw or very lightly steamed. Another salad green, such as MIZUNA, can be used instead if mitzuba is unavailable.

mizuna A salad green of Japanese origin that is becoming increasingly available. Sold in bunches, and often used in mesclun salad mix, it has long, fern-like leaves that taste quite mild and act as a good carrier for dressings.

nigella seeds Small black seeds similar in appearance to black onion seeds and often mistakenly referred to as black cummin. This spice comes from India and is featured widely in many spice blends. Available from Indian spice shops.

nori seaweed sheets Made from laver, a highly nutritious seaweed, and as thin as paper, these are used for making sushi. The greenish sheets have already been toasted, the black ones are untoasted. Toasting nori sheets improves their flavour and texture. To toast, hold a nori sheet with a pair of tongs over a direct flame for a few seconds. Available from Asian food stores. Once the packet has been opened, the sheets should be kept in a sealed, dry container as they deteriorate with moisture.

nuts, roasting and grinding *see* instructions under spices, roasting and grinding

onion, caramelised To prepare, slice brown onions finely and cook in a good quantity of oil in a wide-based frying pan over moderate heat until the onion turns a caramel colour and tastes sweet. Strain from the oil when cooked. Reserve the flavoured oil for other cooking.

passionfruit juice To prepare, remove passionfruit pulp with a spoon, then press the pulp through a fine-mesh sieve, squeezing out as much juice as possible. Discard the seeds. Freeze the juice for future use. Passionfruit juice is not available in instant form, so this process is necessary to achieve the intense flavour of the fruit without the presence of the seeds. It takes about 25 ripe passionfruit to make 250 ml juice.

pepper, sichuan A stock ingredient in Chinese cooking that comes from the prickly ash tree. The berries resemble peppercorns and impart a distinctive, mildly hot flavour.

prawn stock *see* page 165

prawns, dried In fact, small shrimp that have been dried. Reconstitute in warm water before using or DRY-ROAST and grind where required. Available from Asian food stores.

ras el hanout A North African mixture of dried herbs and spices blended by the head of the spice shop according to the region and particular fancies of the blender. It is not readily available in Australia. Refer to *North African Cookery* by Arto der Haroutunian and Jill Norman's *Complete Book of Spices* for a thorough explanation of the many ingredients needed to make the blend, as well as suggestions for its use. There really is no substitute for it, but you could use a mild, yellow, spicy curry powder in its place. This spice mixture is so wonderful and difficult to substitute that I am, in fact, considering importing it.

rice, arborio A variety of Italian rice, slightly starchy with big round grains, used specifically for making risotto. The two varieties available are superfini and semifini, the latter having smaller grains.

rice wine, brown Shaosing wine is a staple ingredient in Chinese cooking and is made from rice brewed with water. The closest substitute is dry sherry, although it won't give the same flavour. Available from Asian food stores.

saffron butter To prepare, heat 50 ml TOMATO ESSENCE until it boils and add 2 g saffron threads and infuse for a few minutes. Whip 250 g softened unsalted butter in a food processor and gradually pour in the saffron liquid until incorporated. Keep stored in a sealed container in the refrigerator. Stir into sauces at the last minute to enrich the flavour.

shallots, fried A deep-fried garnish made from red (Asian) shallots. To prepare, peel the shallots and slice finely lengthwise. Fry over a moderately high heat in quite a deep layer of vegetable oil until golden brown. Remove from the heat immediately, pour the hot oil through a sieve into a stainless steel bowl and spread the fried shallots onto paper towels to cool. Store in a sealed container to keep crisp. Also available ready-made from Asian food stores.

soy sauce, dark I use thick, black soy sauce rather than the thin varieties, and prefer the 'Elephant' brand, which tastes less salty than others and includes some sugar. There is no substitute – be careful never to buy cheap imitation brands. Available from Asian food stores.

spices, roasting and grinding Necessary to develop the oil, aroma and flavour of the spice to avoid it tasting 'raw'. To prepare, heat a cast-iron or heavy-based frying pan until hot and dry-roast (without oil) each spice separately. Toss the pan over a low heat until the spice is aromatic and darker in colour. Allow the spice to cool on a plate before grinding in a spice grinder or mortar and pestle. Once spices have been roasted and ground they are best used immediately as their flavour and intensity becomes weaker when stored. When buying spices, it is best to purchase them in small quantities whole and roast and grind them as you need them. Buy from a shop that does brisk trade, so you won't be buying anything too old.

squab stock *see* page 165

squid ink The fishy-tasting, black liquid from the 'ink' sacs of squid or cuttlefish used to colour pasta or noodles or impart flavour. To obtain, remove the ink sacs and squeeze the ink carefully into whatever you are adding. It is a messy and time-consuming process, but becomes easier and faster with experience. Squid ink is now available frozen; however, few places stock it and quantities suitable for domestic use are uncommon in Australia. Essential Ingredient, a food lover's mecca in Sydney, always has it on hand.

sterilising jars Sterilised jars are necessary for ensuring that preserves do not spoil or become contaminated. Heat kills bacteria and organisms that cause spoilage. To sterilise jars, wash them in boiling water or in a dishwasher and dry in a warm oven until ready for use. The hot food item is put into the hot, dry jars and sealed immediately.

stock *see* pages 164–65

sugar, palm A dense sugar made from the sap of the coconut palm. Available from Asian food stores in block or cake form; there is also a softer variety available in jars. I use a Thai brand – a flat round cake, pale gold in colour – that crumbles easily when cut with a sharp knife.

sugar, rock Less refined than white sugar and available in gold-coloured rock form. It has a mild sweetness and gives a slight glaze to the food with which it is cooked. It needs to be broken up with a mallet as it is quite solid. Don't attempt to use a knife. Available from Asian food stores.

sun-dried tomato paste Used for flavouring and made by blending chopped sun-dried tomatoes with olive oil to form a paste. Australian and imported brands of ready-made paste are available from selected food stores.

syrup, orange An intense syrup used to flavour desserts. To prepare, make a double-strength SUGAR SYRUP (twice as much sugar to water) and add the juice and zest of a few sweet oranges during the cooking. Cook until quite syrupy. Keeps indefinitely, refrigerated.

syrup, sugar Used in the preparation of desserts and made with equal quantities of castor sugar and water. To prepare, bring water to a boil and cook until the sugar has dissolved. 1 litre water and 1 kg sugar yields about 1.5 litres sugar syrup. Keeps indefinitely, refrigerated.

tahini A paste made from crushed sesame seeds commonly used in Lebanese and Middle Eastern cooking. Available from most food stores and supermarkets. Keep refrigerated once opened.

tamarind juice Used as a souring agent and obtained by soaking a block of tamarind pulp, a by-product of the pods of the tamarind tree. To prepare, soak the tamarind pulp in water, bring to a boil and simmer for 1 hour. Tamarind pulp is available from Asian or Indian food stores and some supermarkets.

tangerine peel, dried Used to add a citrus flavour to a wide variety of dishes. To reconstitute, soften in warm water, remove any unwanted pith and mince finely, if the recipe calls for it, or, if adding to a stock for flavouring, add in the whole piece. Available from Asian food stores. To make it yourself, take the peel from fresh tangerines and dry on a wire rack in a warm, dry place. Keep the dried peel in a sealed container.

tatsoi A small green leaf of Japanese origin that grows in clusters and requires very little cooking due to its size and fragility. Related to the Chinese flat cabbage. Usually available from Asian food stores in loose leaf form. Snow pea leaves or bok choy can be used instead if necessary.

tomato essence The liquid that is expelled when pulped ripe tomatoes are left to drain through muslin or a JELLY BAG suspended over a bucket. To keep the essence clear, do not push or force the pulp through the bag. 5 kg tomatoes will yield about 1 litre of essence over a 24-hour period. To make reduced tomato essence, bring the essence to a boil and reduce by half to increase the sweetness slightly and intensify the flavour.

tomato purée Not to be confused with tomato paste, which is thicker and stronger tasting. To prepare, purée chopped ripe tomatoes in a food processor, sieve out the seeds and cook over a low heat for 2 hours until slightly thickened. Keep refrigerated. Also available from supermarkets.

tomatoes, oven-dried To prepare, cut ripe and perfect roma tomatoes in half lengthwise. Arrange on a baking tray cut-side up and sprinkle with a little sea salt and castor sugar. Place the tray in an oven set on 50°C and leave until the tomatoes begin to dry out but still remain quite soft. Best done overnight when the oven is not needed, the process takes 15–20 hours, depending on the moisture content of the tomatoes. Check at regular intervals. Store in a jar, cover with virgin olive oil and spike with a couple of whole garlic cloves, a few basil leaves and some pepper. Keeps for 3 months, refrigerated.

tomatoes, roasting A method of cooking tomatoes whole to soften them and bring out their sweetness before using them in a particular recipe. To prepare, arrange ripe tomatoes in a single layer in a lightly oiled roasting pan and roast in a hot oven for 30 minutes until coloured and soft.

Vietnamese mint A hot-tasting, aromatic mint with long, pointed green leaves with purple markings that is a staple ingredient of Vietnamese cooking. It grows prolifically, especially in warmer humid climates, and constant pruning activates growth. Sprout in water until the stalks strike roots, and plant. Available from Asian food stores, where it is often sold as *rau ram*.

vine leaves Preserved grape vine leaves in brine used to package other food items, particularly in Greek and Middle Eastern cooking. Wash the leaves in cold water to remove any unwanted salty flavour. Available from all food stores.

water chestnut A crunchy sweet vegetable of Chinese origin with a black outer layer that peels away easily with a knife to reveal a white disc with a firm texture. Available fresh for a short time in spring or tinned from Asian food stores and most supermarkets. They can be eaten raw or cooked and keep for 2 weeks in the refrigerator when fresh. Rinse tinned water chestnuts under cold water and blanch briefly in boiling water before use.

STOCK

beef/veal stock

A rich stock made from roasted beef bones, shanks and veal shins that forms the basis of good sauces and soups. Keeps for 4 days, refrigerated.

2 kg beef bones
2 kg shanks, split
2 kg veal knuckles (osso bucco)
1 litre red wine
10 ripe tomatoes
4 brown onions, chopped
2 large carrots, chopped
handful of parsley (including stalks)
1 tablespoon black peppercorns
2 sprigs of thyme

1 Brown the bones in a roasting pan in a hot oven, then put them in a stockpot large enough to hold them with room to spare.

2 Remove any fat from the roasting pan. Deglaze the pan with the wine and add the wine to the stockpot.

3 Roast the tomatoes, onion and carrot in the roasting pan until softened and add to the stockpot. Add the remaining ingredients and cover with cold water. Bring the stockpot to a boil, then reduce the heat and gently simmer for 6 hours. Skim the surface regularly with a mesh spoon to remove any scum.

4 Remove the stockpot from the heat, carefully take out the bones with tongs and pass the stock through a conical sieve and then through a fine-mesh sieve to remove any sediment. Ladle off any fat. Allow to cool completely before refrigerating. Remove any fat from the chilled stock before using or freezing.

chicken stock

A white stock made from chicken bones and meat and used in a multitude of preparations. Keeps for 4 days, refrigerated.

2 chicken carcasses, broken up
  or 1 kg bones
1 chicken
several slices fresh ginger
handful of spring onion tops
1 tablespoon white peppercorns
500 ml white wine

1 Wash the chicken bones in cold water to remove any blood.

2 Put the bones and whole chicken in a stockpot with remaining ingredients. Cover the bones with cold water.

3 Bring the stockpot to a boil over a gentle heat and simmer slowly for 2 hours. Skim the surface regularly with a mesh spoon to remove any scum.

4 Remove the solids carefully and strip the meat from the chicken and keep for another use. Pass the stock through a fine-mesh sieve to remove any sediment. Allow to cool completely before refrigerating. Remove any fat from the chilled stock before using or freezing.

duck stock

Make this when you have used the duck meat for another purpose, as the bones will still have a lot of flavour. It is a good stock base to have on hand for making soup or a sauce and necessary when making Five-spice Duck and Shiitake Mushroom Pies (see page 98). Keeps for 4 days, refrigerated.

4 duck carcasses, broken up
2 brown onions, chopped
1 head of garlic, cut in half
5 spring onions, chopped
1 knob fresh ginger, sliced
a little vegetable oil
2 bay leaves
1 teaspoon black peppercorns
handful of parsley
5 litres CHICKEN STOCK

1 Brown the duck carcasses in a hot oven to render some of their fat.

2 In a large stockpot, sauté the onion, garlic, spring onion and ginger in a little oil until fragrant. Add the bay leaves, peppercorns and parsley and stir. Add the browned duck bones and cover with the chicken stock.

3 Bring the stockpot to a boil, then simmer gently for 3 hours, uncovered. Skim the surface regularly with a mesh spoon to remove any fat and scum.

4 Pass the stock through a conical sieve, pressing firmly on the bones to extract as much juice and flavour as possible. Discard the solids. Pass the stock through a fine-mesh sieve, allow it to settle and remove any fat that comes to the surface as it cools. Allow to cool completely before refrigerating. Remove any fat from the chilled stock before using or freezing.

fish stock

A good stock to have handy as it forms the basis for many soups and sauces. Use good quality, fresh, cleaned fish heads and bones for the best flavour. Keeps for 3 days, refrigerated.

heads and bones of 2 large fish (preferably snapper)
6 spring onions, chopped
1 knob fresh ginger, sliced
1 teaspoon white peppercorns
500 ml white wine

1 Wash the fish heads thoroughly to remove any blood. Make sure the gills have been removed as they will give the stock a sour flavour if left on.

2 Place all the ingredients in a stockpot and cover with cold water. Bring to a boil, then simmer gently for 2 hours. Skim the surface regularly with a mesh spoon to remove any scum.

3 Pass the stock through a conical sieve, pressing the bones to extract as much juice as possible. Discard the solids. Pass the stock through a fine-mesh sieve or muslin to remove any sediment. Allow to cool completely before refrigerating.

prawn stock

Use the heads and shells from fresh green prawns to make this rich, fragrant stock. Once cooled after cooking, it is best kept frozen.

6 tomatoes
1 kg green prawn heads and shells
100 ml Chinese brown rice wine (shaosing)
50 ml vegetable oil
1 brown onion, chopped
6 cloves garlic, sliced
3 slices fresh ginger
2 slices galangal
1 stalk lemongrass, finely sliced
2 red bird's-eye chillies, chopped
1 teaspoon sichuan peppercorns
1 teaspoon fennel seeds
1 star anise
2 kaffir lime leaves, chopped
3 litres FISH STOCK

1 Roast the tomatoes in a hot oven until softened and set aside.

2 Heat a large wok and toss the prawn heads and shells until they start to colour, then add the rice wine and deglaze. Remove from the heat.

3 In a stockpot, heat the oil and sauté the remaining ingredients until they start to colour and become aromatic. Add the cooked prawn heads and their juices, the tomatoes and the fish stock. Bring the stock to a boil and simmer gently for 2 hours. Skim the surface regularly with a mesh spoon to remove any scum. Pass the stock through a conical sieve, pressing to extract as much juice as possible. Discard the solids.

4 Pass the stock through a fine-mesh sieve or muslin to remove any sediment. Allow to cool completely before freezing.

squab stock

A base stock to make when you have a supply of carcasses. Once made and cooled it keeps for 3 days, refrigerated.

10 squab or pigeon carcasses
2 brown onions, chopped
2 leeks, cleaned and sliced
6 large cloves garlic, sliced
1 carrot, sliced
a little vegetable oil
2 sprigs of thyme
handful of parsley
2 teaspoons black peppercorns
2 bay leaves
300 ml red wine
2 litres CHICKEN STOCK

1 Brown the carcasses in a roasting pan in a hot oven. Drain off any fat.

2 Heat a large stockpot and sauté the onion, leeks, garlic and carrot in a little oil until softened.

3 Add the thyme, parsley, peppercorns and bay leaves and stir for a minute or two. Add the wine and allow to boil for a few minutes. Add the chicken stock, bring to a boil and simmer for 3 hours. Skim the surface with a mesh spoon regularly to remove any fat and scum.

4 Pass the stock through a conical sieve, pressing the bones to extract as much juice as possible. Discard the solids. Pass the stock through a fine-mesh sieve or muslin to remove any sediment. Skim any excess fat from the surface with a ladle. Allow to cool completely before refrigerating. Remove any fat from the chilled stock before using or freezing.

Index